THE SCIENCE OF LANGUAGE

THE SCIENCE
OF LANGUAGE

An Introduction to Linguistics

John P. Hughes
St. Peter's College
and
Columbia University

Random House   New York

P
121
.H75 / *38,452*

DILECTIS PARENTIBUS
ET DEFUNCTO ET ADHUC VIVAE
QUI INGENIUM INFANTIS COLUERUNT
ET ADULESCENTEM FIRMAVERUNT
HUNC LIBRUM PRO FAENORE
AUCTOR DEDICAVIT

PREFACE

A scholar who was a wit of sorts once said that the only justification for a scholarly book is the possibility of a second edition. He must have spoken from experience. If my experience is at all typical, anyone who has produced a "learned" work must, as he commits it to print, be painfully aware of its potential shortcomings: detailed explanations that may prove unnecessary, brevity where the reader may want more detail, and above all, a style that may be muddy where it had looked crystal-clear or dull where it had been considered interesting, or—worst of all—that turns out to be *too* readable, for then the book may be termed "slick" and never taken seriously.

I confess my own consciousness of all this, as well as of the fact that not much is said in these pages that has not been said before. However, this was done knowingly, and I trust that my readers, understanding my purpose, will judge the book by the criteria I used in writing it: *completeness* and *teachability*.

The aim of this work is to put into the reader's hands a single volume presenting the fundamentals of all the topics comprised by the science of linguistics. It seeks to be reliable, yet interesting; scholarly, yet not pedantic; readily intelligible, yet not a popularization. It is the outgrowth of more than twenty years of teaching, many of them devoted to linguistics. I trust that this experience is reflected in the organization of the material (which has proved effective with both undergraduate and graduate classes) and that instructors as well as students will find the book a helpful teaching aid.

In order to heighten teachability, important information is often repeated in different contexts and subjects are informally outlined at points preceding those in which they are fully treated. This has been done deliberately because I have found it effective in actual practice. Consequently, the text contains numerous cross-references and a very ample index to facilitate finding all mentions and discussions of a particular topic.

I want to thank Mr. Laurence Urdang and Mrs. Leonore Hauck of Random House for their unfailing patience and helpfulness; Dr. Arthur Abramson and the Haskins Laboratories for their kind co-operation in providing several of the illustrations; the Very Rev. James J. Shanahan, S.J., former President of St. Peter's College, for granting the sabbatical leave without which this book could not have been completed; and my wife, for her constant inspiration.

John P. Hughes

Ardnashee Farm
Ottsville, Pennsylvania

CONTENTS

PART ONE

PART TWO

FIGURES AND ILLUSTRATIONS

THE SCIENCE OF LANGUAGE

PART ONE

Chapter I

Fundamental Notions About Language

Only the most absolutely vital things can be completely ignored. We are conscious when we walk or sit down; yet we could live for decades without doing either. A splinter in the finger may dominate a whole day. But breathing—if any of us went for as much as three minutes without breathing, he would be dead. Do we therefore spend a great deal of time noting and checking the condition of our breathing? We do not. As a matter of fact, we never so much as give breathing a thought. For it is the sort of thing we must either not think of at all, or think of all the time.

Language falls into this category. If not necessary to life, it is certainly necessary to *human* life. Civilization is certainly not possible without it. All sciences depend upon it; all education is conducted through it. It may be necessary for human thought—indeed, some hold that language *is* thought. The material result of all this is, of course, that (until recently, at least) nobody has thought about language. Also, everybody has thought himself an authority on all linguistic matters, which exemplifies another axiom: when there is not —or is not known to be—a formal science of a subject, everyone regards himself as entitled to an opinion, however ill-founded or irrational it might be. Where there are no scientists, there are no laymen.

But it is at last beginning to be generally realized that there *are* professional scholars who devote themselves to the study of what language is and of how it works, and that there *is* a science (albeit one of the younger sciences) concerned with these subjects: a science which has replaced many traditional old wives' tales with a body of experimentally established facts about this most vital of human activities, and which has finally answered questions about it that for a thousand centuries had been asked without receiving serious, well-founded, or proven answers.

This science is beginning more and more frequently in more and more places to be mentioned—sometimes with respect, sometimes with hatred—under the name of "Linguistics."[1] For the workers in this new field no really satisfactory name has yet become current; *linguisticist,* which might seem logical, is not used, while *linguist,* which is widely used, also means merely a person who speaks several languages, whether he studies language scientifically or not.

This book is intended both as a first book for a person who wishes to begin the training necessary to becoming a professional linguist, and as an outline of the subject for the interested amateur who wishes to be better informed about it, but has no intention of entering the field. Fortunately, because of the nature of the science, it is possible to do justice to both classes of readers without slighting either. The subject matter of most sciences, if presented for a serious student, rapidly becomes distant from first-hand experience except for one who can spend many hours in the laboratory and has a thorough grasp of advanced mathematics, but the subject matter of linguistics is really just under everyone's nose (literally and figuratively), once one has been prompted to look.

Thus, to whichever category our reader belongs—be he learned dilettante or future professional linguist—his starting point will be the same. How, indeed, could one begin a science of language except with the question: What is language?

1. The definition of language

The definition of our subject is typical of many parts of it, for it seems like a simple, everyday thing, but upon closer inspection proves quite subtle. We all use the term "language," and feel that we have a clear idea of the sense in which we use it. But the difficulty of arriving at a clear and precise definition becomes apparent when you either collect and compare the definitions given in several dictionaries, or try to write one yourself.

Here are some dictionary definitions of language:

. . . any means of expressing thought. (Charles L. Meader in the *Encyclopedia Americana*)

. . . any means of communication between living beings. . . . In its developed form language is decidedly a human characteristic. (Otto Jespersen in *Encyclopædia Britannica*)

Audible, articulate human speech as produced by the action of the tongue and adjacent vocal organs. . . . The body of words and methods of combining words used and understood by a considerable community, especially when fixed and elaborated by long usage; a tongue. (*Webster's New International Dictionary,* 2nd ed.)

The reader will perhaps agree that none of these gives a really clear concept. But if we turn to the definitions of language offered by linguists, we still do not find the perfect definition, though perhaps we come a little closer. Here are two definitions of language by linguists:

. . . a purely human and non-instinctive method of communicating ideas, emotions and desires by means of a system of voluntarily produced symbols. (These symbols are . . . auditory and . . . produced by the . . . "organs of speech.") (Sapir, *Language,* 1921, Chapter I)

. . . the primary and most highly elaborated form of human symbolic activity. Its symbols are made up of sounds produced by the vocal apparatus, and they are arranged in classes and patterns which make up a complex and symmetrical structure. The entities of language are symbols, that is, they have meaning, but the connection between symbol and thing is arbitrary and socially controlled. The symbols of language are simultaneously substitute stimuli and substitute responses and can call forth further stimuli and responses, so that discourse becomes independent of an immediate physical stimulus. The entities and structure of language are always so elaborated as to give the speaker the possibility of making a linguistic response to any experience. (Archibald A. Hill, *Introduction to Linguistic Structures,* 1958, p. 9)

5

Having weighed—specifically or by implication—several definitions and found them unsatisfactory, it is obviously very poor strategy to come forward with a definition of one's own. Nevertheless, it must be attempted if no other can be adopted. Without undertaking any comparisons, therefore, we merely state that, throughout this book, the term *language* will be understood to mean:

A system of arbitrary vocal symbols by which thought is conveyed from one human being to another.

Please note carefully the elements of this definition:

Language is a *system*. This means that it is a sort of code or set of rules, and each item is what it is by virtue of its place in the system. This concept was expressed by the linguist De Saussure in the term *tout se tient* ("everything hangs together")[2] and has become a basic principle of modern linguistics, in contrast to an older, more atomistic approach[3] under which each linguistic phenomenon was studied in complete isolation. Many important implications follow from De Saussure's principle, as will be shown later.

Language is *arbitrary*. It will be shown in a number of connections (see especially Chapter III, 1) that there is no intrinsic necessity for any word to mean what it does, or for any language to have the structure it has. Certain sequences of sounds have certain meanings only by virtue of the agreement of a certain community, which can, under certain conditions, revoke its consent to established rules and set up new ones. Language is, in fact, always democratic, whatever the form of government under which its speakers live.

Language is *vocal;* that is, it is made up of the sounds which can be produced by the organs of speech[4] in human beings. By putting this term into the definition we arbitrarily rule out of our scope any kind of communication between nonhuman beings (e.g., animals). Now, the writer is a dog owner and dog lover, and will not yield to any of his readers in conviction that his own dogs apparently in some way "understand" certain words (or at least certain sounds within such words), and are able to communicate to him, with uniformity and efficiency, certain "ideas" of theirs. But in the long run the dispassionate observer must admit that the "language" in use between species of animals, or between animals and humans, is fundamentally different from what we refer to as the French or German "language." Let us by all means have as much research into animal "language"—

6

or that of bees—as can be undertaken; but to try to include this, or several other kinds of communication sometimes so called, in a theory of language would force us into extremely superficial and useless generalities. Usually, indeed, the term "language" is applied to these latter, not because the essence of language is recognized in them, but merely to draw an *analogy* with what is originally and properly called *language*, namely, human speech.

Language is *symbolism*. You have seen high-powered cars and trucks come to a screeching stop before a red light. The light has no power to stop them, whatever its color, nor to take any reprisals if they ignore it. But because the drivers recognize the light as a *symbol* of a policeman's command, they obey it—or rather the command which it symbolizes. A runaway horse, not appreciating this symbolism, would not stop. (Would he stop for a policeman? Possibly, in the sense that any man who seized his reins might stop him; but certainly not because the man is a policeman. For the policeman's uniform is a further symbol: it symbolizes the authority which the state has vested in him.) It is clear that symbolism is the philosophic foundation which makes language possible;[5] investigation along this line may do something toward clearing up that age-old riddle, the origin of language. It would seem evident that the power to symbolize and to appreciate symbols is a prerequisite to language, and that any species of beings lacking this power must develop it before they can develop language, properly so called.

Language is a *vehicle of thought*. The most important implication here is that thought is *something distinct from the language used to convey it*. You will find that this is taken for granted by a great many linguists, but denied by many psychologists, who operate on the assumption that both the thought and the word are ultimately the same thing—an electric voltage in the brain, a particular routing of nerve impulses, or some such phenomenon. If this latter view is correct, the acquisition of a new language might call for a whole new set of units and patterns of thought; thus each new language should be harder to learn.

Probably it is this philosophy which underlies the view, long prevalent in American schools, that learning another language is a difficult mental exercise, not to be imposed on youngsters until their minds are well developed—and then only on the exceptional student, lest

7

struggling with several languages preclude or limit mastery in any. Doubtless the psychologists can cite research studies tending to demonstrate this. Yet linguists will take their oath that, whatever learned studies may have been done, such hypotheses are contrary to the facts of their first-hand experience. Many are the linguists born in Europe who from earliest childhood spoke three to five languages, yet today speak English (learned, perhaps, as a sixth language) better than a majority of monolingual American college graduates—as the teachers of the latter would be first to admit. Consider, too, that a merchant sailor named Jozef Korzeniowski learned English well enough to write classic English fiction (under the name Joseph Conrad), and that Oscar Wilde learned French well enough to write a play in that language for Sarah Bernhardt[6]—without apparent detriment to his English style.

The last element of our definition merely reaffirms what has already been pointed out—namely, that we (arbitrarily, if you like) exclude all kinds of communication among animals or other nonhuman beings, as well as any communication among humans that does not employ *vocal* symbols, from the concept of "language" insofar as it is treated in this book.

2. The nature of "meaning"

We are now ready to explore some of the corollaries of the definition of language. First of all, it seems simple enough to equate what we have described as the *thought,* which is distinct from but expressed (or symbolized) by language, and the term "meaning," which is frequently used but not very exact.

What is "meaning"? With very strict observation, you will find that in practice we use the term in two principal ways: If someone asks me "the meaning" of a word in another language, I give him a word in his language which (in my judgment) expresses "the same thing" as that word. If he asks me "the meaning" of an English word, I give him another word or combination of words in English which says "the same thing."

Observe that we never, therefore, know "the meaning" (whatever it may be) directly, but only *through* a symbol—a word or linguistic expression. Hence, I have no way of knowing your meaning except

8

by the language you use to express it; I can't possibly tell what you *mean* except by what you *say*. There is only one exception: when I am the speaker, I presumably know my own thought directly (through consciousness) and can, if I wish, compare it with the means I use to signify it to others. But in the case of other people, I know their thought only by the linguistic forms they have chosen to express it.

Any contrary assumption would be equivalent to assuming the reality of telepathy, which might be defined quite simply as "the communication of thought without the use of language." If such a thing as telepathy exists, it of course lies outside the scope of linguistics.[7] But, even if telepathy is a reality, it cannot be controlled or exercised at will and we must still work out the laws of language without recourse to it. Hence it is surprising to find that the traditional "grammar" as we knew it from English classes in the grades and high school[8] regularly classifies linguistic forms, not by their own characteristics, but (theoretically) according to their *meanings*—persistently, if unconsciously, assuming that it is possible to know the meanings independently of the forms.

When we assume, therefore, that we are classifying the forms of a language by their "meanings," we are really classifying them according to the forms of another language. Even if this were not true, it would be unwise to classify the forms of language according to the structure (if any) of thought. Since it is uncertain whether or how far thought can proceed if not associated with language, and since the language—fully structured in its own way—is presented to each of us before he has done much thinking on his own at all, we must (however reluctantly) admit that language probably shapes thought a good deal more than thought shapes language. The best, indeed the only way to know and study human thought is to observe the expression of the same thought in various languages, until we reach the point where we can allow for and discount the factor of expression.

3. Language and thought

If we avoid the error of thinking that a linguistic form and that amount of thought of which it is the symbol are one and the same, and the opposite error of assuming that we can know the thought directly, independently of the linguistic symbol, we may arrive at a rea-

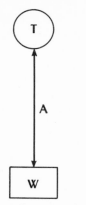

FIGURE 1   Thought and word

T = a segment of thought
A = a psychological association
W = a segment of language
       (e.g. a word)

FIGURE 2   Word and meaning

W_2 is given as "the meaning" of W_1, and may serve for practical purposes, though it *really* symbolizes T_2

sonably sound concept of the relation between language and thought. This is represented diagrammatically in Figure 1, in which the circle is the thought, the square a fragment of language (say a word), and the arrow a psychological association.

Now, as we have seen, when we give someone "the meaning" of a word, we are merely offering another symbol which may be more familiar to him. This may be diagramed by Figure 2, in which W_1 is the word whose meaning was not known—that is, the person in question did not associate it with a specific thought or concept[9]—and W_2 is another word in the same language which is offered to him as "the meaning."

But of course W_2 has a meaning of its own, which is not identical with the meaning of W_1, though the two may overlap almost completely. No language, however, will tolerate two words having exactly the same meaning; that would be a waste of material, and languages are normally highly efficient instruments, the product of centuries of development. That a language will not permit two words to have identical meanings can be shown by the fact that when the situation does accidentally arise—say through the borrowing by one language from another of a word which really means the same as one of its own words—the two words soon differentiate themselves: perhaps one begins to grow obsolete, or each supplants the other in a particular region, or each develops a distinct "shade of meaning."[10]

How, then, do we learn the meanings of new words? A start is made in the manner shown in Figure 2, which gives us an approximation of the meaning; this approximation is then refined by observing the contexts in which W_1 is used, until the specific significance of W_1 is clear.

In other words, the meanings of the other constituents of expressions containing W_1 limit what the meaning of W_1 can be; or, to put this in still another way, the "meaning" of a word is, to a certain extent, *how it can be used*. When you know the linguistic situations in which you can apply this word and those in which you cannot (at least, not without surprising, amusing or confusing native speakers), you know the meaning. Sometimes a person uses a word quite wrongly, thinking the meaning is something quite different from what it really is, yet we know "what he means" from the context in which he uses the word. The lover who said of his sweetheart, "I love her to *diffraction*," did not puzzle his audience, who knew he meant "distraction."

Still another approach to the meaning is the process of *definition*. To convey the meaning of W_1, we supply W_2, whose meaning is similar to or includes the meaning of W_1; then, by additional linguistic expressions, we enlarge or narrow the "meaning" (i.e., applicability) of W_2 until it is identical with that of W_1. "A bear," we say, "is a carnivorous mammal with a massive body and a short tail." Here *bear* is W_1 and *mammal* is W_2. If this definition process is imperfectly carried out, your concept corresponding to W_1 may have varying degrees of vagueness, to the point where any of several words would mean the same thing to you.[11] This is one of the ways in which a native speaker's knowledge of his own language may be improved. (See Chapter XV, 4.)

We generally make the mistake of assuming that human thought is rigidly compartmentalized, and that the language used by a given person reflects this rigid structure in such a way that each unit of the language corresponds to a compartment of the thought. As we have seen, the truth is more likely the reverse of this—that the structure of the language tends to influence the structure of the thought.

A person who cannot really speak more than one language can proceed without challenge on this erroneous assumption; but it leads us into all sorts of difficulties when we endeavor to compare languages.

This can be shown by Figure 3. Let W_1 be a French word, and W_2, W_4 and W_6 be, respectively, the Spanish, German and English words usually given in their respective languages as "the meaning" of the French word. In some cases, as shown by W_2, two words may match so well that it is almost possible to say that one can always and everywhere be translated by the other. Even so, there is almost always some-

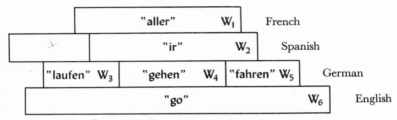

FIGURE 3 Content range among languages

Though *aller* and *ir* match very closely, Spanish says *está bien* where French says *ça va* and German says *es geht*. In English, German or French, "the watch won't *go*" requires W_6, W_4 or $W_?$; but Spanish says *no funciona*.

place where W_2 will not translate W_1, either because W_1 has a meaning not included in the range of meanings of W_2 (using the term "meaning" here in the sense of "potential contexts"), or because W_1 has one or two uses which W_2 would not render.

In our next language, the thought expressed by W_1 is regarded as three distinct concepts, expressed by the words W_3, W_4 and W_5. Hence, writers in this language will say that the French word W_1 has three "meanings," while to the user of French it has only one. But in a third language, a single word may cover all that W_1 covers, and a great deal more besides, including all that W_3 and W_5 express. In this case, it becomes the translator's constant problem to choose whether to translate W_6 by W_3, W_4 or W_5; and this may prompt translators into the language containing W_3, W_4, and W_5 to say that the language containing W_6 has a "poor vocabulary lacking in differentiation."

Because different languages have different structures, a translator cannot hope to reproduce the structure of the original in his translation, using the same number of units (words and sentences) and always translating the same word by the same word. In this sense, the Italian saying *traduttore traditore* ("Every translator is a traitor") is quite right. Because European languages are all closely related, we can often translate from one to another in almost identical structure. It is only by virtue of this circumstance that we have come to feel that the nearer one can get to such a translation the more accurate it is, and, by the same

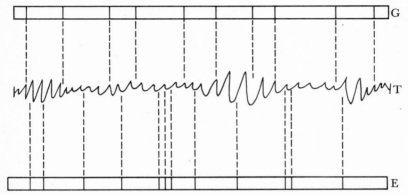

FIGURE 4   Thought, expression, and translation
(The dotted lines represent projection of the segmentation of the language onto the thought.)

G (= German)

E (= English)

T (= thought)

token, that one may be allowed to depart from "literal" translation only when the result is incomprehensible, or English so painful as to be no English at all. Teachers often ask on examinations for a "literal," not an "accurate" translation. When an expression in a given language cannot be translated word by word into ours, we call it an idiom ("peculiarity") of that language.

Let T stand for a certain thought, E for its expression in English, and G for its expression in German (see Fig. 4). The thought, T, is a continuous ebb and flow, not divided nor divisible into parts. Both E and G are faithful expressions of T: Hence E is the translation of G, and *vice versa*. But in this case the mathematical principle that things equal to the same thing are equal to each other does not hold, because the language *represents,* but is not identical with the thought. The speaker of

13

either E or G tends to project the structure of his language on the thought and to presume that this is the only possible structure of his thought. Thus it may be said that many of his notions about thought and reality are suggested and limited by the language he uses—unless, through having learned to use several, he has gained independence of any.

Because E and G happen to be closely related, their structures happen to have a general similarity, and it is possible to make a conversion from G to E without reference to T. From the message so constructed in E, it may be possible to perceive T, and then alter the lame and awkward "translation" into E so as to read better in the latter language. This is the process traditionally taught in schools under the title of "learning German." Many prefer to read foreign classics in this kind of "translation" because, while scarcely worthy of the name of translation, it does give them ideas about the structure of G which they cannot find out in any other way.

The independence and nonstructurability of thought is further shown by the fact that not only can both E and G represent T, but different structures in E (for example, $E_1, E_2, E_3 \ldots$) could also express it, though perhaps not equally well. In the difference between E_1 and E_2 lies the range of *style,* and the distinctions between the English of an average native speaker and the English of a great writer.

4. The nature of words

From all that has preceded, we can derive another formula to show, in graphic form, the precise field and scope of scientific linguistics. In Figure 5 the term *physical element* means the succession of sounds produced by the vocal organs, and the term *semantic element* means the segment of thought (insofar as thought can be conceived as segmented) corresponding to it. Evidently, if we were to study the physical element exclusively, without any reference to the semantic element, we would be studying a branch of physics. Should we limit ourselves to study of the semantic element, we should be studying human thought, and would be in the field of psychology. What the linguist studies is the compound of the two constituents (word in Fig. 5): sounds, *insofar as they express meaning;* concepts, *insofar as they are expressed in language.* The French terms in parentheses are those in which De Saussure

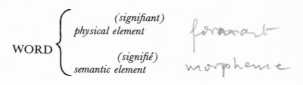

FIGURE 5   The scope of linguistics

expressed this point.[12] The word *signifiant* means "that which signifies," and *signifié* means "that which is signified." Contemporary linguistic terminology would call the physical element the *formant* and the semantic element the *morpheme.*

It is possible for either component of the linguistic unit to change somewhat without destroying the identity of the unit. In this possibility lie the dynamics of language. Thus, the poet Chaucer probably pronounced the word *take* as *tah-kuh* [ta:kə]; the pronunciation (physical element) has changed a good deal, but today's *tayk* evidently occupies approximately the same place in modern English that Chaucer's *tah-kuh* did in his, and we can therefore call it the same word.

On the other hand, the semantic element of a word may change, and we would then say that the word has acquired "a new meaning"; perhaps the original "meaning" will die out, in which case we would say that "the meaning has changed." For example, the word *want* used to mean what we would now express by the word *need* (as it still often does in England; e.g., "Man wants but little here below"), and *nice* used to mean *precise,* which meaning still survives in the phrase "a nice distinction."

Both these processes go on all the time. Indeed, there seems to be an innate tendency for the semantic element to subdivide and multiply itself—reflecting, perhaps, the quicksilver nature of thought. A given language will have a word for a long-necked bird, the *crane.* Then a machine for lifting things is invented, and it will strike people that its tall beam looks something like a long-necked crane; hence, by a "figure of speech," that, too, becomes "a crane." The figure of speech called "metaphor" seems to be found in all languages. Almost all speak of the "foot" of a mountain, the "brow" of a hill, of "headlands" and "guts" (in the maritime sense). We call a faucet a stop*cock* or pet*cock,* German

15

says Wasser*hahn,* French *robinet,* probably because the device bears a faint resemblance to a cock flourishing his comb.

This process is possible because a metaphorical meaning, by the nature of metaphor, is usually applied to something in reality quite different from the original, and the two uses will rarely conflict: who would expect a feathered crane in a shipyard, or a crowing rooster at the end of a water-pipe?

Nonetheless, a case could be made for the point of view that the original word is now two words, homophones. To decide what is a word is really much more difficult than is commonly supposed. Lexicographers follow the principle that as long as they see a possibility that different "senses" could have developed from each other, they have the same word (and often list the meanings in the presumed order of development); otherwise, the words are different, but homophones of each other. Thus *bear* = "to carry" and *bear* = "to give birth" are regarded as the same word, but *bear* = "an animal" is regarded as a different word (though a homophone) and *bare* = "naked" is considered altogether distinct, having a different etymology.

Sometimes words get new "meanings" by a sort of erosion. Prior to 1880, the word *car* in English meant a kind of carriage—as in "jaunting-car"—and *Wagen* in German meant "a farm cart." When the automobile was invented, a term was coined (Greek *autós* "self" and Latin *mōbilis* "movable"), and such expressions as "horseless carriage" and "gas buggy" were also available. In German, logical compounds were made: *Kraftwagen* ("power wagon") for an automobile, *Lastwagen* ("load wagon") for a truck, *Frachtwagen* ("freight wagon") for a railroad freight car.

But soon automobiles became so common that even a three-syllable word was too cumbersome; hence the Germans tacitly dropped the qualifier in each of the words mentioned, leaving *Wagen* to inherit the sense of *Kraftwagen,* thus adding a new sense to the original *Wagen.* As the original sense now began to drop into obsolescence, the change was complete, and *Wagen* has now become the common word for "car."

In the same way, Italian uses *macchina* ("machine") for both "automobile" and "camera" (originally *macchina fotografica*). The latter expression was much too long for everyday use, so the qualifying adjective was dropped and the single word acquired the meaning of the combination. No confusion arises, since you can't fill a photographic *macchina* with gas, nor buy film for a four-wheeled *macchina.*

In a language which borrows freely from other languages one may find two words which really have the same meaning, being the equivalents of each other in the two languages. In such a case the two words will, as we have seen[13], differentiate themselves, and perhaps divide up the field formerly signified by the native word. Thus *military* and *soldierly* are both *militärisch* in German—itself a borrowed word, in the absence of which *warlike, soldierly* and *military* would all be *kriegerisch*.

It is certainly an advantage to a language to have clusters of words like this for different facets of a concept, and English is one of the richest in this respect, having (because of its high tolerance to borrowing) more than twice as many words as most of its European cousins. But there are two limitations: first, free borrowing produces homophones, sometimes to an awkward degree; second, relatively few users of any language employ even a fraction of its resources. Thus, while it is possible to write more precisely and at the same time more colorfully in English than in most other languages, the average speaker of French may probably express himself more precisely than the average speaker of English.

Notes to Chapter I

1. Formerly the science was known as *comparative philology* (see IV, 1); but the term *philologist* is today somewhat out of date, except as referring to a comparative as distinguished from a descriptive linguist. Besides, in Europe the term "philology" includes the study and criticism of literature. For the newer linguistics, the term *phonology* is popular in Europe, but runs counter to an established usage in English restricting it to the study of sounds.

2. De Saussure, *Cours de linguistique générale*, 111.

3. That of the "neo-grammarians." See IV, 2.

4. The "organs of speech" (if we may use that term: see XIII, 3) are the lips, teeth, tongue, palate, uvula, mouth cavity, nasal sinus, fauces, pharynx and larynx with the vocal cords. In a more remote way, the breathing equipment (lungs, etc.) may also be cited.

5. Cf. Susanne Langer, *Philosophy in a New Key,* 99.

6. The play was *Salomé,* which was refused a production license in 1893; see *Dictionary of National Biography,* under "Wilde."

7. Despite quite a good deal of research, notably by J. B. Rhine of Duke University, the existence of telepathy has not yet been demonstrated to the satisfaction of scientists, but some are willing to concede its possibility. It is inter-

esting to note that most of the "ghost stories" and other psychic phenomena—apparitions, visions, and so on—which do not seem to be hoaxes could be explained quite logically with the hypothesis of telepathy. For example, suppose someone plants a thought telepathically in the mind of someone else, and the "receiver" realizes that it is a communication from someone else and not a thought of his own: he would probably think he had heard a voice speaking—in his own language, of course. It would not be a far step to imagine that he saw a human or quasi-human form to go with the voice. Furthermore, if anyone could project his thought telepathically to a polyglot audience, he would no doubt be reported to have been speaking *several languages at once.*

8. See III, 2; cf. Fries, *Structure of English,* 18.

9. For example, many native speakers of English do not have a really clear concept of what is meant by *democracy, education, intolerance,* and similar rather abstract terms. A story is told of a politician who, being asked where he stood on *integration,* replied cautiously that he was "for it in moderation."

10. For illustrations of the first case, we may cite *hale* vs. *whole, savior/healer;* of the second, *bag/sack, underpass/subway, waistcoat/vest;* of the third, *soldiery/militia, ward/guard, guarantee/warranty.* Pairs of words like *ward* and *guard, guarantee* and *warranty*—which are really the same word, now different in form because of different avenues of borrowing—are called *doublets.*

11. Certainly the average speaker does not distinguish colors as, for example, an artist does, so that *russet, carmine, scarlet, oxblood* are to him all substantially identical with *red.*

12. De Saussure, 99 ff., 158–59.

13. See above, pages 10–11.

Supplementary Readings for Chapter I
(Full information is given in the Bibliography)

Fries, *Structure of English,* 1–8.
Gray, *Foundations of Language,* 12–44.
De Saussure, *Cours de linguistique générale,* 23–37, 36–40, 97–99.
Carroll, *The Study of Language,* 83–92, 196–205.
Sturtevant, *Linguistic Change,* 23–24, 85–97.
Sapir, *Language,* 3–23.
Bloomfield, *Language,* 139–157.

Chapter II

FURTHER BASIC
LINGUISTIC CONCEPTS

What has been said regarding the different aspects of the relations between language (or its individual units) and the thought which they express is the foundation for much of the material that follows. At this point it is necessary to define as precisely as possible certain other terms commonly used in linguistics.

1. Native language and first language

Among the terms used to describe language and its operations, "native language" is one of the commonest. Its definition, as applied to most people, is exceedingly simple: it is the first and only language ever acquired. But, if we allow for a degree of linguistic accomplishment not uncommon even in the United States among persons born elsewhere, the situation becomes a good deal more complicated.

It may well happen that a person who started life with one language —say Italian—switches to another. Someone born in Italy is brought to the United States at the age of six; by the time he is sixteen he uses only English, and remembers Italian only vaguely. Which now is his native language, Italian or English? If we say the latter, the essential note of "native" language must be something other than being first; yet how can we call the former his native language, if he barely speaks it, or does not remember it at all?

It is necessary, therefore, to divide this term into two.

First Language. The importance of the *first* language is that it is the only one which we can be sure *was learned without interference from any*

19

other language. This is a matter of great importance, for it appears that the first language learned invariably interferes in some degree with subsequent ones, and introduces a kind of variation from their norms which no native speaker would make.

Even in the exceptional case where no trace of this interference is noticeable, it is rather the result of removal of something once present than of its never having been there. This therefore casts a shadow of possible lack of authenticity—of possible deviation from native tradition—on any but the first language, and thus proportionately enhances the importance of the first.

For any language is essentially the last link in a chain of tradition stretching back thousands of years, perhaps to the very beginning of man; and if that chain is broken in any way, there is no mending it. Even revived Hebrew is essentially a different language from the ancient Hebrew whose existence had ceased except in books. (Modern Gaelic, however, is not necessarily different from ancient Gaelic, for there has never been a period when the native tradition did not continue in a body of monolingual speakers.)

But, as we have seen, the *first* language is not always identical with the language always or generally used, and this introduces another important concept: *the language in which one thinks,* that is, the language which one normally associates with his thinking in the manner already discussed.

Can one think in different languages? Certainly; the only way really to *speak* a language, in fact, is to think in it while speaking it—to associate its words and forms directly with one's concepts and thoughts (G ↔ T in Fig. 4), rather than try to reproduce in its forms the structures of another language. In other words, real "translation" is not translation at all (in the usual sense of that word), but re-expression of the thought in the target language.

Can we think without any language? This would seem *a priori* to be possible; for one thing, it would surely seem that a certain amount of thought independent of language must take place before a baby learns his first language. Since, however, thought is associated with *some* language upwards of 98 per cent of the time, it is probable that we could not think for any long period or in any complicated manner without the support of language. This question is still to be thoroughly investigated.

Language of thought. Even in the case of one who has learned two or more languages, it is not likely that there will be any doubt as to the language in which he thinks when not speaking to anyone, unless he has achieved a proficiency in the use of his acquired language virtually equal to that he exhibits in the use of his first.

If an English speaker is conversing with a Frenchman who speaks English much better than the English speaker does French, common sense suggests that in the interest of efficient communication, English be used; and it is exceedingly unlikely that one would use for one's private, unspoken thought, anything other than the language of which one was most thoroughly master. Should an acquired language become more familiar to a person than his first language, it could, of course, supplant the first as his primary vehicle of thought; but note that, because it *is* an acquired language, he might still have a foreigner's accent in it, and other traces of the fact that he is not genuinely in the tradition of that language.

Hence, if we define the language of thought as the language in which one thinks to oneself, when not speaking to anyone—when, in other words, there is complete freedom of choice as to which language to use—we can call this the second most important language an individual knows and the one which, for practical purposes, is "his language." It would be very rare, even for an accomplished linguist, to have more than one "language of thought" in this sense.[1]

2. "Living" and "dead" languages

It can now be seen that the term *native language,* as commonly used, means *both* the "first language" and the "language of thought," *when these are the same.* What we usually mean by a "native speaker" of a language, therefore, is (since here the *authenticity* of the language is the most important note) a "first speaker." What we really mean by the term *living language,* however, is one which is still the language of thought (not necessarily, in all cases, the first language), of a significant number of people. A language is "dead" when there no longer remains a substantial number (preferably forming a community) who use it as their language of thought—some of them, at least, using it also as a first language.[2]

From the sorting out of linguistic concepts represented by these definitions, we can draw a thought or two about the revival of languages. Irish, for example, is not really a revived language, since there have always been and still are some tens of thousands of people who use it as their language of thought, at least 10 per cent of them using it also as a first language.[3] In linguistic terms, the object of the Irish government's language-revival efforts is to make Irish the *first language* of the population of Ireland (or at least to ensure the production of an increasing number of first speakers), and to have English become a second language; in short, the Irish citizen of the future should be bilingual in Irish and English, with Irish his first language.

This, to be sure, has not yet been accomplished; but many thousands of Irishmen have been made bilingual in English and Irish, with English as the first language. This is certainly a step toward the goal; what needs to be done now is to make sure that Irish is mastered almost as well as English, and to facilitate the occasions when a bilingual group which has been using English, but could use Irish equally well, switches over.

perhaps a renaissance In the case of Hebrew or Latin, however, no genuine "revival" is possible, since there has been a period during which there were no first speakers; hence the tradition is broken, even if some should make either one a language of thought.

3. Linguistic change

To speak of languages as "living" and "dead" introduces a metaphor which can be carried forward. Languages are "born" out of other languages. A language is constantly undergoing change—call this "growth," if you like—and after a certain amount of this change we may find that one language (e.g., Latin) has gradually developed into another (in this case Italian). We shall see later (see Chapter V, 2) that almost all the languages of Europe have developed in this manner out of a single ancestor language spoken before 1500 B.C.

When the linguistic system constituting a language has become so altered as to be in essence a different system, and no one any longer uses the old system as a language of thought—nor are there any more first speakers—we may say that the language has "died." In a sense, though, languages, like old soldiers, don't die but only fade away. The study of the changes that take place in a language over a span of time is often called *historical* or *diachronic* linguistics.

Two other important basic terms of linguistics were originated by the great linguist Ferdinand de Saussure: they are *langue* and *parole*. In French, *langue* means "language" and *parole* means "word" or "speech." As De Saussure used the terms, what is actually spoken is *parole,* while *langue* is the system or code.

No one ever hears *langue* in reality; *langue* is in the long run really an abstraction from innumerable acts of *parole*. Yet each act of *parole* is performed in conformity to the norms and rules of the system called *langue,* for otherwise it would not be meaningful and therefore would not be *parole*. *Langue* is like the rules of a game; they do not in themselves constitute a game, yet no individual contest would be a game if the players were not conforming to a set of rules previously known to each.

4. Dialects and accents

The common opinion about dialects may be summed up pretty well in the proposition that "a dialect is a corrupted form of a language." It is often supposed that dialects arise because "ignorant" and "low-class" people do not "learn to speak correctly" and therefore deform the pure language which they have received into a "dialect" by "drawling" and "swallowing their words" and "articulating carelessly."

The scientific fact is quite different, except insofar as the term "dialect" has to be defined relative to the term "language." No definition of "dialect" can be formulated that will not also be a definition of "language." The best that can be said is that "dialect" is whatever is *not* "language." We seem to be in the position of the eighteenth-century musical dictionary which defined a violin as a "small viola," and then defined a viola as a "large violin."

The whole situation can be greatly simplified by assuming that what people actually *speak* are "dialects"; then, when we observe that a certain number of dialects are very similar to each other, we can group their similarities as a "language." Indeed, what we call a "language" may have achieved the status in precisely this way. To take a simplified illustration: Latin changed, in Italy, into Northern, Central, and

FIGURE 6   Medieval Italian dialect groups

Southern Italian dialects. In the Middle Ages the Northern and South-ern group were so different from each other as to be frequently mutu-ally incomprehensible; but a speaker of the Central group could prob-ably have understood either to the extent of, say, perhaps 75 per cent (see Fig. 6). The area in which all three agreed could be called "the Italian language," but it would have been so limited a concept as to be of little use.

However, as trade revived in the later Middle Ages, a need for communication over a wider area naturally favored the tendency of both Northern and Southern speakers to find a common ground in some Central dialect (Tuscan, as it happened), avoiding those forms of their native dialect used only in the North or South, and acquiring Central forms in their place with little difficulty. A Central dialect thus became the standard "Italian language"—with reference to which the others are dialects.

But a standard language may also arise in another way: any of the individual dialects (i.e., closely related languages) spoken over a given geographical area may be elevated to prominence by prestige or politics, or both. If the greatest writers in the language happen to have written in X dialect, it is likely that X dialect will acquire prestige and become "standard." (When writing the portions of their plays which were to be sung, the Greek dramatists of Attica used to compose deliberately in the dialect of Sparta, because the Doric dialect had so much prestige in that form of composition.)

The speech of the locale of the king's court or the capital of the nation is naturally bound to acquire prestige, to the point where citizens from a locality where people talk differently endeavor to adopt the speech of the big city and erase their local characteristics. In time, perhaps, the whole country will come to consider that dialect the "correct" and "standard" form of the language. Thus, the norm in Spain is by tradition the Castilian dialect as spoken in Madrid, and the "Queen's English," or London dialect, has always been more or less the norm for British speech.

When nationalism enters the picture, what might be regarded as the natural state of linguistic affairs may be still further altered. People speaking a language in no way related to the standard language of their nation may suppose that their native *patois* is somehow a deformation of it. Some of the "dialects" of French might equally well be called dialects of Italian, and probably would be if the border were fifty miles further west. Lowland Scottish would have been a national language if Scotland's national independence had not been extinguished in 1707; indeed, had the fortunes of Mary Stuart been different, London English might today be a dialect of it!

Where there is a strong central government, the national language in whatever is considered its standard form will be taught in all schools, and this may result in the gradual dying out of dialects. But local variation will still remain, since the people of the provinces will not have reproduced the standard perfectly: as long as the dialect is the first language, it will interfere in the learning of the standard, and introduce features which may persist even when the standard (or the local version thereof) becomes the first language.[4]

Language may be a political issue in itself. For example, when one nation conquers another, the language of the conquered people may serve as a re-awakener and sustainer of the national consciousness, and it may become necessary to try to stamp it out—as with Gaelic in Ireland.[5] Conversely, a country which gains independence will also endeavor to develop or re-establish a national language, even going so far as to revive a dead one, as with Hebrew in Israel.

What is called an *isogloss* makes a boundary between adjacent dialects. Isoglosses are plotted by first determining a number of features peculiar to each dialect—for example, the pronunciation of *yes* as *eyuh* and of *thirty* as *thutty,* characteristic of northern New England. For each such feature, a line is drawn connecting the last towns in which it is found to be dominant before the researcher passes into the area where it is not found at all, or only rarely.

Each isogloss plots only one feature; but as a dialect is really an inventory of special features (deviating from the "standard"), isoglosses tend to follow the same paths, so that one dialect (or language) will be clearly marked off from another by a bundle of them. They do not always coincide completely, however; parts of southern New England say *thutty* but not *eyuh.* This gives the researcher the opportunity to draw complicated maps of subdialects (see Fig. 7). Where regional dialects differ very little from each other, perhaps almost exclusively in pronunciation, we would be more likely to speak of an "accent" than a "dialect."

Within the area in which that aggregate of dialects called a language is spoken, not only geographical regions, but also strata of society are reflected in speech. Certain pronunciations, words and expressions, for instance, unknown to the ignorant, are used among the educated. Members of a work-group tend to develop terms specific to themselves—so that we have the jargon of railroad men, restaurant workers, circus people, students, and even teenagers. These latter "dialects" consist mostly in special vocabulary; social levels tend more to

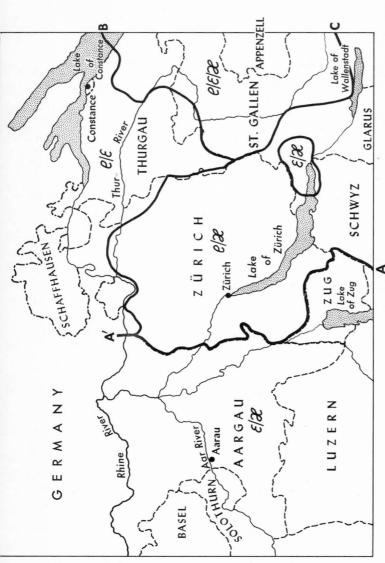

FIGURE 7   Isoglosses and dialect areas

This map reports the number and distribution of short-*e* vowel phonemes in the area mapped. West of the isogloss A-A', *Vetter* and *Wetter* have the same vowel (viz. [ε]), but *Wespe* has [æ]. Between A-A' and B-C, below A'-B, *Wespe* has the same pronunciation, but *Vetter* and *Wetter* are pronounced with [e] (except for an enclave of ε/æ in southwestern St. Gallen). In the area north of A'-B, *Vetter* and *Wetter* are pronounced as in Zürich, but *Wespe* is pronounced with [ε]. East of B-C there is a 3-vowel system, and *Vetter, Wetter* and *Wespe* are distinct, each having its own vowel. (This map is based on W. G. Moulton, "The Vowel Systems of Northern Switzerland," *Word* XVI, 2 – Aug., 1960 – 155-82.)

27

be reflected in differences of pronunciation (though vocabulary differences are also noticeable). The alternative pronunciations of *vase* and *tomato* are supposed to reflect social differences.[6]

Even the same individual will vary his speech slightly, according to the situation in which he finds himself, from *slang* to *colloquial* to *formal*. Each of these could meet the definition of "a language," but they overlap to such a high degree that it is preferable to consider them three dialects—or, in this case, "levels of usage"—of one "language."

Modern linguistics could draw a fairly precise distinction between "language" and "dialect"; but it would not reflect common usage at all. Language is, it will be remembered, a *system*. On this basis we can say that, as long as we have variants of the same system, they are dialects, and we are not concerned with which one is or should be the prestige dialect or "standard"; when the system itself is different, we have a different language. Obviously, by this definition many systems of speech now called languages would be dialects, and *vice versa*. Also, drawing the line in a given case—deciding whether there was a different system or a variant of the same one—could be exceedingly difficult. But this definition would work in time as well as in space, enabling us to tell (if we have sufficient records) when a certain village ceased speaking a dialect of Latin and began speaking a dialect of Italian.

Why do we have dialects? Wouldn't it be simpler and more efficient if everyone spoke alike? Simpler and more efficient, certainly, but (such is the perversity of human nature) hardly natural. It is well known that every natural phenomenon is characterized by bewildering variety; no two snowflakes are exactly alike; and it is a principle of philosophy that everything which exists in reality is absolutely unique. Language, too, has its built-in dynamics resulting in constant change: the meanings of words shift or subdivide (see Chapter I, 4); sounds are modified to permit more rapid speech; this interferes with grammatical patterns, and some are altered to restore consistency, and so on. Furthermore, it seems probable that no one reproduces a language exactly as it was spoken by the persons from whom he learned it.

The character of the language of a given person in given circumstances in a given locality is thus the resultant of a balance of innumerable exceedingly complex forces. On the one hand, there is a tendency to individualize language and make it unique; on the other is the limitation that, if it becomes so personal as to belong to one individual alone, it is no longer language, for it is not a means of communication. The compromise is to develop (or retain when developed) features unique within relatively small communities, which tend to accentuate the feeling of membership and to exclude outsiders; but to eliminate peculiarities (however acquired) that tend to impede the desired amount of communication with the world at large.

Social mobility evidently works as a centripetal force in language: the wider the circle within which communication is needed, the more local and class individuality must be suppressed; the narrower it is, the more individualism may be permitted. It is no surprise, therefore, that during the Middle Ages, when few ever traveled far beyond their birthplace, dialects proliferated; whereas, during the present century, when social and physical mobility are both at a record high, the tendency is to adopt standards or find speech compromises, and local dialects subside—even in places like Germany and France, where a rich variety of dialects is a historical heritage.

If three brothers married to three sisters—all first and native speakers of the same language—were to settle a previously uninhabited land, there would still be the nucleus of future dialects. The three brothers might speak a form of the language slightly different from that spoken by the three sisters; each brother and sister could be shown to have—in infinitesimal degree, of course—a slightly different way of speaking from his or her siblings. The children of these couples will not reproduce their parents' speech exactly. After scores of generations have passed, the descendants who migrated across the mountains might have lost contact with those who stayed behind, and might have developed localisms unknown in the older province, and the others would probably by then have developed some of their own not heard beyond the mountains.

The actual history of any language would be a lengthy continuation of these processes and many others, and would clearly show that the linguistic situation over any geographical area is an exceedingly complex picture, the result of dozens, if not hundreds of influences. It is naive to suppose that each speaker or group of speakers has deviated from the same norm. But if there is a manifest or demonstrable relationship among all the forms of speech in use over this area, it means that all of them must derive ultimately from one language or dialect—not a "standard" or "correct" language recently elevated to that prestige by kings or schoolmasters, but a true linguistic ancestor of long before, perhaps more than a thousand years before, which was probably in its turn a dialect of some language then current, possibly (but not necessarily) the prestige dialect or "standard."

In the long run, then, the reason for dialects is linguistic fission—the fact that, for many reasons, a single language inevitably develops into several or many languages (or dialects). This process is apparently of the nature of language, and has operated for thousands of years. It has naturally occurred to many scholars to wonder whether it is not a clue to the ultimate origin of language.

5. The origin of language

It has been pointed out[7] that a bylaw of the Linguistic Society of Paris constitutes anyone *ipso facto* out of order who wishes to read before it a paper on the origin of language. This is a scientifically sound attitude for, whenever and however language originated, one thing is sure: it was at a time so remote that there is not a shred of evidence on which to reconstruct any part of the story. But a word or two should be said in any serious linguistic work to counter the arrant nonsense on this subject which is still circulated in Sunday-supplement science features.

According to this pseudo-evolutionary foolishness, based on nothing but rampant imagination, language originated among our caveman ancestors when someone tried to tell the hitherto speechless tribe about the wolf he had killed, and was forced to give an imitation of the wolf, so that *owoo-owoo* became the word for "wolf" (this is called the "bow-wow" theory); or when he hit his thumb with the mallet while shaping a stone spear, so that *ouch* became the word for "pain" (the "ouch-ouch" theory); and similar fairy stories.

What needs to be pointed out is that there *is* evidence against several of these hypotheses. For one thing, we are *not* descended from the cave man—if by the cave man we mean those prehistoric people whose remains were found in caves in France and Germany. (To assume that the whole human race went through a cave-dwelling stage is another inadequately founded hypothesis.) We know that the Indo-Europeans, from whom most Europeans and their languages are descended, entered Europe proper later than 3000 B.C.; how then could they be descendants of people who had lived in France some thousands of years before? The Basques *could* be descendants of the cave man, likewise the *Tuatha Dé Danann* of old Irish legend, and the people who built Stonehenge and the dolmens and menhirs of Brittany; but not any other present-day Europeans.

As to onomatopoeic theories of the origin of language, note first that in no language is a dog called a "bow-wow" or a cat a "meow." Secondly, it can easily be shown that we hear and imitate the sounds of nature *within the limitations of our first language;* in fact, we cannot reproduce a sound of nature with a sound that is not used in our own language. Thus, to speakers of English it seems obvious that the sound of a bell is *ding-dong;* but to speakers of French, which has no *ng* sound, it cannot be—and as *dindon* is a turkey, a bell is more commonly *tam-tam.* The Spanish hear the same sound as *tín-tín,* the Germans as *bim-bam-bum.* The sound a cat makes is *meow* to us, but *minou-minou* to a French child. In Germany, the cock does not crow *cock-a-doodle-doo,* but *kikeriki;* the dog does not go *bow-wow,* but *wau-wau* (in which the *w* is pronounced as *v* in obedience to German spelling). Since onomatopoeia is influenced by language, it obviously cannot be the source of language.

There is an *a priori* notion that language must have originated from "primitive grunts," and that consequently the tersest and most disjointed expressions we use today represent an earlier stage in the development of the language. Here again, however, scientific study of language reveals that all such expressions are merely fragments from more elaborate expressions containing all the structure of the fully developed language. Thus, when a Frenchman colloquially says *dac,* it is an abbreviation of *d'accord,* which is in turn an abbreviation of *je suis d'accord.* When a German says *guten Tag,* the adjective has an accusative form, showing that it comes from a sentence *ich wünsche Ihnen einen guten Tag;* a polite exclamation like *bitte* is in the first person singular—because it is abbreviated from *ich bitte Ihnen (dass Sie davon nicht sprechen).* Since short forms presuppose developed ones, they cannot be the nucleus of the latter's development.

If we leave off pursuit of these will-o'-the-wisps, originally loosed across our path by, probably, Herbert Spencer, and set ourselves to seeing how far sound reasoning would carry us (undiscouraged by the fact that it will not carry us very far), we find ourselves in possession of three or four solid facts.

First of all, as far back as we can trace the process, every language ever spoken has originated from a previous language, and the lines usually converge: several languages in use at a given time derive from one in use some centuries before. It is therefore not impossible that all the languages of the world descend from a single language; though it is improbable that we shall ever have the data to prove this.

Second, as far as we can ascertain, each first speaker of any language has learned it from his parents, or, in rare cases, from other mature individuals who were already in full possession of its total structure. This poses us a problem analogous to the old riddle, "Which came first, the chicken or the egg?" Before anyone can learn a language, someone has to have learned it.

Third, there is some indication that "immediate" speech preceded "referred" or "displaced" speech (for a full explanation of these terms, see Chapter IX). This would seem to justify what we would assume *a priori*, that language arose from the need of human beings to signal to each other, and from their mental capacity to appreciate symbolism and to construct a system of symbols. The moment they could, by this means, manipulate phenomena not present to the eye, we may say that human language was born. But this leaves us one dilemma—if they were not living in society they would not need language; and how could they have commenced to live in society without it?

Here the data run out, and science abandons us. From here on, any hypothesis is equally possible—and equally unprovable. Let each choose his favorite, and find whither it leads him.

Notes to Chapter II

1. Some would wish to establish the language in which one *dreams* as the "language of thought." It is evident, however, that this is to base the definition on something quite beyond the scope of objective observation, even on the part of the dreamer himself. Of course, we cannot observe objectively the language in which a person is thinking, either; but the subject's own testimony on that point is usually sufficiently reliable, unless he is so proficient in two or more languages as to be really uncertain which one he is using (cf. Weinreich, *Languages in Contact,* 69): but this, also, he can testify to.

2. Cf. Weinreich, *Languages in Contact*, 84; Jackson, *Contributions to the Study of Manx Phonology*, 1–4.

3. Brian O'Cuív, *Irish Dialects and Irish-Speaking Districts*, 31–32.

4. Cf. a forthcoming paper by J. P. Hughes, to be titled "The Irish Language and the Brogue," in *American Speech*.

5. The infamous "Statutes of Kilkenny," enacted by the Anglo-Irish Parliament in 1366, made it a capital offense for an English subject to speak the Irish language. Cf. O'Faoláin, *The Story of Ireland*, 18.

6. It may be said that in the United States [ve^{i}s] and [tə'me^{i}to^u] are the more common pronunciations, and [vɑ:z] and [tə'mɑ:to^u] are generally regarded as somewhat affected.

7. Sturtevant, *Introduction to Linguistic Science*, 40.

Supplementary Readings for Chapter II

De Saussure, *Cours de linguistique générale*, 36–39, 193–97.
Gray, *Foundations of Language*, 40–41.
Weinreich, *Languages in Contact*, 74–82.
Sturtevant, *Linguistic Change*, 146–58.
Sturtevant, *Introduction to Linguistic Science*, 32–37.
Langer, *Philosophy in a New Key*, 94–127.
Whitney, *Life and Growth of Language*, 278–300.

Chapter III

A Brief History of the Study of Language, I: The Pre-Scientific Period

We have already observed (Chapter I) that every man is naturally interested in the questions which linguistics investigates scientifically; what is more, we find that he always has been, at least as far back into the past as records will take us.

To give a complete, detailed account of man's endeavors along this line, therefore, would probably require two sizable volumes—one devoted to the pre-scientific period, and a second to the history of *scientific* linguistics. We shall proceed to try to cover this ground within the confines of two chapters, not, of course, giving anything like a detailed account, but (in keeping with the general aim of this book) seeking only to provide a sort of Baedeker's guide of the route: mentioning very briefly all the important landmarks, and providing references which will enable the reader interested in deepening his knowledge to fill in the details at his leisure, and to the degree of depth he desires.

1. Ancient peoples: Hebrews, Hindus, Greeks and Romans

Probably the oldest record we have, insofar as it is a historical document—and it unquestionably is, to some extent—is the Bible. And in numerous Old Testament passages we see evidences of linguistic curiosity—most frequently concerned with etymology. How often does the Sacred Scribe pause to observe, "and it was called thus because . . . ," followed by the supposed etymology of the name.[1] Indeed, the writers of the Bible were the world's first punsters (testimony, perhaps, to the Lord's approval of, or at least forgiveness for punning), and the Sacred Books unquestionably contain some of the world's first (and possibly worst) puns.

The name of Adam (which means "a man": Hebrew ʔādām) may not have been an intentional pun; it may, in fact, have been a mistranslation to make it a name. But when Moses asked who was in the burning bush (*Exodus* iii, 14), the answer *'eHYeH'aSHeR'eHYeH* ("I am that I am" or "I am One Who is") was certainly an intentional anagram of "Jehovah" (YaHWeH), the unspeakable name of God: what the voice actually said—though perhaps Moses, too grave to be a punster, missed the implication—was "I am Jehovah"—"I am God." (Upon this passage a religion has been founded, the *I Am* religion.)

Nor is this sort of thing confined to the Old Testament: did not Christ say, "Thou art a rock, and upon this Rock I will build my church"? The pun in Aramaic on the name *Kefas* (Caiaphas) continues in Greek, Latin and French (πέτρος, Πέτρον; petram, Petrum; pierre, Pierre), but finally disappears in English.[2]

The Bible is literally full of such passages, and though many have been obscured by ages of translation and retranslation, anyone devoted to his Scripture can find a large number of them, even when reading the text in a modern language.

However, the interest of the ancient Hebrews was, as we have seen, directed mainly toward matters of etymology, and it was to be very long before the conditions necessary for accurate etymology would come into being. It was otherwise with the ancient Hindus, who were, perhaps, the most scientific grammarians we shall meet with until modern times. These people, among the first of the Indo-Europeans to emigrate from the original homeland of that nation, probably arrived in India about 1500 B.C. and overcame a native population (of whom the inhabitants of southern India today are probably the descendants). The attention of their scholars (whose title was *pandit*, whence the English word "pundit") was inevitably directed to the ancient religious rituals which they had preserved by oral tradition from the time when they first arrived in India, rituals whose increasing archaism more and more demanded explanation.

The "pundits" devised for the writing of Sanskrit a syllabic script—later an alphabet—based on the Semitic syllabary (see VII, 3). Unlike the other nations which adopted this script, however, they did not follow a policy of making only unavoidable modifications, but shaped it into the most accurate description of the sound system of a language to be available for more than two thousand years. The Sanskrit alphabet (Fig. 21, page 131) is, indeed, very nearly a statement of the phonology of the Indo-European language.

The Hindus seem not to have been much given to speculation on the philosophy of language; *their* orientation was rather, as we have said, toward description of classic usage and elucidation of the discrepancies between it and contemporary speech, both as a guide to understanding the classical texts, and as an aid to approximating their style in one's own composition. The *Sūtras* ("Instructions") of Pāṇini (fourth century B.C.) constitute the first known formal "grammar" of any language, being a detailed analysis of classical Sanskrit which at once became— and still remains—authoritative. (Like another great summary of a very different subject, however—the *Summa theologica* of St. Thomas Aquinas—it was originally written in a form so highly abbreviated as to be practically a code, and can be understood only with the help of a commentary on Pāṇini, the *Mahābhāṣya,* compiled by Patañjali about 150 B.C.)

A very early linguistic experiment, presumably carried out in Egypt in the ninth or tenth century B.C., is recorded by the Greek historian Herodotus, who tells (ii. 2–15) how King Psammetichus of Egypt disagreed with the Phrygians over which of their nations and national languages was older. According to the story, the king of Egypt had two babies taken from their mother at birth and brought to a shepherd's mountain hut, where they were left to develop through their first weeks of life with no company save that of the flock of sheep which provided milk for their nourishment, and the occasional visits of the shepherd who came to attend to their wants—but he, as the king had carefully arranged, was mute. The shepherd was instructed to report to the king at once the first time the baby boys made any sounds that seemed to be an effort to communicate by speech.

After some time, the shepherd came excitedly to relate that, as he entered the hut, both children had stretched out their hands to him and cried, "bekos; bekos." This word meant nothing in Egyptian, but the Phrygians claimed it meant "bread" in their language, so Psammetichus conceded their claim. He need not have done so. True, the

36

children had never encountered any human being from whom they could have learned the word. But think—what had the *sheep* been saying all the time?

The Egyptian king is to be praised for his spirit of experimentation, and still more for his willingness to abide by the result of a scientific experiment—which must have been hard for a man to whom no human being dared offer denial. But the question of the origin of language will not be solved in this way. Either the child will speak the language of whoever first takes care of it, or, if *not* cared for, it will die. This, we are told, is what happened when Emperor Frederick the Second (1194–1250) of Germany and the Holy Roman Empire tried the same experiment.

The same considerations apply to the cases occasionally reported of children found in a wilderness, presumably raised by friendly animals—by wolves or apes—and presumably speaking the "language" of these animals. The fact that they survived presupposes that they were cared for by some human being long enough to have learned his or her language—perhaps imperfectly and not recognizably, perhaps partially forgotten since last contact—but at all events a preexisting, fully developed language, never one originated by the child itself; still less any "animal language," no such thing having ever been demonstrated by any proof worthy of belief.

It was the Greeks, however, who more than any other ancient people were responsible for the main outlines of a body of teaching about language. This comprised a more or less scientific classification of observed facts about the Greek language, and a good deal of philosophical speculation on the nature of language, which by a series of accidents came to be enshrined as *the* "science of language," authoritative, all-inclusive and final, not subject to addition or correction: to challenge it in any part was both to reveal ignorance and to strike a blow for the forces of darkness and evil.

The Greeks, we will remember, were the first great philosophers of the West; Greek thought on language starts in the first instance from the speculation of philosophers on questions involving language, and on the nature of language itself.

But the Greeks, like the Hindus, also had a heritage of ancient classics—chiefly the *Iliad* and *Odyssey*—which similarly occasioned much commentary, criticism and analysis. Finally, since the reading, study and appreciation of these classics became the basis of what might be called the "liberal arts" curriculum in both Greek and Roman civilization, both these currents of thought ultimately merged in a stream of school tradition, in which bold speculations and brilliant critical insights were frozen into cut-and-dried definitions and administered in prescribed, unvarying doses to the school children of a thousand generations.

The first question that invited the cogitations of the Greek philosophers was on the ultimate nature of language; and two schools of thought soon formed, one or the other of which enlisted almost all who considered the subject for several centuries. Specifically, the question was: In virtue of what does a word have its meaning? Why do we call a horse a "horse," and not a "glop"? Or, why does the succession of sounds [hɔrs] refer to a horse and not a zebra?

The philosophers reasoned that a word must have its meaning either by *nature,* or by *convention.* Either there is something in the nature of a horse that makes "horse" the proper word for the animal, or there is no natural connection between word and meaning, and the animal is designated "horse" only because a certain number of people have agreed on this designation; tomorrow they could make a new agreement to call it thenceforth a "glop." Evidently, this investigation quickly becomes a search for that perennial will-o'-the-wisp, how language originated (see Chapter II, 5).

The two points of view may be called the "nature" school (Greek φύσει, "by nature") and the "convention" school (Greek συνθήκη, "by convention"). The "nature" school has the problem of explaining why different nations have different words for the horse; while the "convention" school has to show how people could have reached agreement on a name-giving convention if language had not already been invented.

The "convention" school usually met its difficulty by postulating a "first name-giver"—some individual who, at some particular time, began the "convention" by arbitrarily assigning the various sound-sequences which we call "words" to their various meanings. (It will be noted that the Bible accounts for the origin of language by making Adam the first name-giver; but, since "Adam" means "man," this is merely equivalent to saying that "mankind made a convention by which words have their meanings," which is obviously true.)

The "nature" school accounted for the different languages of the world by assuming that originally all mankind used the same "natural" word for each concept, but that all nations (except, of course, the Greeks) had somehow, through laziness and ignorance, "corrupted" the words until they became unrecognizable. This view probably underlies the Greek word *barbaros,* similar to Latin *balbulus* and meaning "someone who speaks incomprehensibly," or, for practical purposes, "one who does not speak Greek." (By the original definition of the word, therefore, we are *all* "barbarians.")

The great philosopher Plato belonged, on the whole, to the "nature" school, except that he had a characteristically original version of the "first name-giver" device—the famous cave (*Republic* vii. 514 ff.) which we visit before birth, where we behold the original, archetypal horse, and recognize the imitation in each horse we encounter in the world. Plato states the other viewpoint, however, in the views of Hermogenes in *Cratylus* (384c, 401c).

Actually, both schools were right, of course: language is certainly a system of conventional symbols, and a "horse" could just as well be a "glop," and some day might be; but from the point of view of each individual speaker, the meanings of words are immutably fixed as if by nature—each receives the system fully developed, and cannot make more than infinitesimal changes without incurring the penalty of incomprehensibility. (The accumulation of infinitesimal changes, of course, might ultimately result in a new language.)

Now, this naturally entails the question: If each speaker of a language received it fully developed, what about the first human being ever to use language—whence and how did *he* get it? But this is, evidently, the insoluble problem of the origin of language and indeed the problem of the chicken and the egg—the problem of creation—and perhaps the idea of a First Name-Giver is the most plausible solution after all. (We have shown elsewhere—see Chapter II, 5—that no evolutionary postulate will account for the known facts in the development of language.)

Contemporaries of Plato (for example, Protagoras, 481–411 B.C.) wrestled with the problem of grammatical "gender." But it is in the work of Aristotle (notably his *Rhetorica*) that a really scientific attack upon the problems of language begins to get under way. Less inclined than Plato to speculate on ultimate fundamental but insoluble questions, Aristotle began sorting words into classes—the first beginnings of a technique of analysis (the "parsing" of a text, i.e., distributing its words into categories or "parts of speech"), which is in use to the present day.[3] This is in itself, of course, no proof that the technique either is or is not the best or only possible one. As a matter of fact, Aristotle founded his work on two postulates which have since been shown to be incorrect.

First, he assumed that a language is spoken *word by word:* hence, to explain each word, and to ascertain the principle by which the words are selected and put in order, is to give an adequate scientific description of the language. But it is now known that language is learned in clumps of words[4] and only later, by comparing these clumps, do we discover the identity of the units called words, and thence arrive at the concept of the word. Some languages (quite unknown to Aristotle, of course) have never gone this far—have never developed this concept, and consequently *do not have words at all.* Hence this approach was erroneous, but because of Aristotle's tremendous prestige, it became a strait jacket for the study of language for over two thousand years.

Second, Aristotle, as a philosopher, was really more interested in human thought than in the language which expresses it: he really classified, not words, but the concepts they represented. (It is to be remembered that Aristotle was a great logician, and as such a profound authority on thought processes; he also organized rhetorical argument along the lines of his system of logic.) Accordingly, he classified words on the basis of what they "*meant*," not on the basis of any observable characteristics of the word as a physical phenomenon. But, as we have pointed out elsewhere (Chapter I, 2), this is circular reasoning, essentially quite unscientific. Yet all works on language until about thirty years ago followed Aristotle in this.[5]

Aristotle defined the linguistic structure which we call a *sentence* in logician's terms, as "the expression of a proposition." The sentence must name something, he stated, and then "predicate" something about it. (Grammarians have consequently assumed that structures like imperatives—see Chapter X, 3—have "understood" subjects.) Hence, Aristotle divided words into two classes—names (ὀνόματα, nouns) and words which "made a statement" or "predicated" (ῥήματα, verba). All other words were "connectives" (σύνδεσμοι, conjunctions). Thus, in Aristotle's science of grammar, there were only three parts of speech. Aristotle also first noted the expression of time contained in his "predicate words," which was absent in the "names."

The great philosopher's chief successors in the field of grammar were the Stoics, who, teaching that there were four states of being, wanted four parts of speech, and therefore set up a new category for the article (a feature which the Roman grammarians dutifully copied, although Latin did not have articles).

The Stoics invented the term *declension*: the term πτῶσις, "declination" (in the sense of "deviation from a base line") had been used for a word derived from another, but they first restricted it to the variations of form which expressed case function. (We shall see later—Chapter VIII, 5—what the real difference is.) The Stoics also originated the term *participle* (μετόχη) for words which "participated" in the character of *both* of the basic categories, verb and noun. The Stoics also first distinguished the voices and the moods, and indeed left the linguistic description of the verb very much in the form in which it remained almost to the present day.

The scholars of Alexandria were the next to advance the work.[6] They were particularly interested in editing, criticizing and annotating Homer and other classic authors, and were no doubt the first to look upon grammar as *normative*—as a means of analyzing classic writing and guiding contemporaries to approximate this model. Here, perhaps, is the origin of the pernicious notion that the true "grammarian" is not one who scientifically ascertains what language *is*, but one who dictates what it *should be*. The Alexandrians enlarged the roster of "parts of speech" to eight, and in the outline of Greek grammar by Dionysius Thrax it is not hard to recognize the beginning of a formula for the description of a language which, until about twenty years ago, was the latest and only one available to anyone seeking to present a language to persons desirous of learning it (see Fig. 8).

In matters linguistic, the Romans were, generally speaking, little more than translators (sometimes mis-translators) of what the Greeks had developed. An exception, perhaps the most original Roman thinker in this field, was Publius Terentius Varro (116–28 B.C.), who declared that he thought there were only four "parts of speech" in Latin: (1) words inflected like nouns, (2) words inflected like verbs, (3) words inflected like both (participles), (4) words not inflected like either (all indeclinables, including prepositions, adverbs, interjections,

FIGURE 8   Development of the formula for describing a language

DIONYSIUS THRAX (1st cent. B.C.)	DONATUS (350 A.D.)	PRISCIAN (450 A.D.)	A MODERN GRAMMAR (published 1955)*
Values of the letters	Functions of the letters	1. Sounds	*Introduction:* the alphabet; pronunciation
Syllables	Syllable, meter, accent	2. Syllables	
Parts of speech	Parts of speech	3-4. Comparatives and denominatives	
		5. Gender	
Noun (paradigms)		6, 7. The *noun*	Chapter I: The noun. Gender, nominative case. II-IV: The verb
Verb (paradigms)		8-10. The *verb:* its conjugations	
Participle (paradigms)		11. The *participle*	
Article; *Pronoun*		12-13. The *pronoun*	V: Genitive; *pronouns* VI: Numbers, telling time
Preposition		14. The *preposition*	
Adverb		15. Adverb and interjection	
			VII-VIII: Adjectives IX-X: Noun declensions XI-XV: Verb conjugations
Conjunction		16. The *conjunction*	XVI: Conjunctions and relative pronouns XVII: Word Order XVIII: Passive Voice XIX-XXI: Subjunctive
(There was probably a section on Syntax which does not survive)	Sentences not to be imitated. Model sentences	17-18. Order of the parts of speech (i.e. syntax)	APPENDICES Tables of paradigms Vocabulary

*(Note that the 1955 book is clearly following Priscian, 1000 years earlier)

etc.).[7] Note that this classification of words was based on their *form*, not their meaning. Had the Roman grammatical writers been original enough to see the merit of Varro's method (without necessarily following his classification), Aristotle's fundamental mistake might have been corrected at an early date, and linguistic science might have continued to take the seven-league forward strides it had been making for the previous two or three centuries. But already the chill of traditionalism was setting in. All Varro's successors, over-awed by the prestige of the Greeks, preferred to follow Aristotle, and thus reinforced the strait jacket into which Western thought on language was being forced.

Julius Caesar and Sallust are reported to have done some writing on grammar, but their works do not survive. Cicero, a great artist in the use of Latin, did not advance the theory of language, but his *De oratore* is no mean contribution to Latin stylistics, and his philosophical writings (largely translated from Greek sources) gave Latin the technical and scientific vocabulary which it bequeathed to many modern languages. The emperor Claudius, we are told,[8] dabbled in linguistics; but the currency of his ideas was more or less coterminous with his reign.

In summary, Roman work on language was much like the Romans' role in Western culture: they originated little, but organized and disseminated what others had discovered. The grammatical terms in use today are, generally speaking, the Latin translations of terms originated by the Greeks. All that had been learned about language in general, and Latin in particular, up to their time, was summed up in the writings of Aelius Donatus (fourth century A.D.) and Priscian (A.D. 512–560). The former used the linguistic science of his day as a tool for the analysis of the language of classic authors, particularly Vergil. The "Grammatical Commentaries" of the latter became a textbook for Roman schools of "rhetoric." To appreciate the aim and viewpoint of this profoundly important work, it is necessary to say a word about the late Roman educational system.

Education in the later Roman empire was, of course, only for children of the patricians and the well-to-do upper middle class. Such children usually had had, even before attending school, a personal slave called a *paidagogos,* who was generally a cultivated Greek. Besides acting as the boy's valet, he was also supposed to teach his charge

Greek and coach him in his school work. This latter began with the classes of a *grammaticus,* who, as the name implies, probably taught the "three R's," and later introduced his pupils to Greek and Latin literature.

It was after completing the classes of the *grammaticus* that the Roman boy studied with the rhetorician, who tried mainly to develop the pupil's ability to express himself elegantly, forcefully and effectively, both orally and in writing. This was the "liberal arts curriculum" of ancient times: the "practical" value of learning to be a good public speaker was, to the Roman mind, a small part of what the course was supposed to do for the student, which was nothing less than to make him a cultured gentleman.

Under the general heading of teaching oratory, the rhetorical schools ranged over what we should now consider the "subject fields" of history, natural science, law, literary criticism, psychology, and many others. The *rhetoricus* was the revered educator of Greco-Roman society, and many individuals of this class became wealthy and famous (e.g., Quintilian, and Seneca, who was the Emperor Nero's *rhetoricus*). After his rhetorical education, the well-brought-up young man went on to the study of philosophy, often journeying to Athens for this. The whole curriculum was probably descended from, if not identical with, the famed ἐγκύκλιος παιδεία.[9]

In the rhetorical schools the "science of grammar" was studied as a means of analyzing the best Latin writing and thus enabling the educated Roman youth to speak and write his native language more elegantly. But by the time of Donatus and Priscian, progress in the study of language had ceased; the most illustrious names were those of pedagogues who found better ways to transmit what others had discovered. Presently even this much originality faded out, and rigid formulae were imposed with little change on generation after generation of pupils. The matter taught, and the method of teaching it, solidified about A.D. 500 and underwent no substantial change for more than one thousand years. This appalling mental stagnation was justified by claiming that the "science of grammar" was complete, that within its framework all linguistic phenomena in all languages, known or to be discovered, could be adequately handled—and anything which could not be was dismissed as either a mistake due to ignorance, or a barbarism beneath notice. A vested interest came into being which strove—and still strives—to perpetuate itself forever.

Crucial as is the role of the educator in society, the age-old hatred of and contempt for the mere schoolmaster is not ill-founded. Even today, we may well beware any school above the most elementary level which abjures the first duty of an educational institution—to strive to add to the sum of human knowledge—ostensibly to concentrate on the second, the transmission of knowledge already accumulated. This usually results in the type of school, so often described, which repels all the best minds and confirms all the most petty in their narrow-mindedness, prejudice, and self-satisfaction.

The world will never have enough scholars, so we must be satisfied to leave education for the most part in the hands of schoolmasters. If education is not to become stagnant and sterile, however, it must keep frustrating the constant efforts of schoolmasters to freeze out scholars so as to make the schools safe for their own kind.

2. The Middle Ages, the Renaissance, and the Eighteenth Century

For the reasons just mentioned, formal school education, insofar as it survived at all in the Middle Ages, continued to follow the Roman pattern very closely. Its place in society changed, of course: to the ruling class—the nobility—only the profession of arms was deserving of the young squire's time, and the prince who learned "clerkish" arts was suspect as a leader of government. Until the seventeenth century a king was expected, in time of war, to take the field at the head of the nation's troops, and it is said that the first sovereign of England capable of signing his own name was Henry the Eighth.

Since the peasantry had neither duty, right, nor time to do anything but work from sunrise to sundown, scholarship became the concern and prerogative of the Church alone. (One unfortunate result of this was that anyone desirous of learning had to become a clergyman, whether or not he had any real calling to that state of life, and this was the cause of much mischief.) Whatever progress in science—including the study of language—was achieved during the medieval period, it was within the framework of medieval schools (all of them Church controlled) and occasionally the medieval monastery. The social conditions of the period were not favorable to the progress of science (experimentation and exchange of information among scholars, for example, were for all practical purposes impossible), and some will maintain that Church control of all schools can also be an obstacle. On the other hand, had the Church been hostile to learning, the time would have been one of complete barbarism.

The sequence of studies comprising medieval elementary and secondary education was "the seven arts" (the ancestors of the areas of study which we call "the liberal arts" today), often subdivided into a group of three (the *trivium*) and a group of four (the *quadrivium*). The first subgroup was the Roman sequence of grammar, "rhetoric," and "dialectic"—the beginnings of philosophy. To this had been added four sciences which had developed to a fair degree of maturity during the later Roman empire: *scientia arithmetica, scientia geometrica, scientia astronomica,* and *scientia musica* (the last, by the way, really meant acoustic physics). Except for the earliest level of *ars grammatica,* which boys got either from tutors or from the chantry schools, these studies were offered by the faculty of arts at the medieval university, as the base of general education preliminary to professional training in the faculty of law, the faculty of medicine, or the faculty of theology.[10]

Now, the Roman curriculum had assumed that the student beginning it was a native speaker of Latin. It did not occur to the clergymen who were the schoolmasters in the Middle Ages to make any modifications, even when the native language of the student was French or Italian. (One reason for this was that the earliest Romance speakers were slow to realize that they were not still speaking Latin, albeit quite carelessly and colloquially; even today, the Italian schoolboy regards Latin as a sort of archaic Italian, and can get the gist of it without special instruction.) From this accident two remarkable consequences followed.

First, until the late nineteenth century, each nation pronounced Latin according to the rules for pronouncing its own language: just listen to an Irish and a French priest read, consecutively, the same Latin text. Second, a plan of instruction based on an infant science and originally intended merely to help a native Latin speaker improve and polish his usage perforce became a (most inadequate and ineffective) method for teaching Latin to people who did not know it, and was regarded as the complete, definitive science of language. So sanctified by tradition did this "science of grammar" become that alteration or addition of any jot or tittle came to seem to the medieval (and to many a modern) schoolmaster, as unthinkable as sacrilege or heresy.

So we may say that the study of language made no appreciable progress in the Middle Ages—none in the schools; and, although all the universities were profoundly devoted to philosophy, medieval philosophers, who did quite often speculate on fundamental questions concerning the nature of language, achieved no important new insights nor any real advances over the Greeks. In some cases, indeed, they reasoned themselves into errors as monumental as Quintilian's derivation of the Latin word *lūcus,* "a grove of (sacred) trees," from the word *lūx* (light), "because there is *no* light there." The expression "a *lūcus ā nōn lūcendō* etymology" is still used.

What mainly prevented progress in the study of language during the medieval period—aside from the fact that what we today call "scientific method" had not yet been invented—seems to have been the fact that investigation of fundamental linguistic principles was regarded as exclusively the task of the philosopher, while any dealings with the actual forms of Latin or any other particular language were considered to be in the province of the schoolmaster. Thus the philosopher theorized without having to base his theories on observed facts, and the grammarian taught what he (and his grandfather) had been taught, without ever asking "why." This most unprofitable division of labor has tended to continue to the present day, and it is often precisely those who speak only one language who feel most qualified to pontificate on the use, usage and workings of language in general.

During the course of the fifteenth century the vernacular languages began to rise in stature and importance, and this occasioned the collection of material about many contemporary languages which had long been ignored or neglected. Of course, the only method known for describing the facts of a language was Priscian's textbook on Latin orthoëpy—a rather Procrustean bed into which to force such languages as Mozarabic and Hungarian; but at least "grammars," however inadequate, of these and many other languages now began to be written and—thanks to Gutenberg's recent invention—circulated in printed form. Grammars of most of the European languages appeared before 1500; by 1600 grammars of Hebrew, contemporary Greek, Ethiopian, Syriac, Basque, and Welsh had appeared; and the list was lengthened still more in the seventeenth century. Collections of short specimens from many languages around the world, like Megiser's examples from forty languages (in the edition of 1603, fifty) were circulating by 1600.

All these works went on the assumption that to describe a language it was only necessary to list "paradigms" of inflections for each of the "parts of speech" and rules for the arrangement of words into sentences, and to supply a lexicon. Nothing was normally said about how to pronounce the language, because there had been no treatment of this subject in Priscian (after all, he was writing for native speakers).[11] It was soon discovered that such books were not much help to a person seeking a real, usable command of a language. Hence the sixteenth century witnessed the first appearance of the "dialogue" type of language textbook—still popular today—in which someone who really spoke the language fluently composed short dialogues representing typical conversations such as a traveler or resident in the country might frequently fall into, and published them in parallel columns with a translation. A book of this sort in Latin and French was apparently already a very popular elementary Latin textbook in 1530,[12] and other examples of the type are Van Torre's *Dialogi* and Heyden's *Colloquia*.[13]

To pursue this aspect of language activity during the Renaissance would lead into the history of methods of teaching foreign languages, which has always been regarded (perhaps unfortunately) as quite distinct from linguistic science. These books deserve mention here, however, insofar as they were—intentionally or not—methods of describing a language alternative to the traditional Priscianic formula. The data of the language were neither analyzed nor explained, to be sure; but they were authentic data accurately presented, never distorted to fit preconceived categories. It is interesting, therefore, to note that the appearance of this type of book began a sort of running battle—which continues to the present day—between innovators struggling to originate and circulate books which would be of real use in the study of foreign languages, and schoolmasters seeking to crush such impertinence under tons of academic scorn and hoary tradition. Complaints against the sterility of the traditional approach were registered by Michel de

Montaigne in 1580,[14] John Locke in 1693,[15] J. J. Rousseau in 1763.[16] Innovators along the lines mentioned were Comenius (1592–1670), Basedow (1723–1790), François Gouin (1880). But in each case the complaints were ignored and the innovators frustrated. Upon reading their books, one is surprised at the "modernity" of their point of view; the newest methods of the most alert teachers we know today tend to be rediscoveries of ideas first proposed—and dismissed—two centuries or more ago.

To sum up developments of the three centuries following the end of the fifteenth century, we may say that (1) much reasonably sound and accurate information gradually became available about a good many languages; and (2) a number of scholarly writers attempted to discover relationships among languages, and upon this basis to classify them. These efforts provided the material for, and pointed the aims of a new science, just at the time (the middle and latter third of the eighteenth century) when centuries of fumbling were crystallizing into the highly professional natural sciences as we know them today. Scientific linguistics, properly so called, was on the point of being born.

Notes to Chapter III

1. A number are cited in Gray, *Foundations of Language,* 420.

2. Cf. Matthew xvi, 18. Jesus had previously changed Peter's name from Simon to Kefas, possibly with this application in mind: cf. John, i, 42.

3. See L. H. Robins, *Ancient and Medieval Grammatical Theory in Europe,* 19–20.

4. This is the ultimate implication of most reports of children's linguistic behavior, e.g., Sturtevant, *Introduction to Linguistic Science,* 97, where the boy probably knew "irrigate," not as a word, but as a "clump," which contained *ear* but might turn out to have any possible structure. A choir-boy of our acquaintance, having been taught to sing *qui tollis peccata mundi,* eventually became convinced (no doubt after much subconscious commutation) that the text was "We told Liz we caught her Monday."

5. Cf. Fries, *Structure of English,* 18–19.

6. The possibility of some influences from the grammarians of India on the work of Alexandrian scholars is not to be discounted. Since the conquests of Alexander, some contact between the two countries had been maintained, and it is probable that some Indian works were known at Alexandria in Greek translation.

7. Varro, *De lingua latina* x. 17.

8. Cf. Suetonius *Claudius* 41; Tacitus *Annales* xi. 13.

9. Cf. Quintilian *Institutiones oratoricae* I x. 1.

10. Cf. J. P. Hughes, "What Are the Liberal Arts?" *Association of American Colleges Bulletin*, XLI, 4 (December 1955), 614 ff.

11. This is why, almost to the present day, grammars of a foreign language disposed of pronunciation in a few pages not numbered as part of the text.

12. Cordier's *Colloquia*. See Gans, *St. Ignatius' Idea of a Jesuit University*, 91.

13. *Ibid.*, 101.

14. Montaigne, *Essais*, I, 26 (to Diane de Foix, comtesse de Gurson).

15. Locke, *Locke on Education*, 138–48.

16. Rousseau, *Emile*, 55, 72.

Supplementary Readings for Chapter III

Aristotle, *Rhetorica*.
Gray, *Foundations of Language*, 25.
Robins, *Ancient and Medieval Grammatical Theory in Europe*, 3–25.
Freeman, *Schools of Hellas*, 79–117, 157.
Girard, *L'éducation athénienne*, 100–160, 221–252.
Haarhoff, *Schools of Gaul*, 52–92.
Rashdall, *Universities of Europe in the Middle Ages*, I, 157 ff.; III, 79–117.
Gouin, *L'art d'enseigner et d'étudier les langues étrangères*.
Mallinson, *Teaching a Modern Language*, 2–17.

Chapter IV

A Brief History of the Study of Language, II: The Periods of Scientific Linguistics

To give a definite date for the beginning of the modern science of linguistics, we may fix upon the year 1786. In that year, Sir William Jones, a British civil servant, who occupied the post of Chief Justice in Bengal in India, and who had studied Hindustani in order to be better able to follow the cases tried before him, made a speech before a learned society in London, in which he declared that the Sanskrit language bore to both Greek and Latin "a stronger affinity, both in the roots of verbs and in the forms of grammar, than could possibly have been produced by accident; so strong, indeed, that no philologer could examine all three without believing them to have sprung from some common source which, perhaps no longer exists."[1] Here, in a sentence, was laid out the work of linguistic science for almost a century.

1. "Comparative Philology"—1786–1870

Like most important milestones in the history of thought, Sir William Jones's revolutionary proposition did not burst upon the world unheralded. Several grammars of Sanskrit had been published in Europe, some of the literature of India had been translated, and the need for classifying languages and determining their interrelationships, if any—even the thought that many or all languages might have descended from a single original one—all this had preceded his speech. But his speech proved to be the spark that touched off the intellectual explosion in the world of British scholarship. Perhaps it was the drama inherent in the idea that in distant India, in the heart of the mysterious East—a land but newly discovered and still largely unexplored—the native language, exotic to the ear and written in a script that had all the strange intricacy of Far Eastern temple ornament, should turn out to be a first cousin to the familiar Latin and Greek, so thoroughly entwined with the roots of Western culture.

At any rate, there followed immediately a period during which British and European linguistic scholars began feverishly studying Sanskrit and comparing Latin, Greek, and later other European languages with it. The close genetic connection was soon evident, and the conviction began to grow that Sanskrit was the mother language from which the chief European languages had sprung: in short, that it was the language which we now call Indo-European.

Although the British had the most immediate access to India, it was the scholars of Germany who first took important steps in the new science, even though they were hampered by the Napoleonic Wars and often had to go to Paris to find the necessary materials for study. In 1808, Friedrich von Schlegel published a book, *Ueber die Sprache und Weisheit der Inder,* in which he used the term *vergleichende Grammatik* ("comparative grammar") which was to become standard and fundamental. Franz Bopp, in a work published in 1816,[2] compared the verb conjugations of Sanskrit, Persian, Greek, Latin and German. Rasmus Rask, a Dane, in 1818 published the first actual "comparative grammar," a remarkable work outlining comparatively the Scandinavian languages and noting their relationships to each other.[3] This book foreshadowed most of the methods and discoveries of the next half-century but was less influential than it should have been because it was written in a language not widely read.

A milestone in the early history of linguistics is the publication (1819, later editions 1822, 1840) of the *Deutsche Grammatik* ("Grammar of the Germanic Languages") of Jakob Ludwig Karl Grimm (1785–1863)—who, it happens, was one of the Grimm brothers of fairy-tale fame.[4] He had studied Sanskrit in Paris, and later held professorships at Göttingen and Berlin. The main aim of his book was to be simply what its title announced—a comparative grammar of the Germanic languages; but what made it monumental was its achievement in showing how Germanic languages could be descended from Sanskrit (as the hypothesis then was) and still show the striking differences of form from Latin and Greek which they often did. In other words, if the Sanskrit word for "he moves, carries" was *vahati,* and the Latin one was *vehit,* it is not difficult to postulate a relationship; but if the German equivalent is *er bewegt,* it is hard to see how this form, too, belongs to the family. Likewise, we are incredulous when first told that English *hundred* and Latin *centum* are essentially the same word. Grimm showed, however, that differences of this sort fell into a systematic pattern, German always (well, nearly always) having *h* where Latin and Greek had *k,* and so on. The statement of these regular correspondences became famous as *Grimm's Law.*

Grimm's Law states, for example, that where Latin and Greek words have *p, t* or *k,* Germanic cognates[5] have *f, th, h*: thus the Latin word for "father" (*pater*) corresponds to the Germanic word *Vater* (the *v* pronounced as *f*); Latin *frater* corresponds to English *brother*; Latin *cornu* to English and German *horn*. In the same way Latin *b, d, g* will be *p, t, k* in Germanic: Latin *lubricus,* English *slippery;* Latin *domo,* English *tame;* Latin *genu,* English *knee* (where the *k* was once pronounced, as it still is in German *Knie*). The law embraces several other sets of such equivalents (see Fig. 9).

Grimm's Law is, of course, a "law" only in the sense in which we speak of the "law" of gravity; it is a statement of regular patterns of behavior observed in the phenomena under study. It implies, however, that during some period—estimated to have begun about 300 B.C. and to have continued for about three centuries—there was a regular sound shift throughout a certain group or community of Indo-European speakers (those known as the Germanic tribes), transforming all (or practically all) *p*'s into *f*'s, and so on. Since this sound shift did not happen to take place among other tribes (known as Romans and Greeks), we find the latter saying *pater* where we (English being a Germanic language) say *father.*

Such regular sound shifts are familiar phenomena in all languages, and are part of the evolutionary processes of language (see Chapter II, 3). In English, the words *sea, tea* and *me* (and thousands of others) were once pronounced *say, tay* and *may,* so that there was a regular sound shift (occurring in about the fifteenth and sixteenth centuries) of *ay* ([e]) to *ee* ([i]). At the same time, words like *house* and *mouse* assumed approximately their present pronunciation, having formerly been *hoose* and *moose*; in Scotland, however, this change did not take place, and

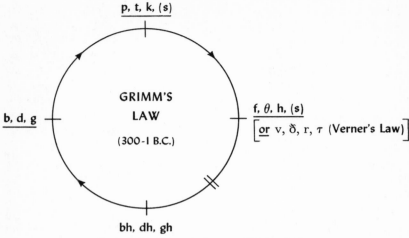

FIGURE 9   Grimm's Law and Verner's Law

Indo-European (hence Latin and Sanskrit) p̱, ṯ, ḵ, shift to Germanic f̱, ꞨΘ, ẖ, while Indo-European ḇ, ḏ, g̱, shift to Germanic p̱, ṯ, ḵ, and Indo-European bh, dh, gh, shift to Germanic ḇ, ḏ, g̱. The circle revolves only once; Germanic ḇ, ḏ, g̱ derived from Indo-European bh, dh, gh does not subsequently shift to p̱, ṯ, ḵ, and so on.

ILLUSTRATIONS

Latin p̱ater	English father	Latin boletus	German P̱ilz (mushroom)
Latin ṯres	English ṯhree	Latin ḏentes	English ṯeeth
Latin c̱ornu	English ẖorn	Latin g̱elidus	English c̱old

Sanskrit ḇharati   English ḇear
Sanskrit rudhiras   English reḏ
Sanskrit han̄sas*   English g̱oose

* In Sanskrit, initial gh became ẖ

the "braid Scots" still refers to a "wee hoosie." Another such shift is responsible for the Scot reciting the old saying as "stecks an' stanes will brak me banes." Fundamental as these sound shifts are, they had never previously been scientifically studied and formulated; and this fact lent additional importance and influence to Grimm's "Law."

During the next few decades, the milestones of development of the science of linguistics—then generally referred to as "comparative philology"—were the comparative grammars of subfamily after subfamily of the Indo-European languages, and even some non-Indo-European families. Between 1836 and 1844, Frederick Diez (1794–1876) published the three volumes of his *Grammatik der romanischen Sprachen* for the Romance group, and in 1853 Johann Kaspar Zeuss, in his *Grammatica celtica,* proved that the Celtic languages were related to Latin and Greek—hence to Indo-European—which had not previously been the opinion of scholars. From 1874 to 1879 Franz Miklosich brought out his long-awaited *Vergleichende Grammatik der slawischen Sprachen.* A comparative grammar of Dravidian languages appeared in 1856, of Polynesian in 1858.

It became clearer and clearer that virtually all the languages spoken in Europe, as well as many in the Near East and India, were descendants of a single language spoken some thousands of years before. Scholars had begun to suspect that Sanskrit was not itself that language, but considered it the earliest descendant, and therefore most similar to the original. The time was ripe for seeking to reconstruct the original from its descendants; from the beginning it had been inevitable that comparison would culminate in efforts at reconstruction. This is one of the most fascinating aspects of linguistics; it is a sort of detective work with words. Just as Sherlock Holmes collected clues left behind—a footprint, a bit of cigar ash, an unfinished word—and reconstructed the story of the crime, so the comparative philologist collects all the words in contemporary languages which have evolved from the same word in the ancestor language and surmises what the original word must have been. This basic technique of the comparative linguist is illustrated in Figure 10.

The first book, therefore, which—consciously or not—sought to be a grammar of Indo-European itself was Franz Bopp's *Vergleichende Grammatik des Sanskrit, Zend* (= Old Iranian), *Griechischen, Lateinischen, Litauischen, Gotischen und Deutschen* (Berlin, 1833–1852). The second work of this type was A. Schleicher's *Compendium der vergleichenden Grammatik der indogermanischen Sprachen* (Weimar, 1861). In this book Schleicher originated what has become a standard usage in linguistics, marking reconstructed forms, not quotable from written documents, with an asterisk: e.g., **kmtom, *swopnos* in Figure 10.[6] A little later, Schleicher attempted to write a short passage in Indo-European.[7] The fact that Schleicher's "Indo-European" looked very much like Sanskrit reflects the position of comparative philology during the mid-nineteenth century.

What ultimately changed this point of view was a growth of inter-

INDO-EUROPEAN *swep-, *swop-(no-s) 'sleep'

IRISH	OLD ENGLISH	LATIN	GREEK	RUSSIAN	SANSKRIT
suan	swefen	somnus	ὕπνος	spat′	svapnas
(Eng. "swoon")			ʜʏᴘɴᴏ		

INDO-EUROPEAN *gnē-, *gnō- 'know'

IRISH	OLD GERMAN	LATIN	GREEK	RUSSIAN	SANSKRIT
fíos	knāan	gnōscō	γιγνώσκω	znat′	jñatum
(Eng. "know")			gignósko		

INDO-EUROPEAN *km′tom 'hundred'

IRISH	GERMAN	LATIN	GREEK	RUSSIAN	SANSKRIT
céad	hundert	centum	ἕκατον	sto	çata
			h		

INDO-EUROPEAN *pelə-, *pol-, plē-(no-s) 'full'

IRISH	GOTHIC	LATIN	GREEK	RUSSIAN	SANSKRIT	ARMENIAN
lán	filu	plēnus	πολύs	polny	pūrnáh	li
(German viel, Eng. "full")						

FIGURE 10   Indo-European reconstructions

est among comparative philologists in what is called *ablaut*. This is regarded as a formidable concept by some, yet every speaker of English is thoroughly familiar with it in verb forms like *sing, sang, sung; drive, drove, driven*. Students of German meet it in the principal parts of strong verbs: *sterben, starb, gestorben; fliegen, flog, geflogen*. Ablaut is, in short, a systematic alternation of vowels in a root. In English and German, for instance, the more common way of putting a verb into the past tense is to add a past-tense ending to the root—*walk* becomes *walk-ed*; but the other way is to change a vowel *within* the root—*sing* becomes *sang*. A vowel alternation of this type is "ablaut."

Ablaut is less systematic in Latin and Greek than in Germanic, but is found there also: cf. *tego/toga*. No doubt all these languages inherited ablaut from the parent language. A. Holtzmann, in a treatise *Ueber den Ablaut* (Karlsruhe, 1844), first demonstrated that the ablaut must have arisen in Indo-European accidentally, as a result of shifts of accent.

This line of reasoning naturally awakened interest in the nature and position of the Indo-European accent, as evidenced in works like that of L. Bendoew, *De l'accentuation dans les langues indo-européennes tant anciennes que modernes* (Paris, 1847), and led to a new "phonetic law": Verner's Law, first proposed by Karl Verner in 1877.[8] Verner's Law seeks to account for certain exceptions to Grimm's Law, such as cases where Germanic shows *voiced* stops where Grimm's Law calls for *voiceless* spirants (in other words, *d* where *th* would be expected): e.g., according to Grimm's Law, the number 100 (Sanskrit *çata*, Greek ἕκατον, Latin *centum*) should be *hunthred*. Verner showed that this voicing occurred when the Indo-European accent had come on a syllable *following* the sound in question. Under the same conditions, *s* changed to *r* (this change is called *rhotacism*), and this is why we have *s* in *was* but *r* in *were* (the latter descended from some such form as **wasón*; German has introduced the *r* into the singular—*war*—by analogy).

Another original contribution of Schleicher's must be mentioned here: the Stammbaum or "genealogical" theory of how Indo-European evolved into the languages descended from it. According to this theory, dialects began to develop in the Indo-European homeland (wherever it was)[9] which might be called proto-Celtic, proto-Italic, and so on. Then when the break-up and emigration came, one such group migrated to one part of Europe, another to another; and in their new homes each continued to develop its dialect in accordance with individual trends already established; thus arose Common Celtic, Common Germanic, and so on.

J. Schmidt in 1872[10] proposed a different theory, the *Wellentheorie* ("wave theory"), according to which changes in Indo-European moved in more or less successive waves toward the outer perimeter of Indo-European settlement. According to this theory we should imagine that groups migrating from the perimeter preserved stages of Indo-European effaced by subsequent "waves."

Neither of these theories is an entirely satisfactory explanation of the facts. It was really too soon to venture one, and still is, until more data are available—not only from linguistics, but from history, archaeology, and other areas of research.

57

In this period of linguistic science, also, began the history of a type of reference work which is basic for all workers in the field. A. Fick published at Göttingen in 1863 a *Wörterbuch der indogermanischen Sprache in ihrem Bestande vor der Völkertrennung:* a dictionary of Indo-European— which is to say, of course, an alphabetical list of Indo-European roots as reconstructed. This book had a second edition in 1870–71, with a changed title (now *Vergleichendes Wörterbuch der indogermanischen Sprachen*), a third in 1874–76, and a fourth which appeared between 1890 and 1923, under the editorship of Fick and others.

Another "phonetic law" was contributed in 1863 by Hermann Grassmann. Grassmann's Law is that when reduplication or other processes resulted in two aspirated consonants in one Indo-European root, one—usually the first—is de-aspirated. Thus the Greek root θε- is reduplicated in the present tense of the verb "I place," but *θίθημι becomes τίθημι; *θρίχs becomes θρίξ, but the genitive *θρίχos becomes τρίχos.

Mention should be made here of two writers who, while not them-selves originators of great new advances in linguistics, were interpreters of the new science to the wider, nonprofessional public and as such were better known and more influential than many who are "great names" only to the initiate. The first is Friedrich Maximilian Müller, better known as F. Max Müller (1823–1900), a godson of the com-poser Mendelssohn, a pupil of Bopp and a distinguished Sanskritist in his own right (his *Sacred Books of the East* still circulates). Born in Germany, he went to England in 1846 and became a master and fel-low at Oxford and a British subject (despite which, however, he failed of his most cherished ambition, to succeed to the chair of Sanskrit at Oxford when it became vacant in 1860). His books *The Science of Lan-guage* and *Chips from a German Workshop* are still the only books on lin-guistics to be found in the libraries of many colleges.

The other writer was William Dwight Whitney, an American San-skritist and a Harvard professor, whose books *Language and the Study of Language* (1867) and *The Life and Growth of Language* (1874) are still to be met with, and are still good introductions to linguistics, if one keeps in mind how much has happened in the science since they ap-peared.

If the reader cares at this point to make a list of the books men-tioned in this section as milestones of linguistics between 1786 and

1870, he will at once see how indispensable it is for research in this science to be able to read German. Of course, one should not consider a career in linguistics at all before at least laying the foundations of a mastery of several languages, and German would probably be one of them.

2. The "Neogrammarians"—1870–1925

We can conveniently begin the second period of linguistics with the appearance of an Italian scholar's contribution—G. Ascoli's *Corso di glottologia* (Florence, 1870). In this most important work Ascoli demonstrated that in certain places Sanskrit had changed what must originally have been a *k*-sound to an *s*- or *sh*-sound: The word for "hundred," for instance, was *centum* in Latin, ἕκατον in Greek, *cét* in Old Irish, and (by Grimm's Law) *hundert* in German; yet it was *çata* in Sanskrit, *satem* in Old Iranian.

It is not infrequently observed that languages in the course of their evolution change gutturals to sibilants, generally because of a following palatal vowel—the "palatal" vowels are *e* and *i* (see Chapter XIII) —and consequent palatalization; but no case is known of a guttural developing from a sibilant. In general, the western descendants of Indo-European kept the *k*, while the eastern ones changed it: and the Indo-European languages were therefore divided into the *centum* and *satem* language groups. The discovery of a *centum* language (Tokharian) far to the East, in Chinese Turkestan, diminished the significance of this division.

Ascoli's discovery spelled the end of the belief that Sanskrit was either identical with Indo-European, or the descendant most like the parent language (in the sense in which Italian is undoubtedly the most like Latin of all the Romance languages, though some have preserved features of Latin which Italian has altered). Ascoli's work also made it clear that *two* series of gutturals must be postulated for Indo-European: in other words, it did not have merely p, t, k, but must have had p, t, k_1, k_2—the k_1 series being those which altered in the "satem" languages, while the k_2 series (eventually called "labiovelars" and often written k^w, etc.) remained unchanged.

The new point of view also required revision of the concept current up to that time of the vowel system of Indo-European. Sanskrit had no *e* or *o* (the *e* and *o* of classical Sanskrit are derived from older *ai* and *au*, as shown by their place in the *devanagari* alphabet, where they are the short counterparts of *āi* and *āu*). Hence it had been assumed that the vowels of Indo-European had been *a*, *i*, *u*, and that the *e/o* ablaut so frequently noticed in other Indo-European languages was developed from diphthongs, although a great classicist, G. Curtius, had already (in his *Grundzüge der griechischen Etymologie*, Leipzig, 1858) questioned this assumption. V. Thomsen in 1877 announced the *palatal law*, by which he accounted for the conditions under which Indo-European gutturals had been palatalized. And a young French linguist, Ferdinand de Saussure (1857–1914)—destined later to become one of the great names in the science—with his first important work, *Mémoire sur le système primitif des voyelles dans les langues indo-européennes* (Leipzig, 1878), contributed to the re-evaluation of Indo-European vocalism.

De Saussure's monograph had the unexpected and unintended result of starting a new school in linguistics. The noted classical scholar, Georg Curtius of the University of Göttingen, fell out over it with his outstanding pupil Karl Brugmann. It is perhaps characteristic of scholars, who may comprehend abstractions better than the average men, that they can come to blows over, for example, whether Tokharian (extinct for over a thousand years) had an *h*; and Brugmann founded a new linguistic journal, *Morphologische Untersuchungen*, which became the voice of his faction.

In this journal Brugmann maintained the position that phonetic "laws" like Grimm's are exactly like the laws enunciated in the natural sciences: in other words, the kind of sound shift summarized in Grimm's Law is, according to Brugmann, a physical phenomenon like that described in the law of gravity—hence it has no exceptions, any apparent cases of deviation from the law being due to data or laws not yet discovered. The war cry of the Brugmann camp, therefore, was, "Phonetic laws are natural laws and have no exceptions." (It is evident, of course, that this point of view was a reflection in linguistics of the ascendancy of natural science at the end of the nineteenth century—the influence called "positivism" in literary criticism. Even natural science does not maintain precisely this point of view today.)

Since Brugmann was junior to Curtius, and since most of Brugmann's followers were younger and less conservative than their opponents, the faction was popularly labeled *die Junggrammatiker,* not quite correctly translated "the neogrammarians."[11] Since Brugmann became a professor at Leipzig, his school is also referred to as "the Leipzig school," the opposition being "the Berlin and Göttingen school."

This controversy raged in German philological circles during the last quarter of the nineteenth century, and migrated sooner or later to adjacent countries; and the neogrammarians may be said to have won, in the sense that a majority of linguists of that time eventually came around to essentially their point of view. When Brugmann and Delbrück brought out the *magnum opus* of the school—a work entitled *Grundriss der vergleichenden Grammatik der indogermanischen Sprachen* (three volumes, Strassburg, 1886–1900; second edition, revised and much enlarged, 1897–1916)—it was universally recognized as the authoritative textbook on comparative linguistics.[12] Even today, this great work, while a little dated, is not yet obsolete. A somewhat modernized compendium is A. Meillet's *Introduction à l'étude comparative des langues indo-européennes* (Paris, eighth edition, 1937); but Meillet's work in no sense supersedes Brugmann's, nor was it intended to.

The burgeoning of natural science at the end of the nineteenth century had another most important effect on our field: the study of the sounds of which speech is made up—hitherto full of the most preposterous notions and the wildest of stupidities—finally adopted scientific method and emerged as an authoritative science of *phonetics.* A sketch of the development of phonetics is given later (Chapter XIII, 1).

Although the Germans had been in the lead since the beginning in all branches of linguistics, the year 1906 marked the appearance of a non-German constellation in the linguistic firmament. That was the year in which Ferdinand de Saussure was appointed to a professorship at the University of Geneva; and his courses in general linguistics from that year on were greatly admired by a wide audience. Unfortunately, De Saussure published but little, and had not embodied his influential and highly original teaching in a book up to the moment of his untimely death; but a group of his enthusiastic students, headed by Charles Bally and Albert Sèchehaye, prepared one based on their notes of his lectures, and published it in 1916 under the title *Cours de linguistique générale.* This posthumous book had the greatest possible influence on the study of linguistics in all French-speaking countries, and became the cornerstone of the "phonemic" school.

Between 1900 and 1914, archaeological expeditions working in northeastern Asia Minor discovered a quantity of documents, some written in Babylonian cuneiform and others written in hieroglyphs, but in a language which was neither Akkadian nor Egyptian. It was eventually identified as the language of the Hittites, a shadowy early people mentioned in the Bible (Genesis x, xxiii, xxvi; Numbers xiii; Second Kings xi, etc.) and in Egyptian chronicles; and, when it was deciphered,[13] it proved to belong definitely in the Indo-European family.

This discovery was all the more exciting because the relationship of the new-found language to Indo-European was by no means obvious: on first inspection, in fact, Hittite seemed much more like its Semitic neighbors than like any of the Indo-European languages already known. Evidently its development must have diverged from that of the others at a very early date.

These facts gave rise to all sorts of interesting speculations. Was Hittite the original Indo-European language, discovered at last? Or was it the link between Indo-European and Semitic, pointing the way to the reconstruction of a language spoken some five thousand years ago, the common ancestor of both Indo-European *and* Semitic? Will it enable us to decipher other ancient inscriptions in Asia Minor which are still a riddle? Linguistic science has not up to the present time arrived at final answers to all possible questions.

One major recent development in linguistics can, however, be credited in part to the discovery of Hittite. The study of that language— certainly destined to be as important to the comparative linguist as Sanskrit[14]—tends to confirm a theory which had long been taking shape among scholars: that at an early period of its history, Indo-European had had a few consonantal phonemes which ultimately were eliminated—leaving traces, however, that are still discernible. It was surmised, for instance, that long vowels in Indo-European which had not been lengthened from earlier short vowels were the result of the lengthening (by "compensation," according to a prevalent theory) of a short vowel when one of the consonantal phonemes just mentioned dropped out. This theory—still in the process of development—is called the "laryngeal" theory.[15]

To summarize the neogrammarian period, we may say that it began with the establishment of the fact that Sanskrit was neither Indo-European itself, nor the most like it of its descendants. The next important step was the proposal and ultimate acceptance of the thesis that "phonetic laws are like physical laws and have no exceptions." The third major development of the period was the discovery of Hittite, and the consequent re-evaluation of the basic outlines of comparative Indo-European linguistics.

It should be noted that, to the end of this period, "linguistic science" was for practical purposes equated with *comparative* linguistics; and the latter in turn was practically equated with the comparison of Indo-European languages and the reconstruction of Indo-European. For the scientific description of languages to be compared, the age-old, Greco-Roman "grammar" was still used; nor had it occurred to anyone as yet that this was in need of revision.

The neogrammarian point of view seems to lead to focusing on minutiae, to amassing large amounts of data, and to proliferating rules. In comparative work the neogrammarian will take, say, Latin long *ā*, and trace each of its derivatives in the various Romance languages, without thinking to speak of the relationship between long *ā* and short *ă*, between long *ā* and the other phonemes in the language, or between it and the language as a whole—forgetting that long *ā* exists only in virtue of short *ă* (for if there were only one *a* in the language, its length would be immaterial).

In school grammars, the neogrammarian approach is seen in the setting up of many declensions and conjugations, in complex paradigms, and in the statement of numerous rules to govern each individual phenomenon in the language, without any general picture. The situation in education being what it is, approximately 75 to 80 per cent of foreign-language instruction in American schools, as this is written, remains neogrammarian in its philosophy and outlook.

3. The Structuralists—1925–1950

After World War I, *descriptive* linguistics began to develop rapidly—at first, probably, in connection with an interest in and fairly intensive study of dialects, which commenced around the turn of the century and led to the publication of the first linguistic atlases.[16] The rapid development of phonetics, already noted, no doubt also played a part; and the great improvements in transportation at the end of the nineteenth century brought Europeans into more frequent contact with a wider range of languages than the Continent displayed—which could also be cited as a reason for the commencement, around this time, of the first really scientific efforts at establishing the etymology of place names.[17]

The new movements in linguistics in this period are, therefore, all in the descriptive field. Comparative linguistics did not languish nor fall behind, but it began to lose its pre-eminence, as another branch of the science began to equal it in importance.

Perhaps the most important name during this period is that of Nikolai S. Troubetzkoy (1890–1938).[18] Son of a Russian prince who was a professor of philosophy at Moscow University, he became interested as a boy in ethnography and ethnology; at the age of fifteen he published articles on the Finnish tribes living in Russia, and then turned to the study of Caucasian languages, on which he ultimately became an authority. He majored in linguistics at Moscow University, and later studied under Brugmann at Leipzig, where he took a doctorate in 1915, afterward returning to Russia to teach at Moscow University.

Becoming interested in Slavic comparative linguistics, Troubetzkoy found himself profoundly dissatisfied with the theories and prevailing methods in that field, and began to search for better methods of reconstruction and historical linguistics. The direction of his thinking was strongly influenced by the teaching of Ferdinand de Saussure and by a near-contemporary, Baudouin de Courtenay, and to some extent by the methods of a school of literary criticism then popular in Russia.[19]

Troubetzkoy's work was of course interrupted by World War I, and the vicissitudes of those years found him holding brief professorships at Rostov and Sofia. Despite many difficulties, he continued to work on his new approach to comparative Slavic linguistics. In 1922 he was invited to assume the chair of Slavic philology at the University of Vienna, where he remained for the fertile last sixteen years of his life (he died at the early age of 48). His old friend Roman Jakobson was by then located at Charles University in Prague, and during this decade and a half the two scholars carried on a sort of Schiller-Goethe correspondence full of sparkling new ideas in linguistics.

At Prague, moreover, Jakobson founded a society of scholars, the Prague Linguistics Club (*Cercle linguistique de Prague*), which published a journal, *Travaux du cercle linguistique de Prague*, in which, during its ten-year existence, a wholly new approach to linguistic description was outlined. This came to be known as the Prague or "phonemic" school of linguistics, also as "structuralism" and "functionalism." Its principles were presented to the scientific world at the First International Linguistic Congress at The Hague in 1928, and the first International Congress of Slavic Philologists at Prague in 1929, where they made their first great impact on the scholarly world in general. After the appearance of preliminary studies, Troubetzkoy's *magnum opus,* his *Grundzüge der Phonologie,* appeared (1939), and became, to a large extent, the Bible of the movement.

The position of the "phonemicists" may be summarized as follows. First, they were more interested in system than in detail: they did not wish to study each atom of a language individually and successively, but wanted first to conceive the structure of the whole—what kind of *system* it formed. This implied that each detail was to be examined first as a part of a system; Troubetzkoy made elaborate studies and classifications of the relations of each unit to the whole and to each other unit in the system. It is probably for this reason that the phonemicists were the first to study and report on the *distribution* of linguistic units—whether a speech sound occurs with equal frequency initially, medially and finally in the syllable or word; what *sequences* of speech sounds occur; the structure of the syllable, in terms of whether and in what sequence and number phonemes occur before and after the vowel or syllable-nucleus; and similar questions, the answers to which are all highly characteristic for each language, but which it would not occur to the neogrammarian, with his isolationist approach, even to ask; thus was the method of describing a language improved.

The phonemicists also devoted a large part of their attention to defining and isolating the phoneme (see Chapter XIV, 1); the technique of describing grammatical structure, in fact, was in its early infancy at the time of Troubetzkoy's death, and a completely developed structuralistic approach to the description of grammatical phenomena has not yet evolved. But even outside the Prague school, forces were working toward the development of the phonemic concept. By the middle twenties, the most advanced phoneticians were already coming to the realization that the unit of description of the sound system (phonology) of a language must be a *concept* rather than a physical entity; for, as the tools of observation and measurement developed, it became clear that instruments could distinguish twelve different *p*'s, twenty *t*'s, and so on, in any language—yet all of these might, from the point of view of *function in the structure,* constitute only one unit (as in English).[20]

Thus two groups of scholars—the Prague school and the phoneticians—were gravitating toward the position that, regardless what actual *sounds* or "phones" were emitted by a speaker on a given occasion, the unit of *language* was not the "phone" but the "phoneme" (a term which is fully explained later—see Chapter XIV, 1). This gave a close correspondence, as regards a basic unit of linguistic description, to Ferdinand de Saussure's general distinction between *langue* and *parole* (see Chapter II, 3): the phoneme being the unit of *langue,* and the phone of *parole.*

The evolution of the point of view just stated may be taken as a touchstone in the field of linguistics. No one who has not yet appreciated its truth can be regarded as a really *modern* linguist. And yet it would appear that a majority of those concerned with the study and teaching of languages have not yet become aware even of the existence of this position. Evidently there is some failure here of that mechanism of intercommunication among scholars which is part of the basic framework of modern science.

There are at least two apparent causes for this. On the one hand, it is true that a certain minority of linguists have seemed to want, or at least not to be adverse to, a development of linguistics into a narrow cult, within which scholars write only for each other and are not only incomprehensible to the general scholarly world, but really prefer to keep the mysteries unknown save to a choice few initiates.

On the other hand, we may blame the extreme compartmentalization of the contemporary university and the scholarly fields therein represented, the result of which is that in a university which has both a department of linguistics and a department of English, it is certain to be decades before a profound discovery in the former is heard of by those in the latter, and decades more before the latest research in either is reflected in public education on the primary and secondary levels.

While the developments just chronicled were unfolding, another set of circumstances was working on the other side of the Atlantic in a different way toward the growth of linguistics—especially in its descriptive branch. Here the names of Leonard Bloomfield (1887–1949) and Edward Sapir (1884–1939)—each of whom wrote a book destined to become basic in the field—are among the most outstanding.

Bloomfield first qualified himself as an expert in the field of comparative Germanic linguistics; but later the pursuit of a curiosity about American Indian languages (he did some basic work on Cree)[21] led him to consider the general principles underlying all languages, and ultimately resulted in his best-known work, titled simply *Language* (New York: Holt, 1933). This classic, full of original insights and approaches, may be regarded as having founded an American school of linguistics. Bloomfield went to Yale University in 1940 to found its Department of Linguistics, which has ever since been a center of the "American school" in linguistic science.

Sapir, linguist and anthropologist, in the course of his studies of the American Indian became an expert on Indian languages. The utter inadequacy of the techniques of linguistics, as known and practiced in his youth, to handle the description of languages so different from those in the Indo-European family, led him to consideration of basic linguistic principles. His book, earlier than Bloomfield's but identically titled *Language* (New York: Harcourt, Brace, 1921), has remained popular as a readable introduction to the subject, and has probably done much to attract people to the study of linguistics.

Other factors which contributed to the development of linguistics in the United States were, first, the work of various missionary groups, both with American Indians and with African peoples. These, too, having found that traditional "grammar" got them nowhere in describing and teaching these languages, turned to linguistics for help and, finding it there in abundance, continued to have a keen interest in the progress of the science. It is probably through some such connection that the Wycliffe Institute and the Hartford Seminary Foundation organized departments of linguistics—the former well known for its work in American Indian tongues, especially those of Mexico and central America; the latter for African dialects.

Second, the teachers of English to non-native speakers, especially within the United States, found that only approaches based upon the scientific findings of linguistics enabled them to accomplish any real improvement with their students, and they too—a rapidly increasing group—became students and promoters of linguistic science. (The fact that most students of French and German in the United States did *not* learn to speak, read, write or understand any French or German, bothered nobody; schools were expected to give nothing but "practical" instruction, yet in "humanities" subjects—probably because they were considered hopelessly impractical to start with—apparently no such result was looked for.) The interest in linguistics on the part of teachers of English as a second language led to establishment of courses in linguistics in some teacher-training institutions—notably Teachers College, Columbia University.

Third, the need arising suddenly during World War II to provide men in military service with training in the languages of countries where they were to be stationed—languages which had never been taught in American schools—again ultimately led the relevant authorities to have recourse to linguists, as elsewhere detailed (see Chapter XV, 2).

All the most important developments favoring the growth of linguistics in the United States, it is clear, worked toward the development of the descriptive branch, as had also been the case in Europe during the period under consideration. At the present time, therefore, we may picture descriptive linguistics as divided into an "American school"—those linguistic scholars who regard themselves, or can justly be regarded, as followers of Sapir, Bloomfield, and Kenneth Pike—and the "Prague" or European school, those who were professed or *de facto* followers of Troubetzkoy, Jakobson and André Martinet. American descriptive linguists (there are no clearly marked schools among contemporary comparative linguists) tend naturally to belong to the American school, but some Americans and most European linguists follow the Prague school. The two schools are reflected in the two leading professional societies: the *Linguistic Society of America* in general represents the American point of view, the *Linguistic Circle of New York* (named in conscious reminiscence of the *Cercle lin-*

guistique de Prague), the European. There are, besides, many scholars in the field (both in the United States and in Europe) who, whether or not formerly affiliated with either school, are now best classified as independent.[22]

The differences between the two schools are not great and tend to appear only at the higher levels; certainly almost all linguists would agree on fundamentals such as are presented in this work. In the author's opinion, one of the most notable differences is the phenomenon called "juncture" by the American school. This will be more fully explained later (Chapter XIV, 5), but here it may be said that the sort of pause or break in the flow of speech represented by punctuation marks is regarded by the Americans as a phoneme and is classified along with and on the same level as the phonemes, while the Prague linguists emphasize it somewhat less and prefer to treat it in another category, that of "boundary signals."

The American school is like the Prague school in not having a fully elaborated approach to the description of grammatical phenomena, so the various approaches that have been experimentally proposed (including that outlined in Chapters VIII to XI of this book) cannot be regarded as characteristic of one school rather than another. Many American linguists wish to carry out analysis in this area by the methods and procedures of mathematical analysis; but this is probably suggested by the existence of computers and their possible use in mechanical translation (see page 271), and need not be regarded as characteristically American.

The progress of linguistics in the Soviet Union and eastern Europe has tended to be somewhat self-contained because of political conditions, and because so many American scholars cannot read Russian; but the linguistic scene is by no means concealed from one who has the ability and willingness to follow Soviet journals. Naturally, there was an exodus of scholars from Russia in 1917, and about the only linguist of repute who remained was N. Y. Marr—known for his "Japhetic Theory"[23]—whose influence was dominant in Russian linguistics for many years, until the "Soviet Linguistic Controversy" in 1950. About this we cannot go into detail, but as might be expected from the political climate, Stalin's decision that the "younger comrades" were right would have spelled oblivion for Marr, had he not already been dead, and meant that all contemporaries would have been well advised to adopt opinions similar to those of V. V. Vino-gradov, R. I. Avanesov, and other leaders of the newer school. Soviet linguistics is naturally much occupied with descriptive, historical and comparative Slavic linguistic questions, and with the description of the lesser-known languages of the Soviet Union.

Thus, from its beginnings in an age-old basic human curiosity about the mechanics of that indispensable device, language, we find that in four thousand years a full-grown and mature science, with branches and divisions, fundamental postulates and proved hypotheses, has come into being. It provides the student with much to occupy him—much to master—but has still not lost its ancient, fundamental fascination.

Notes to Chapter IV

1. Gray, *Foundations of Language,* 459. Cf. also Jones's observations in a private letter dated 27 September, 1787; see *Dictionary of National Biography* under "Jones."

2. *Ueber das Konjugationssystem der Sanskritsprache in Vergleichung mit jenem der griechischen, lateinischen, persischen und germanischen Sprachen* (Frankfurt, 1816).

3. *Undersögelse om dat gamle nordiske eller islandske sprogsoprindelse* (Copenhagen, 1818).

4. He and his brother, Wilhelm Karl (1786–1859), who was also a philologist, made their collection of fairy tales as a basis for folkloristic study.

5. A *cognate* is a word in a given language which closely resembles, both in form and in meaning, a word in another language, because each of the pair is derived from the *same* word in a third language which is the parent of the other two. Thus, German *Fuss* and English *foot* are cognates, and either is cognate with Latin *pes, pedis.*

6. It should not be assumed that a reconstructed form is identical with a word which once existed; the reconstruction serves its purpose merely as a formula summarizing sound-changes and other developmental trends in a group of languages. But where the possibility exists that the actual word might some day be found in a document—as in the case of Romance philology, where extensive records of the ancestor language exist—a scholars' reconstruction has not infrequently been found to be identical with the real word.

7. In the journal *Beiträge zur vergleichenden Sprachforschung V* (1868), 206–8.

8. Karl Verner, "Eine Ausnahme der ersten Lautverschiebung," *Zeitschrift für*

vergleichende Sprachforschung auf dem Gebiete der indogermanischen Sprachen XXIII, 97–130.

9. There has been much speculation on this topic, but evidence for any firm conclusion is insufficient. Among the locations generally favored are (1) eastern central Asia Minor, (2) the southeastern Ukraine.

10. J. Schmidt, *Die Verwandschaftsverhältnisse der indogermanischen Sprachen* (1872).

11. The English term suggests, not that they were the "younger philologists" (which is what the German term means), but that they were "the believers in neo-Grammar," just as neo-Platonists are followers of neo-Platonism.

12. An abridged edition, originally published in 1897, still circulates.

13. By B. Hrozný: cf. his *Die Sprache der Hethiter* (1916) and E. Sturtevant, *Comparative Grammar of the Hittite Language* (Philadelphia, 1933).

14. Despite which fact it is taught at only two or three universities in the entire United States.

15. It was thought probable that these vanished phonemes might have been deep gutturals or "laryngeals" (see Chapter XIII) such as are encountered in Semitic languages—hence the name "laryngeal theory." Jerzy Kuryłowicz of the University of Krakow, a pupil of Meillet's, has been a leader in the development of this theory.

16. E. g., J. Gilliéron and E. Edmont, *Atlas linguistique de la France* (Paris, 1902–10); F. Wrede, *Deutscher Sprachatlas* (Marburg, 1926–   ).

17. Cf. Albert Dauzat, *Les noms de lieux* (Paris, 1926); Isaac Taylor, *Names and Places* (London, 1864; 2nd ed. 1865); P. Joyce, *Origin and History of Irish Names of Places* (3d ed., Dublin, 1896–1913).

18. Cf. the memoir of Troubetzkoy by R. Jakobson in the French edition of Troubetzkoy's book (*Principes de phonologie,* tr. J. Cantineau, Paris, 1949, xv–xxxiv).

19. This point may be pursued further in the works of Jean Baudouin de Courtenay (1845–1929).

20. For purposes of phonology, we must say that English "has only one *p.*" Yet an extremely simple experiment will show that it has at least two *p-sounds.* Let a match be lighted and held in front of the mouth while the word *pot* is pronounced. The puff of air after the *p* will blow out the match. If the word *spot* be used, the match will not go out. Thus we can clearly distinguish *p* and *ph* physically. Yet, in English, the two variants comprise only one phonemic unit.

21. Cf. his *Sacred Stories of the Sweet Grass Cree,* National Museum of Canada Bulletin No. 60 (Ottawa, 1930).

22. Among these may be mentioned, as worthy of special note, Louis Hjelmslev of Denmark, the proponent of "glossematics"—a highly original approach to the philosophy of language as well as to the methods of describing it. See his *Principes de grammaire générale,* Copenhagen, 1928.

23. According to which the pre-Indo-European languages of Europe were all related to each other and spoken by a single race or racial group, which he called "Japhetic" after Noah's other son. Quite a case can be made for this theory.

Supplementary Readings to Chapter IV

Whitney, *Life and Growth of Language,* 57–58.
Gray, *Foundations of Language,* 79–82.
Sturtevant, *Introduction to Linguistic Science,* 32–37,150–53.
H. Pedersen, *Linguistic Science in the 19th Century, passim.*
Schultz, Sieg and Siegling, *Tocharische Grammatik.*
Mary R. Haas, "The Linguist as Teacher of Languages."
Meillet, *Introduction à l'étude comparative des langues indo-européennes,* 453–83.
John V. Murra, R. M. Hankin, and F. Holling, *The Soviet Linguistic Controversy,* 9–19.

Chapter V

THE WORLD'S LANGUAGES:
EUROPE AND ASIA

The first step in the scientific study of anything is to gather and classify all available data: on this basis theories may be postulated, tested, and proved or disproved. In the field of language it would seem to follow that a basic concern should be to collect exhaustive information on all possible languages, and to set about sorting out all these into groups and categories, before making generalizations about the operations of language.

In practice, however, the stage of theorization cannot be delayed until research is completed, because—to mention only the first obstacle—the amount of data that can be gathered is normally infinite, and research can go on forever. The best that can be done is to avoid beginning theorization before a sufficient amount of data is available for the fundamental principles to emerge.

In this respect, the study of language has been somewhat unfortunate. While it seems obvious that even the most learned European or American has neither first- nor second-hand knowledge about fully two thirds of the languages spoken in the world, there *was* at hand, when the first steps in the science were taken, a large amount of knowledge about a considerable number of languages—those of Europe. It was not then realized that these were all related to one another, and it was assumed that these data were adequate—that study of additional languages would only provide additional illustrations of the same or essentially similar patterns of construction. In other words, it was incorrectly but not unreasonably believed that enough material had been gathered for theorization. Thus, a rather fully developed "science of philology" was elaborated at what was, in reality, too early a time.

After 1900, when scholars began more generally to become acquainted with African, Arctic, Asiatic and American Indian languages (too easily dismissed in the days of Herbert Spencer as "primitive," merely early stages in the "evolution" of language), the impact was to unsettle the very foundations of what in 1880 had been called, with assurance, the "science of grammar." One result is that today many sincere scholars look upon the work of those who seek to give validity and scientific method to the study of grammatical phenomena as somehow subversive.[1]

More than ever, then, it is the duty of modern linguistics to address itself to the task—never yet done both completely and scientifically[2]—not only of taking a census of the world's languages and gathering significant, useful data about as many as possible, but of describing more accurately, in accordance with the latest developments of linguistics, most of those already studied. This task is still in its early stages; but as the present century has advanced and exploration has reduced to relatively small areas those regions of the world (many of them uninhabited, and hence linguistically not significant) about which we have no information, we may begin to feel some confidence that at last all the main types of languages have come to our attention.

1. Geographical and genetic bases of language classification

The first problem in reviewing the world's languages is to decide what to count as a language. We have already dealt with this question (Chapter II, 4); but it really does not affect our present purpose, except insofar as we are interested in the precise number of languages there are in the world. And this, of course, is ultimately a self-contradiction: like the number of words in English or the number of people in the United States, no truly precise figure can ever be ascertained —and certainly not when so little accurate information is obtainable about so many languages. We may take the estimate of the French Academy,[3] that there are about 2,796 distinct languages spoken on earth, as close enough for all practical purposes. More significant is the fact that half a dozen of these are spoken by almost two billion people; in other words, two-tenths of one per cent of the world's languages provide speech to some two-thirds of the world's population. From these figures, incidentally, it will be clear that, in attempting to deal with all the languages of the world in two chapters, we can give only a very cursory mention to the principal families. We shall attempt no more than to classify each family typologically, and suggest its most notable characteristics.

There are three ways in which languages can be classified: geographically, genetically, and typologically. The first of these is used when we really do not know enough about the languages in question to categorize them according to their characteristics; in that case, we merely determine the maximum area over which what may be called "the same language" is spoken, and adopt the geographical divisions of that area as divisions of the language. Thus, if we knew nothing whatever about American Indian languages, we might divide them into North American and South American, Eastern North American and Western North American, and so on.

When no better procedure is possible, it can be argued that the geography of the country may possibly be reflected in its language— physically separated areas having developed different dialects, and other localisms. It seems superfluous to say that this is by no means necessarily so, yet many students of language insist on trying to see in their data genetic boundaries corresponding to long-used geographical ones. Thus, all textbooks distinguish Scottish from Irish Gaelic, but actually there is more difference between the Irish of Munster and that of Donegal than between the latter and that of the Isles. (It would be more nearly correct to say that there are six main dialects of Gaelic: Munster, Connacht, Ulster, Manx, Hebridean, and Highland.)

Where it is known that a number of languages have all descended from a common ancestor, it is of course much preferable to group them according to the *families* they form. Generally, as our knowledge of the languages in a given area improves, we perceive genetic relationships among at least some of them which allow us to postulate family groups and subgroups. Thus, within the last fifteen years, the classification of American Indian languages has shifted from a geographical to a family basis, and we no longer speak of "an Eastern North American Indian language," but of "a language of the Algonkian group." After various languages have been accurately described, the task of comparing them and establishing family relationships belongs to that branch of our science known as *comparative linguistics.*

2. Typological bases of language classification

The third basis of classification, the *typological,* becomes possible only when our knowledge of the languages in question is fairly complete. It is not necessarily preferable to the genetic classification, nor does it supplant the genetic classification (as the latter does the geographic). The typological classification is based on the internal structure of the language, so naturally languages genetically related will tend to fall into the same typological category.

A preliminary sort of typological classification began to develop the better part of a century ago, and from that period we inherit a few terms whose use we shall here continue, while endeavoring to redefine them more clearly and precisely. In older textbooks we find the statement that all languages can be fitted into one or another of three categories—*inflecting, analytic,* or *agglutinative.* To these we shall add the term *polysynthetic*—an old term employed by Edward Sapir (see his *Language,* Chapter VI), to characterize the structure of American Indian and similar languages—and venture the proposition that these four terms can be so defined as to constitute a system capable of embracing all languages. (Other systems have been proposed.)

The first criterion of typological classification is whether the language in question does or does not have a level of structure below that of the sentence: which is to say, *whether or not it has words.*

Traditional grammar took it for granted that all languages had words; language was defined as "a system of words and rules for combining words,"[4] so that the terms "language" and "words" were assumed to be synonymous, and it was regarded as impossible to conceive of a language that was not made up of words. But languages have by now been discovered and studied which manage quite well without the kind of structure to which our term "word" (see Chapter I, 4) could, even with maximum extension, apply. There are some grammarians even today, however, whose attitude on this question is like that of the rustic who, upon seeing a giraffe for the first time in a zoo, averred: "They cain't fool me, by gum; there *ain't* no such animule!"

Though difficult for us to conceive, the situation does not require an especially complex explanation. In languages familiar to us, the word is the first level of structure (first in logic, that is, not necessarily in time): first, words are built up, then sentences are built out of words and word groups.[5] The immediate constituents of the sentence are words (and word groups); the immediate constituents of the words are the formants (see Chapter I, 4). If there were not these two levels of structure, the sentence would be formed directly from the formants—and there would be no words (or, if one insists on calling the resulting structures words, there would be no sentences, but each word of the language could be used in situations which in English, for example, would require a sentence). Very simply put, in a language of this type you cannot make (under normal conditions: cf. Chapters IX, 1 and X, *passim*) an utterance which is not complete enough to be a sentence.

The "wordless" languages are those we shall classify as *polysynthetic*. Examples are the American Indian languages, including Eskimo, and probably many others which are as yet little investigated. (Frequently the real structure of this type of language is not evident from the earliest descriptions, done by traditional grammarians determined to find in them the structure of English or Latin.) Languages which *do* have the concept of the word can then be divided into the three categories *agglutinating, inflecting,* and *analytic.* (See Fig. 11)

The languages we call *agglutinating* can be characterized as very much like polysynthetic languages, except that groups of formants are clearly marked off from adjacent segments of the chain of speech as words; hence a formant must first have a place in a word before it can have a place in a sentence. The word-unit does not yet, however, exert much structural polarity: beyond being required to belong to a word, the formants seem still to have a great deal of independence.

Their "freedom" in fact, is precisely our next typological criterion. As we shall see later in the usage of this book a "free" form is a formant or group of formants which can occur as a word, while a "bound" form is a formant which cannot occur on the word's structural level, but can only occur as part of a word. In agglutinative languages, the tendency is for all formants to be free, in the sense that what can be recognized as the same formant, in essentially the same shape, can be found in almost any position in different words; and a formant within

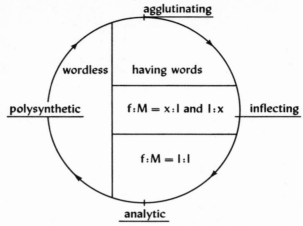

FIGURE 11   Typological classification

a word might also turn up as a root or as an independent word. (Here remember that we are speaking of the essential *tendency,* not describing the actual state of affairs in any particular language.) In this type of language, grouping of formants in words is only a marriage of convenience: aside from having boundaries, the word has little identity or structural organization of its own.

Closely connected with this is what we may call the *morpheme-formant ratio,* another characteristic which helps to define the typological affinities of a language. The formant is any bit of linguistic material —usually, but not necessarily, a sound or syllable—which expresses something. The morpheme is what it expresses. In agglutinative languages, the ratio tends to be one-to-one, that is, the same morpheme (for instance, for plurality) would normally be expressed always by one and the same formant, while a given formant would rarely express more than one morpheme.

But here is perhaps the outstanding characteristic of the *inflecting* languages. In strong contrast to the agglutinative, they regularly show a morpheme-formant ratio of $x : 1$ and $1 : x$; that is, the same morpheme might be expressed by several different formants (e.g., in Latin, the plurality of a noun is indicated by such different endings as -*ae*, -*ī, -a,* and -*ēs*), and one formant expresses several morphemes (e.g., in

78

English, -*s* expresses the plural and the genitive in nouns, but the singular in verbs). As a result, there is a tendency for these polymorphemic formants to crystallize into rigid, invariable systems (declensions and conjugations), and the elements within a word thereupon assume identity as roots, stems or endings (see Chapter VIII, 3; also XII, 5). A list of the fixed, interlocked combinations of formants in one of these systems of bound forms is called a *paradigm*. About two thousand years ago, when Latin was in its heyday, most of the languages of Europe were of the inflecting type; and for many centuries it was assumed that a listing of all the paradigms was a complete description of the grammar of a given language.

The *analytic* type of language is characterized by a tendency toward a morpheme-formant ratio of 1 : 1, and by a resistance to tautology, which tends to develop in inflecting languages (for example, in a Latin phrase like *in omnibus hīs locīs,* the morphemes "ablative" and "plural" have been expressed three times). Because of these characteristics, analytic languages tend to have shorter words than inflecting languages, since the independent identity of the formant is much greater, the formant becoming an independent word. In an analytic language, separate short words have the function of a bound-form system in an inflecting language; thus Latin said *cultellō* where English says "with a knife," *ībam* where English says "I used to go." The ultimate in this direction is a language like Chinese, in which each syllable is a word, and there are no paradigms—all structural information being conveyed syntactically, that is, by groupings of words in the sentence.

Having established these categories of classification, it naturally occurs to the student of language to wonder whether there might be some developmental relationship between one and another. It can be said that there certainly does seem to be a tendency for inflecting languages to develop toward the analytic type, for we have seen just this development in most of the languages of Europe during the course of the last thousand years; and it appears also that Chinese was once inflecting in structure. We might even be tempted to state it as a principle that analytic languages result from the operation on inflecting languages of a tendency toward economy.

Then, too, as more and more data about the history of the Indo-European languages are discovered, reconstructed and elicited, we seem to see vestiges in highly inflecting Indo-European of agglutinative structure, lingering from a period just beyond the frontier of our investigations. Highly analytic Chinese today shows signs of developing in the direction of agglutination. In contemporary Chinese there are many word-combinations which are used together so regularly as to suggest that they have really agglutinated into a single disyllabic (or even trisyllabic) word. On the other hand, it was probably Bopp who first pointed out the similarity between the personal endings of the verb in Indo-European and the personal pronouns and third-person demonstratives (cf. Greek ἐσ-μί, ἐσ-σί, ἐσ-τί and μέ, σύ, τού), which suggest that they might possibly have resulted from an agglutination. (The similarity between ἐσ-σί and σύ, however, is accidental.)

Not enough is yet known about the polysynthetic languages to surmise from what sort of structure they developed; but we can speculate *a priori* that the first development *from* a polysynthetic structure would be the invention of words, probably through the sort of tautology that already arises in such languages, that is, starting with a sentence-word defined by names—"loving-someone-he or she-does-it /John/ Jane" (i.e., "John loves Jane")—the sentence complex may, because of the tautology, lose its self-contained character and become "loves John Jane," whereupon it might become also possible to say "loves he her," the structure now having three distinct words, none of them equivalent to a sentence. (It is interesting to note that a Latin form like *amat* was originally equivalent to a sentence, meaning "he loves someone," until the persons were defined by tautological words: *amat Ioannes Ioannam*). But a polysynthetic language which developed words would probably then be classifiable as agglutinating.

A hypothetical illustration might make clearer the way in which a language of one structural type could develop into another. Let us suppose that, in some Creolized dialect of English, the indication of subject and object by position in the sentence was imperfectly understood, and it became customary to use pronouns for clarity: "This man calls that man" might become "This man, he call him that man," or "Man he call man him." This would be *analytic* structure, with "he" and "him" counting as formants expressing structural morphemes, but having the status of free forms (i.e., independent words). In time, however, these words might coalesce (agglutinate) with the word "man"; however, as long as they were easily recognizable, occurred elsewhere as free forms, and coalesced in different combinations in other words, the structure of the language would be *agglutinating*. But eventually they might lose identity except as endings, and we would say that the "paradigm" of the "declension" of the word *man* was:

Nom. mani
Gen. manz
Dat. mantu
Acc. manim

We might then have sentences like *mani kill bossim, give bossiz money other mantu,* and the language would have become *inflecting*.

All in all, the investigator who is not hampered by Spencerian pseudo-evolutionism may well be inclined to imagine that change in language goes in a great cycle which makes one revolution every five or six thousand years, as represented graphically in Figure 11. The span of recorded history would coincide with the movement from *Inflecting* to *Analytic* among the languages of Europe.

3. Indo-European and its descendants

We have already seen (page 51) how the discovery that tongues so little in contact as Sanskrit and Latin were descended from the same tongue provided the impetus that started the scientific study of language. The task of finding out all the descendants of that language and ascertaining the line of their descent was, as we have seen, the main occupation of linguistics for most of the nineteenth century and indeed still continues (see Chapter XV). It makes, in fact, a sort of detective story, and if it were told in the classic detective-story sequence—from the result back to the ultimate origins of the crime—it might have a considerable amount of suspense and excitement. But it will probably be clearer if we do it the other way and, summarizing all that has been discovered so far, tell the story from its beginning to its consequences in the present day. (Bear in mind that many details are still moot, and that in such cases what is presented here is the author's conclusion as to the most probable theory on each such disputed point.)

It would appear that a very long time ago—about 2500 to 2000 B.C. to be a little more exact—there lived in the interior of eastern Asia

Minor[6] a people who called themselves something like *Arya* (the Sanskrit form: the root is found also in *Ir*-an, *Ar*-menia, *Ire*-land), but who are referred to nowadays most generally as *Indo-Europeans*.[7] We are not sure whether the whole nation was of the same race—for linguistic unity does not presume racial unity, as almost any nation can demonstrate—but there probably *was* an "Indo-European race" which dominated the nation.

Though already in use in Egypt, the art of writing (see Chapter VII, 3–4) had not yet reached the Indo-Europeans, and so they left no written documents, which are, after all, the chief basis of history. What we know of the Indo-Europeans is therefore based mainly on inferences from their language: It is presumed that a word which has a descendant in all or most of the languages derived from Indo-European designated a concept which was at least known to the Indo-Europeans, not discovered later by one of their descendant tribes.

On this evidence it would seem that they did not live near the water, but among forests; that they had such domestic animals as the horse and dog; that kinship was featured prominently in their social organization. They were hunters and raisers of dairy stock and may have kept kitchen gardens, but were not "dirt farmers." Their religion was probably pantheistic.[8] From their conquests it is safe to conclude that they were especially valiant warriors.

We may learn something about them, too, by studying the oldest customs of their oldest descendants—especially those which are paralleled by similar customs among other Indo-European peoples whose history we can trace back equally or almost as far. Thus, the use of cattle for money is found among the early Irish and among the early Romans; the tactic of fighting from chariots is common to the Irish and the Persians. Indo-European society undoubtedly had a class of bards or rhapsodes, and from comparison of the earliest legends of the Indo-European peoples, we have a more than sketchy idea of the repertoire of these artists.

No doubt the Indo-Europeans were mentioned in Egyptian chronicles and in the oral annals, later written down, of the Hebrews; but the problem is to identify *which* non-Egyptian and non-Semitic race appearing in these sources were the Indo-Europeans. Some think that the Hittites or Hethites of the Bible (the *Khatti* of Egyptian records)[9] may have been the Indo-Europeans, and it is established that their language was of the Indo-European family; but no contemporary linguists believe it was *the* Indo-European language. The Indo-Europeans might also have been the Scythians described by Herodotus.[10]

At all events, it seems clear that shortly after 2000 B.C., the Indo-European nation was subjected to such extreme pressure by tribes moving into Asia Minor from the plains of Asia[11] that it broke up, left the homeland, and migrated in many different directions. Some of its members moved directly westward, arrived at the coast of the Ionian Sea, and their descendants a few centuries later appear in history as the Ionian Greeks. Some apparently followed the same coastline around to Greece, and *their* descendants are known to us as Attic Greeks. Some appear to have continued to the Adriatic coast and made their way into Italy, while others moved through central Europe—then, perhaps, a largely uninhabited land of great primeval forests—until they ultimately reached the British Isles. Some crossed the Ionian Sea to Crete, where they overthrew the Minoan civilization, and later its colony in Sparta.

One or more divisions seem to have gone northward and eastward, circling the Black Sea until they reached the fertile Ukrainian plains. And one adventurous branch struck out to the southeast, eventually, after traversing arid deserts and great mountains, to reach India—but not before leaving colonies which were to grow into the nations of Persia and Afghanistan. Considering how far they spread, how many pre-existing populations they must have overcome, and how many great cultures developed among their descendants, we cannot resist the conclusion that the Indo-Europeans were quite a remarkable people. The fact that they are unmentioned in conventional history books is a lesson not to use these latter as an "argument from silence."

These migrations are known to us from linguistic evidence, not historical, but—except in details—they are not less certain for that. They are arrived at by the simple yet perfectly sound process of plotting the present location of languages proved to be descended from Indo-European, and then surmising what migrations and what point of origin could best account for the present distribution of the languages of the Indo-European family.

Figures 12 and 13 summarize all this information in the form of a

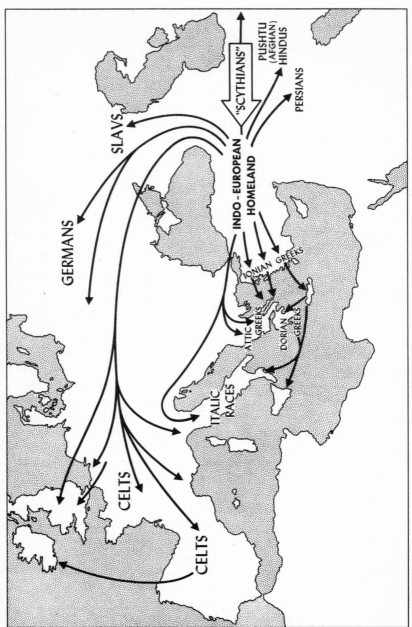

FIGURE 12 Indo-European migrations

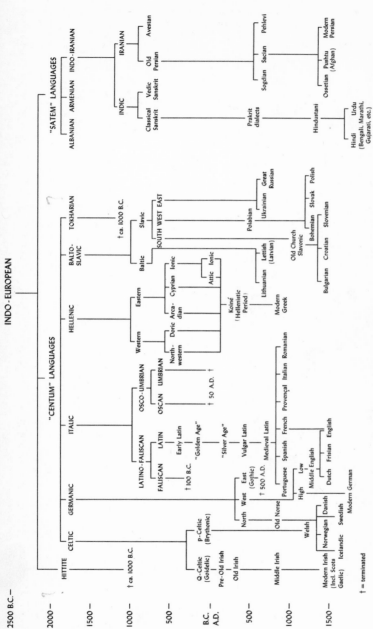

FIGURE 13   Indo-European and its descendants

The proliferation of languages from Indo-European is here laid out to suggest the time spans involved. Languages are entered at the approximate time when they came into existence (exactness in such dating is, of course, out of the question), and are presumed to continue unless shown to terminate (like Hittite and Gothic). It has not been possible to enter all the periods into which any given language could be subdivided.

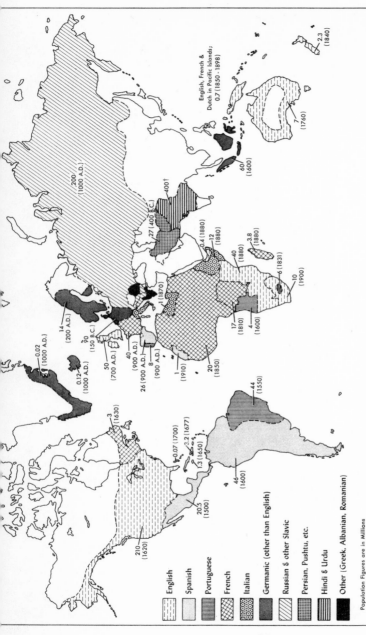

FIGURE 14   Superimposition of Indo-European languages*

* This map shows areas where, at the present day, the dominant or official language is an Indo-European one which has, in recent centuries, been superimposed on an earlier language or languages. The approximate date when this superimposition began is given. The population figures are contemporary totals, and may include many who do not speak the superimposed language. In some cases, this information is omitted for lack of space.

† In India, Hindi and Urdu represent a superimposition of Indo-European about 1000 to 1500 B.C. Beginning about 1750, English was superimposed on the whole country.

86

map and genealogical chart. The topmost level represents the immediate descendants of Indo-European languages which came into being about or shortly after 1500 B.C.; the bottom one, the languages of Indo-European descent in the world today. Note that the so-called "Romance" languages (French, Spanish, Italian, Romanian, and their dialects) are not descended directly from Indo-European, but from Latin which itself was a direct descendant. Naturally some of the finer points of the relationships of these languages to each other, and their consequent location on the chart, are still subject to discussion and revision.

This scheme of classification will account for all the languages today spoken in Europe (excepting only those to be described in the next section) and, of course, for the dominant languages of many countries in North America and elsewhere, where Indo-European tongues have become established in the last three centuries. Figure 14 presents a plotting of what might be called the "colonies" of the Indo-European languages, with the approximate number of native speakers and the approximate time when they were first brought to each area, frequently suppressing local indigenous languages. Of course, before Indo-European speech spread across Europe there were many earlier languages, about some of which (e.g., Basque, Etruscan) we know more than a little, while others are only names preserved in history. But we have not space here to recount what is known about the linguistic picture of pre-Indo-European Europe.

The Indo-European language, and its first descendants, were of the highly inflecting type—indeed, almost any of them might serve as a model for the category. But, during the last thousand years, a tendency toward economy has operated upon them in different degrees until the present-day descendants of Indo-European are all more or less squarely in the analytic column. Compare the analyses of Latin and English structure in Figure 15.

4. Non-Indo-European languages of Europe and India

We have seen that all the languages now spoken in Europe, with only four exceptions, are each and all descended from the language of our remote ancestors, the Indo-Europeans. One cannot help developing respect for those doughty people who, four thousand years after

LATIN	ENGLISH
cant/a/bo —one 3-syllable word *-bo* = 4 morphemes (first person; singular; future; active) *cant-* = root, *canta-* = stem	*I/shall/sing* —3 one-syllable words —each formant one word and one morpheme —*sing* = root, stem and word
libr/i —*i* one of many ways of indicating plural —*i* also indicates "gender," and implies the singular form —note root alternation: *liber, libr-* (cf. German *unser, unsr-*)	*book/s, the book/s* —*s* one of only two ways of indicating plural —because English has an article, plurals can be definite vs. indefinite
homin/is —genitive morpheme expressed by a bound form (ending *-is*) —note root alternation: *homo, homin-*	*man's, of a man, of the man* —genitive morpheme expressed by ending in 1 case, by word in 2
serv/o —2 formants, 1 message (the root), 1 structural (the ending)	*to a slave; I/serve* —each morpheme expressed by a separate formant is a separate word

FIGURE 15   Inflecting and analytic structure

being forced from their homeland, are not only still represented in history, but represented over such a wide area and by such noteworthy cultures. More than a billion people have inherited or adopted one or another of the Indo-European-descended languages and these include some of those most advanced in civilization. Surely, our ancestors must have been people of considerable prowess, possessed of a strain of genius which has continued to reappear in their remotest descendants.

The four languages which are indigenous to Europe but not Indo-European are Finnish, Estonian, Hungarian and Basque. Since the first three belong to the Finno-Ugric family, to which we shall devote a special section, our task here is only to describe Basque and the non-Indo-European languages of India.

Basque and the non-Indo-European languages of India. The Basque language is so little known that many well-educated persons have never heard of it; yet upon inquiry both the language and the people who speak it prove to be quite fascinating. The people call themselves *Euskara,* which might possibly mean "the left-handed ones" (Basque *esker,* Spanish *izquierdo*). An older form of the name seems to have had the root *e-wesk-* or *e-wask-,* whence the Spanish *los Vascos* (pronounced *Baskos*) and the English name, and the French *Gascon* (from *Guascon*). The Basques live on both sides of the French-Spanish border, but the majority are in the Spanish province (once nation) of Navarre. As of 1950, there were estimated to be 750,000 native speakers of the Basque language (of whom at least 80 per cent are bilingual in Basque and Spanish or French, or both), but the nation has had an influence on the Spanish people and on the history of Spain quite out of proportion to its size—and it used to be much larger. (Basque place names are found in Spain almost as far south as Madrid, and such well-known Spanish personal names as Mendoza, Vázquez, Vasconcelos, Urrutia, Aguirre, Echeverría are originally Basque.)

Despite many efforts, no connection between the Basque language and any other has ever been proved. The conclusion seems inescapable that it was already there when the Indo-Europeans arrived in Spain—and place names show that the Basques must have at one time controlled the whole northern half of the country. Basque is, therefore, the sole survivor of the languages spoken in western Europe before the Indo-Europeans entered it. It might well be a descendant of the language spoken by the so-called "cave men."

No thoroughgoing study of Basque according to the principles and methods of modern scientific linguistics is yet available; and in its absence, even a summary description of the language cannot be made with complete confidence, since in the case of a language of this type, traditional studies invariably obscure the actual structure by persistently interpreting all phenomena of the language either in terms of Greco-Latin "grammar" or of some contemporary Indo-European language.

Basque is undoubtedly agglutinative—possibly polysynthetic, but there seem to be genuine words. The formants, however, have great independence—much more than in an inflecting language. The phonemic system proves to be quite like that of Spanish, which is not surprising when we remember that Basque is the substratum[12] of Spanish. (Basque has two *s*-phonemes, written "-s" and "-z," a fact which may underlie Spanish *ceceismo*.) It is said that the verbal system has a characteristic tendency to become passive and nominal (for example, *Joanesek etxe bat erosi du,* 'John has bought a house,' literally 'by-John house one bought is'), but such statements have to be interpreted in the light of the fact that in agglutinative languages, where the same suffixes often attach as easily to what other languages translate as "nouns" as they do to what we would call "verbs," these two word classes may not be completely distinct from each other.

Our count of only four non-Indo-European languages in Europe will not be upset by the Caucasian tongues, spoken largely in the all but inaccessible glens of the Caucasus Mountains, between the Black Sea and the Caspian, between Europe and Asia. They, like Basque, are probably a remnant of the languages spoken in Europe before the arrival of the Indo-Europeans, although attempts to link them with Basque have not been successful. There are a dozen or more, including Abkhaz, Circassian, and others whose speakers have provided Russia with some of that nation's fiercest cavalrymen. Most of the Caucasian languages are spoken by only a few thousand people; but one fairly sizable exception is the group of three related languages, Georgian, Mingrelian and Laz, which among them count 2,000,000 speakers. (A particularly famous one was the late Josef Stalin, a Georgian.) Georgia is undoubtedly the land to which Jason of Greek legend journeyed, and the "Golden Fleece" may have been the product of prehistoric gold mines.[13] These languages appear to be of the inflecting type, and are characterized by clusters of many consonants, including sequences not admitted in most other languages, e.g., *mkv-*.

Turning now to the situation in India, it seems evident that the Indo-European conquest of that great peninsula extended only to the vicinity of a line drawn from Goa to Hyderabad, and thence to the coast. North of this line (that is, in Pakistan and the northern half of India) the indigenous languages (including such widespread tongues as Gujarati, spoken around Bombay, Bengali, Marathi, Singhalese) are all derivatives of the ancient Sanskrit—with the exception of some isolated enclaves of non-Indo-European speech, and these appear to be of the same stock as the languages below the Goa-Hyderabad line.

In lower India and most of Ceylon the many native tongues are non-Indo-European, but they all seem to belong to one family, to which the name Dravidian is given (from Sanskrit *Dravida*). Noteworthy languages in the Dravidian group are Tamil, Telugu and Malayalam. The languages of this family have not been by any means adequately explored, and very little generalization about them is justified, but it is clear that they are agglutinating in structure and tend to very long words. The island of Ceylon is divided about half and half between Indo-European and Dravidian. Portuguese' is, of course, spoken as a colonial language in Goa.

A curious derivative of the Indo-European languages of India is the Gypsy language. The details have not been worked out, but the gypsies apparently migrated from India westward during the Middle Ages, and each European nation thought they came from the East ("Gypsy" is from Egyptian; the French call them *Bohèmes*, 'Bohemians'; the Germans, Italians and Slavs call them *Zigeuner, zingaro, zigan*).

A word might be said about Hindustani, which a century ago was considered almost the universal language of India, and now has no official existence. This paradox is explained by the fact that Hindustani was a *lingua franca* based on a dialect much like most of the descendants of Sanskrit;[14] it was understandable to almost all Indo-European speakers, in India, but not spoken in what might be called its "classic" form by anyone.

Today we find Hindi listed as the official language of India, and Urdu as that of Pakistan. The former is written in the ancient Sanskrit characters (*devanagari*) and the latter in Arabic script; but it is at first surprising to find that when one hears them spoken, they sound very much alike, and both much like the old Hindustani. The explanation is (to simplify the situation radically) that Hindi is Hindustani filled out with borrowings from Sanskrit, while Urdu is Hindustani filled out with borrowings from Persian and Arabic—conforming to the religious orientation of the two nations.

We must not omit to mention that English, though a second language for almost all natives of India and Pakistan, because of historical conditions that need not be detailed is so widespread there as to be more universal than any native language. Hence it is essential to the deliberations of government and to the operation of all government services, and will probably continue to be, willy-nilly, an indispensable monument to British involvement in India for many decades to come.

Finno-Ugric and Altaic. The remaining European languages which are not Indo-European are Finnish, Estonian, and Hungarian; these form the group conventionally referred to as Finno-Ugric. They are closely related to each other—though not mutually comprehensible—and may also be related, although much more distantly, to Turkish and the Altaic family of which Turkish is the best-known language.

Finnish is, of course, the national language of Finland (though Swedish is almost equally widespread), and we are here considering such languages as Permian, Mordvinian, Livonian, Cheremiss and the language of the Lapps (which is also spoken in the extreme north of Sweden and Norway) as related to dialects of Finnish. We name Estonian as distinct largely because it has been a national language, although Russia has again swallowed up Estonia.

Hungarian and Turkish have been thought related somewhat as are Irish and Russian, and there are languages very similar to, and probably—in many cases certainly—related to Turkish, strung out from eastern Asia Minor across central Asia as far as the western provinces of China: such languages as Tatar, Kalmuck, Uzbek, Turkoman, Mongol, and Manchu. Many of them are spoken by very small tribes in very inaccessible areas, and are only sketchily known. It is probable that they are the last remnants of that vast westward surge of people whose first impact on Europe caused the break-up of the Indo-Europeans around 2000 B.C., and which did not subside and come to rest until after the Battle of Lepanto in A.D. 1571—a span of almost four thousand years, encompassing the rise and fall of many great empires.

All the languages of the Finno-Ugric and Altaic groups have the agglutinating structure, and are characterized by "vowel harmony"; that is, the vowels are regarded as belonging to one of two or three groups (front, back, neutral), and in each word the vowels of the suffixes or postpositions must match the quality of the vowels of the root. Thus, Hungarian often makes the plural with the suffix *-vowel* + *k,* the vowel varying with the harmony, so that the plural of *ház,* 'house' is *házak*; but the plural of *ember*, 'man' has to be *emberek*, since the suffix has to have a palatal vowel to join a palatal root. This gives the spoken language a surprising liquidity and melodiousness.

Other features common to these languages are an invariable word accent (in Hungarian and Finnish, always on the first syllable; in Turkish, always on the last), and no forms expressing "gender." The words are sometimes quite long, due to the accumulation of postpositions, but the vowel harmony and accent serve to maintain their identity.

Finnish has genuine long vowels and double consonants, whereas in Hungarian the so-called "long" vowels differ in quality from their theoretical short counterparts, and in Turkish there is no such correlation. The languages differ, too, in the number of "cases" (Finnish is supposed to have fifteen), but this is probably largely due to variation in description; for while languages of this type have no "cases" at all in the sense of Latin or Greek—they really have as many cases as they have postpositions.

Another feature of agglutinating languages is, as we have said, the relative freedom of suffixes: sequences of three or four in one word do not stiffen into standardized "endings," so new combinations can theoretically be created at any time, and in fact, probably often are. (As soon as the users of the language restrict themselves to a few standardized combinations, the language is on the way to becoming inflectional.) This can be illustrated as follows: in Turkish, *baba* is 'a father'; *baban*, 'a father's'; *babam* is 'my father,' so *babamin* is 'my father's'; *babalar* is 'fathers,' *babalarim* 'my fathers,' *babalarimin* 'of my fathers.' Theoretically, a root (see Chapter XII, 5) plus any combination of suffixes can in turn be taken as a root to which are applied all the same suffixes or combinations thereof.

The agglutinating languages have great resources of expressiveness, and it is estimated that sixty million people speak languages of the Finno-Ugric and Altaic groups. Anyone who seeks to learn the fundamental principles of language should master at least one of this type.

5. The Sino-Tibetan languages

Vast as the continent of Asia is, it is not nearly as congested linguistically as Europe or Africa (or even the Caucasus), for large stretches are sparsely populated, while in the populous areas—and they, indeed, are teeming—a single language-family will encompass an almost incredible number of people. Thus, languages of the Sino-Tibetan family (which includes not only Chinese and Tibetan, but also Thai, Burmese, and Vietnamese) are spoken by approximately five hundred million people. (Thai is now often excluded.)

Chinese is a perfect example—indeed, might be taken as the pro-totype—of the *analytic* type of language structure. It is at the oppo-site pole from polysynthetic languages (where no syllable or group of syllables is a word) in that *every* syllable is a word—and conversely, therefore, all words are monosyllabic. Thus, there is no morphology in languages of this type, since there is no principle governing the or-ganization of formants within words: everything is syntax, since it comes under the principle of the organization of words within the sentence.

In practice, to be sure, two or more monosyllabic words are often taken together to express a concept for which another language might use one word (e.g., *hsia⁴ wu,³* 'bottom noon' = 'afternoon';[15] *chung¹ kuo²* 'center country' = "China";[16] sometimes one of the words is not translatable into another language, e.g., *hai² tzu³* 'child,' originally 'this child'); but although such word groups are common, the sepa-rate words remain truly distinct, as in the English phrase "repeat per-formance" or the French *compte rendu*. (Some linguists deny this.)

As a result of this type of structure, some morphemic concepts that seem to us essential play no part in Chinese. Thus, there is naturally neither gender, number nor case. Plurals, for instance, are expressed by a number, or a word meaning *'many'*: *pa¹ jen²* = 'many man' = 'men.' An expression like 'the man's house' would be rendered 'house this man belong.' (It will be noticed that Chinese, literally trans-lated, sounds rather like Pidgin English. This is because Pidgin Eng-lish is in large measure, English vocabulary with Chinese grammar.) A verbal expression like 'he wrote' is *ch'i² wen² liao⁴*, i.e., ('he) write finish.'

Limiting the word structure to monosyllables results in a relatively small supply of words, especially as many Chinese dialects permit no final consonants except *-n* and *-ng*. In some dialects only about 400 words are possible. It may well be this which has led to another out-standing feature of the Sino-Tibetan family—the *tones*. Each syllable may be pronounced in one of four ways—level, rising, falling-rising, and falling; a roughly equivalent cadence, it has been suggested,[17] may be heard in English in (1) *ding* (as in ding-dong-bell), (2) what? (3) well? (4) now! Thus, *shi*[1] is 'to lose,' *shi*[2] 'ten,' *shi*[3] 'history,' and *shi*[4] 'market.' This, of course, quadruples the possibilities, but 1,600 to 1,700 words are still not many (the average speaker of English is estimated to know up to 70,000),[18] and Chinese often has to contend with ambiguities, though of course all concepts get expressed in some way.

There are many dialects of Chinese, some with several million speakers, and a few which would probably be counted as distinct languages if it were not for the political unity of China. A standard Chinese called *kuo*[2] *yü*[4] (nation-language) is gradually becoming widely adopted; it is based on North Mandarin, the dialect of Peiping, and seems to be suppressing other dialects and to have, or to be acquiring, the necessary prestige to establish itself. The spread of literacy with the standard writing system, *Wen*[2]-*Li*[4] tends to spread the *kuo*[2] *yü*[4] of which it is the expression. But literacy is slow to spread because *Wen*[2]-*Li*[4] is a complicated graphic system (see Chapter VII), and a close transcription (e.g., into Roman letters) would destroy cultural unity.

The other languages mentioned above are very much like Chinese. Thai (Siamese) has five tones, and Tibetan is in many ways somewhat more archaic than Chinese. The scientific reconstruction of earlier stages of Chinese has a long way yet to go, but the amount of change that has taken place since Marco Polo's time can be seen in the word *tea*, which was evidently pronounced *tay* when borrowed from Chinese in the thirteenth century, but is *ch'a* in contemporary Chinese.

6. Japanese

It is often thought that the Japanese and Chinese languages are closely related, but in fact they are not even similar. It is true, however, that cultural relations between the two countries have been close since the fourth century A.D.; the Japanese have used the Chinese script since then, and many Chinese words have been borrowed into Japanese. But the situation is like that between Persian and Arabic, which also are unrelated linguistically despite the fact that Arabic culture has long held a most prominent place in Persian life.

So far is Japanese from Chinese, indeed, that in one feature they are exact opposites: Chinese has *l* but no *r*, while Japanese has *r* but no *l*. Actually, this is most probably an oversimplification: each language has a single phoneme (neither has the *l/r* distinction) which to the American or English ear sounds now as *r*, now as *l*.[19]

Japanese appears to be essentially agglutinative in structure, or at a stage between analytic and agglutinating. The words are regularly more than one syllable, and the roots appear to be modified by affixes, which, however, are treated (perhaps under the influence of Chinese) as separate words—they are independently stressed—and yet are not really independent words, for they cannot in turn be roots. Thus, *uchi ni* means "in the house," *hoteru e* means "to the hotel." Consider this sentence: *Kono mono wa nani ni tsukaimasu ka?* ("What is this used for?") Here *kono-mono-wa* means "This-thing-concerning"; *nani-ni* = "what-for"; *tsukaimasu-ka* "use question." (We could just as well write *konomonowa nanini tsukaimska*. Note that unaccented *i* and *u* are frequently dropped out.) Verbs are distinguished from nouns by a different set of formants which are considered part of the word—unlike the noun's postpositions—but are easily distinguished from it. In the case of verbs, there are alternate series of endings for *familiar, polite* or *honorific* situations. This is unique in Japanese and certain other Far Eastern languages, where special provision is made in the basic structure of the language for recognition of the social status of the person addressed. (Such recognition is made to a greater or less extent in other languages too, of course—including Indo-European languages—but usually by style or vocabulary. Nevertheless we do have German *duzen* and *siezen,* French *tutoyer*.)

The Japanese language is easily written in Roman letters and, for English speakers, quite easy to learn if so written. (In these respects again it is distinct from Chinese.) The language is spoken as a native tongue by at least a hundred million people, and with remarkable uniformity, for there are no clearly differentiated dialects.

7. Other languages of Asia

The language families thus far characterized include all languages spoken in Asia (excluding Semitic and the Asiatic islands except the Japanese), with two exceptions. One of these, Korean, has long been assumed to be closely related to Japanese; in fact, the linguistic family is often listed as "Japanese-Korean." But there are some grounds for suspecting that this assumption, founded mainly on the fact that the country was for centuries ruled by Japan, is not entirely valid. (Before that it was ruled for an equal length of time by China.) Most of the literature about Korean is in Japanese, making it difficult of access in the West. Also, the facts are often disguised by the assumption that Korean is ignorantly spoken Japanese. The phonology of Korean is similar to that of both Japanese and Chinese—perhaps slightly favoring the latter—with the noteworthy differences that Korean has both *l* and *r*, and in final position permits both *m* and *n* (in place names like Panmunjom, for example). The structure is less like Chinese—words appear to be polysyllabic, although naturally much of the vocabularly is borrowed from Japanese—but it seems to differ in fundamental respects from Japanese also. In any event, it seems to be agglutinating. Korean has a twenty-four letter alphabet of its own (called *onmun*), invented specifically for it in the fifteenth century, which is more efficient than either Wen^2-Li^4 or Japanese *kana*—at least for writing Korean.

More study of Korean is evidently needed, and the same can be said even more emphatically for Ainu, the remaining Asian language—like Basque, one of the world's most fascinating linguistic mysteries. There are only about 20,000 Ainus. They live in conditions somewhat similar to those of the Indians of the United States, in certain areas on the Japanese islands, and are evidently the remnant of the people who inhabited the island empire before the Japanese came. Anthropologically, they seem to be related to the races of Europe: they certainly do not have the characteristics of the Japanese, Chinese or Manchurian races; they are fair-skinned and their eyes are not "slanted." Their language is definitely unrelated to Japanese, but no one has suggested what language family, if any, it *is* related to. Information on it is too sparse for us to venture a characterization—except that the word *ainu,* meaning "man," "a human being," strikes us as resembling the word *inyu* of several American Indian languages with the same meaning.[20] The Ainus are spoken of as living in primitive conditions, but "primitive" here may mean merely that, dwelling in remote and unfrequented districts, they preserve ancient customs and social organization quite different from those familiar to us, and are, of course, unacquainted with modern technology. All sorts of interesting theories could be launched to account for the Ainu, but in the absence of fuller evidence, they would all be equally unfounded.

In this chapter we have reviewed, by families, the languages of two continents and of approximately 1,750,000,000 people, of which the Indo-European family includes slightly more than half, say 60 per cent. Here is certainly a vast storehouse of data from which to build a science of language. Individuals who have in hand any significant fraction of these data are, unfortunately, rare indeed. As a matter of fact, American and most European schools teach no language from outside the Indo-European group, except on the most advanced levels at the largest universities.

It would seem a truism that to be a linguist (scientific or otherwise) one must first learn to speak *many* languages. One sees today, however, some evidence of a tendency among some professed linguists and more linguists-to-be to theorize *about* language without a real grasp or fluent command of more than one or two (if that many) besides the native one; so that native speakers, when available, complain that the theories are founded on forms or principles not actually in use. The student who wishes to become a professional linguist should speak at least two or three languages (not including his own) as well, or almost as well as a native, and should acquire this skill before, or at least concomitantly with, his training in linguistics. He should know in this way at least one non-Indo-European language—preferably one of each of the four basic structural types.

These requirements make the road to real scholarship in linguistics seem an exceedingly arduous one—too steep, undoubtedly, for a majority of those who might otherwise favor this as a profession. But these requirements, like most ideals, are seldom completely achieved. Anything less, however, risks the great waste of building up a false science of language. As this has already been done once, it is to be hoped it will not be done again.

Notes to Chapter V

1. Cf. L. A. Waters, S. J., "Progressivist Attack on Grammar," *America* XCIX (April 12, 1958), 56–58; J. Donald Adams in *New York Times Book Review*, Jan. 31, 1960, 2.

2. The nearest approach is Meillet, A., and M. Cohen, *Les langues du monde,* 2d ed., Paris, 1952.

3. Cited in Gray, *Foundations of Language,* 417.

4. *Webster's New International Dictionary,* under "language."

5. The reason for the existence of words is probably the psychological difficulty of perceiving accurately a sequence of more than four or five syllables. See Chapter XII, 1.

6. See Chapter IV, Note 9, and C. W. Ceram (pseud.), *The Secret of the Hittites,* New York, Alfred A. Knopf, 1958, 77.

7. The terms *Indo-Aryan* and *Indo-Germanic* are now falling into disuse, although German writers still prefer *Indogermanisch.*

8. Some fairly probable surmises about the religion of the Indo-Europeans can be made on the basis of comparison of the pre-Christian religions of their oldest descendants. Some work along this line has been done by Georges Dumézil of the University of Paris and Myles Dillon of the Dublin Institute for Advanced Studies.

9. Cf. Ceram, *op. cit.,* 56, 26.

10. Herodotus *Historiae* i. 15, 103–6.

11. This was the beginning of a pressure on Europe from the east which continued, with varying intensity, for about 3500 years. See page 92.

12. When the language of an area is replaced by another language, linguists say that the former is the *substratum* of the latter. The lingering, though dwindling influence of the substratum may affect the new language in various ways to varying degrees.

13. The late Prince Troubetzkoy (see pages 64–65) was a student of Caucasian languages, and author of the *Encyclopaedia Britannica* article on them (12th edition). A contemporary authority on Caucasian is Dr. Aert Kuipers of Columbia University.

14. It is clear that the names *Hindu, Hindi, Indus, India* and *Sindh* have the same root.

15. The superscript numbers represent "tones," for which see page 95.

16. America is called *mei*[3] *kuo*[1], which is an attempt to approximate the English word, but happens to mean "beautiful country."

17. See Hsi-en Chen, T., and Chung-chen, W., *Elementary Chinese Reader and Grammar,* South Pasadena, Calif., P. and I. Perkins, 1945, viii.

18. Cf. M. Pei, *The Story of Language,* 96, and A. Ellegård, "Estimating Vocabulary Size," *Word* XVI, 2 (August 1960), 219–44.

19. An ancient parallel is found in the Bible, Judges xii. 6: The Hebrew language had the sound *sh,* the Ephraimite dialect did not—hence *shibboleth* made a good password. It was because Greek and Latin did not have *sh* either that Hebrew place names containing the word *shalom* ("peace") are given in the Bible as we know it under the spelling *Salem.* For the same reason, *Jesus* and *Joshua* became distinct names.

20. If any Indian language encountered by Columbus was related to Algonquian the similarity of *inyu* (really a contraction of *iyinyu;* a cognate, *ilinyu,* gave the State of Illinois its name) to Spanish *indio* could be responsible for Columbus' belief that he had arrived in India, rather than any notion that the course he had sailed would have taken him to that country; for it was *China* he wanted to reach.

Supplementary Readings to Chapter V

The *Encyclopaedia Britannica* article on each language mentioned.
Pei, *The World's Chief Languages, passim.*
Meillet and Cohen, *Les langues du monde, passim.*
Gray, *Foundations of Language,* 295–418.
Sapir, *Language,* 120 ff.
Bloomfield, *Language,* 199–200.
Whitney, *Life and Growth of Language,* 179–212.

Chapter VI

THE WORLD'S LANGUAGES:
AFRICA, THE PACIFIC, THE AMERICAS

We now turn to the languages of other continents and archipelagoes. In the two continents so far considered, relatively few languages are spoken by very large numbers of people; in the areas now to be reviewed, the opposite is true—each of a large number of distinct languages is, with some exceptions, spoken by a small, sometimes a very small community.

The first linguistic family which we shall examine is of prime importance, not only from the linguistic point of view, but also for historical, archeological, religious and many other considerations. There are records in these languages back to three and four thousand years B.C., and Western culture and civilization unquestionably originated among the peoples of whose culture these ancient languages were the vehicle.

1. The Semitic languages

At the time of the oldest existing records, we find the earliest known representatives of this family spoken at the eastern end of the Mediterranean, south of Asia Minor and westward into northern Africa. From before the beginning of recorded history the Semitic peoples inhabited the Arabian desert, and from time to time one or more of these tribes would make their way into the fertile plains at the desert's edge and there settle down to an agricultural life, abandoning their original nomadic culture. Thus, beginning about 3000 B.C., the Hebrews started to move into the land of Canaan (essentially modern Palestine); the Akkadians moved into the plain of Shinar, inhabited by the Sumerians, and founded the city of Babylon; and the Assyrians, further north along the Tigris, occupied the upland of Assur (where they were often harried by the Hittites). Already at this time Egypt had reached a high level of civilization, and between Egypt and Sumeria there was regular communication—no doubt over well-marked caravan routes, which may in themselves have attracted Semitic desert raiders.

When the Akkadians adopted the cuneiform writing of the Sumerians, the first known records were made in a Semitic language—using the term "Semitic" in the narrower sense, with reference only to the languages of the tribes of the Arabian desert. (The latest researches suggest that to consider Egyptian and the related languages of northern Africa a distinct subgroup, more closely related to each other than to the Semitic languages, is to perpetuate an unjustified geographical classification; according to this view, some other term, such as "Afro-Asiatic," should be found to designate all the languages, without subgroups.) But it was certainly not much later that the Old Semitic syllabic script was originated, probably from the Egyptian writing (see Chapter VII, 5), and was first put into use by the Phoenicians, northerly cousins of the Hebrews and inhabitants of what is now Lebanon.

Through many centuries of ancient and medieval history, different peoples of the Semitic stock succeeded each other in playing major roles in the development of civilization in the "cradle of Western culture." The Phoenicians traded all over the Mediterranean, and founded Carthage, the nation on the site of contemporary Tunisia which was the early rival of Rome. The Arameans, about 1500 B.C., emerged from the desert and occupied Syria (until recently merged with Egypt as the United Arab Republic), where they founded the storied city of Damascus. Their language, Aramaic, eventually displaced many other Semitic dialects and became the general language in the region between the Mediterranean shore and the desert, between Egypt and central Asia Minor. By the time of Christ, even Hebrew had yielded to Aramaic, and it was that language which Christ and his disciples spoke.[1] In later times, Aramaic developed into Syriac, and sacred literature in Syriac is still preserved; but Syriac itself ultimately gave way to Arabic. On the Persian Gulf, the Chaldaeans overran the Assyrians and Babylonians. Meantime the migration of the Indo-Europeans was taking place, so that even as the Assyrian empire fell (seventh century B.C.), the Persian empire was rising to dominance in Asia Minor.

What we may regard as the last of these waves of Semitic people washing in from the desert and displacing their predecessors was begun with the foundation of the Mohammedan religion in 622 A.D., and the subsequent spread of Islam and the Arabian people, language and culture all over the southern Mediterranean and even into Spain and Portugal. At the present time, Arabic is the chief Semitic language (with widely varying dialects, ranging from very archaic to what, but for tradition, might be called new languages developed from classical Arabic); but Hebrew has apparently been successfully revived in Israel—though Israeli Hebrew, too, is something quite different from that spoken in ancient times.

Besides the languages so far named, we must also mention the dialects of southern Arabia, and four languages spoken in Ethiopia—Tigre and Tigriña, Amharic (the national language), and the older Geez, the liturgical language.

The phonology of the Semitic languages is quite a bit different from the familiar phonemic systems of the Indo-European group: it includes several phonemes—especially in the guttural category—which are unknown in European languages, and systems of correlations are found which are unknown or at least rare in the more familiar tongues.

As regards structure, the Semitic languages exhibit a curious dualism. Striking, and with only distant analogies in other languages, is the feature of consonantal triliteral roots conveying the message information, and arrangements of the vowels interspersed in this framework conveying the structural information, resulting in what might be called 'two-dimensional-words' (for more data, see Chapter VII, 4). This type of structure is found more predominantly in the Semitic verb (cf. Arabic *šāf,* 'he saw,' *yišūf,* 'he is seeing,' *šāyif* 'seeing,' *šōf,* 'the seeing'), but it can also be found in nouns in the so-called "broken plurals" (cf. *kitāb,* 'book,' plural *kutūb; bint,* 'girl,' plural *banāt*).

On the other hand, this structure comprises only about half, or less than half, of the grammar of a Semitic language; the other half seems to fall into the familiar and conventional *inflectional* category (cf. *tōrōbēza*, 'table,' *tōrōbēzāt*, 'tables,' *tōrobēzen*, 'two tables'). The verb shows signs of nominal character; the "person endings" are the same as the possessive suffixes of the noun.

The comparative study of Semitic languages (as, indeed, of all language families other than Indo-European) is still in its infancy: perhaps when it has developed further we shall be able to reconcile these two structural principles in one inclusive view.

2. The "Hamitic" languages

Turning to the so-called "Hamitic" subgroup, the first and most important language is, of course, ancient Egyptian. Records were made in this language almost 3,000 years before the birth of Christ— but as the script was syllabic, and no living language of today is descended from Egyptian, we have no adequate knowledge of the vowel-phonemes or vocalic system; one school of Egyptologists (e.g., Petrie) simply substitutes an *e* for every unknown vowel, and would transcribe a name as, e.g., *Akhenaten,* while another (e.g., Breasted) follows Coptic and would render the same name as *Ikhnaton*. This lack of knowledge hampers us in forming an idea of the language; no one has attempted a phonemic description of ancient Egyptian, but it seems clear that its basic structure is similar to that of Arabic and Hebrew. The very age of the records in this language may work to conceal the basic relationship between it and Semitic as we know the latter; for in effect we have to compare Egyptian of 2500 B.C. with Arabic of more than two thousand years later. Linguistic development in that interval might well have obscured a relationship originally much more evident.

The Coptic language, spoken in Egypt and Ethiopia down to the sixteenth century, was the descendant of ancient Egyptian (the name probably preserves the native name of the Egyptian language, for Egypt was called "the house of Ptah," *heka Ptah*) and, although no longer a living language, is still used (like Latin in Europe) as a liturgical language of Ethiopian Christians.

The next main component of the "Hamitic" group is the various languages spoken widely over northern Africa by the Berbers and Tuaregs, the wandering tribes of the Sahara desert: such languages as Cabyle and Shilkh come under this heading, but they, like so many languages of Africa, have been imperfectly investigated.

Arabic and Berber—with, of course, a slight overlay of the languages of colonizing countries, such as Spanish, French and Italian—account for the speech of all of the upper third of Africa, north of a line drawn from Senegal on the Atlantic coast to Eritrea on the Red Sea. In Abyssinia, as we have seen, Hamito-Semitic languages are spoken, and also in the Somalilands; the languages of these latter regions—Somali, Galla and Beja—have been regarded as a special subgroup of Hamito-Semitic, and named Cushitic (the ancient Egyptians called this area Cush). Last in this family is a group of languages spoken south of our line, in Nigeria and around Lake Chad. Noteworthy among the Chad languages is Haussa, rather widely used as a trade language.

3. Central and southern African languages

While it is not geographically accurate, for our present purposes we shall define "central Africa" as that part of the Dark Continent between one line drawn from Senegal to Eritrea (about 14° north latitude), and another drawn from the Atlantic coast along the southern border of Angola to the Mozambique strait (at about 16° south latitude). This will include Ghana, Liberia, Nigeria, the Congo, Kenya, Uganda, Rhodesia and Tanganyika. This is the region of equatorial forest, primitive tribes, and exotic wild life—of elephants, pygmies, gorillas, headhunters and cannibals.

Over this whole area, the so-called Niger-Congo language family is dominant—which is a way of saying that there seems to be enough evidence to justify the conclusion that the many languages spoken over this wide area all belong to a single family, which we label the Niger-Congo family. The languages of Sierra Leone, Senegal, Liberia, Ghana, coastal Nigeria, and the Cameroons come under this heading. The largest subgroup of the Niger-Congo family is the Bantu languages, including Swahili in the Congo and in eastern Africa, Kikuyu in Kenya, and Zulu in South Africa.

Excluding the Niger-Congo family, there remain in central Africa only (1) a few languages here and there which are either undescribed or which cannot be proved related to any other, and (2) one other group—the Upper Nile group, spoken along the headwaters of the Nile in the Sudan, and also extending westward into what was formerly French Equatorial Africa and southeastward into Uganda, Kenya and Tanganyika. This group includes the Masai and Nuba languages.

The remainder of the African continent can be covered in a brief compass. Here European colonization has gone on for a long time, and Indo-European languages—first Afrikaans (Dutch), later English—have become well established, as the languages of as much as a third of the population and as the official languages of the governments of the Cape colonies. As regards the native African languages in these nations, it seems that in relatively recent times tribes of the Bantu speech overran an earlier stock represented by Hottentot and Bushman in South Africa, by Hatsa and Sandawe in Tanganyika. These four appear to be related and have been called the Khoisan group. Several Indo-European languages of northern India are rather widely spoken in Africa, due to migration.

As to the structure of the languages of Africa, the "Hamitic" languages are, as has been stated, similar to the Semitic. About the vast Niger-Congo group it is difficult to make statements which will be both substantially true of all the various languages, and not so sweepingly general as to be of little practical use. It can be said, however, that these languages frequently feature phonemes which are unknown or excessively rare in both Indo-European and Hamito-Semitic, such as partially nasalized stops (Mboya, Ngayo, ba-Ntu) and implosive sounds, or "clicks"[2]; in addition, many of them are tone languages (cf. Chapter V, 4). The majority would appear to be either agglutinative or polysynthetic; but as may be imagined, considering that a really accurate description of a language can only be given by someone who speaks it fluently, our descriptive data for most African languages is none too reliable. Here is another of the many vast untilled fields which linguistic science offers to the ambitious young scholar.

Geographically, the island of Madagascar (now, officially, the Malagasy Republic) would presumably be regarded as part of Africa. Linguistically, however, something peculiar has happened: the languages spoken on the island do not belong to any of the African linguistic families, or even to those of India: they are members of a group whose nearest representative is Malayan, thousands of miles away in the Malay peninsula. Herein lies, certainly, the result of some highly significant migrational movement unrecorded in history because of the absence of any written record. (In the study of linguistics one often finds evidence of historical events unknown to the science of history, which is so often derived exclusively from written documents in the writer's own language.) We cannot here pursue the historical or anthropological implications, and must simply take the facts as they are and consider Madagascar under our next heading.

4. The Malayo-Polynesian languages

Probably no family of languages is spoken as original (i.e., not "superimposed") over a wider area than that which now comes under our consideration. From the island of Madagascar, as we have seen, to the Malay peninsula (that tail of Asia with Singapore at its tip), to the East Indies and thence across the vast Pacific to Hawaii, this group of languages prevails over an area stretching more than halfway around the world.

The point along this great circumference at which the family originated is very hard to identify. Although Heyerdahl proved that the Pacific islands *could* have been settled from South America,[3] linguistic evidence does not support the proposition that they *were*, for no languages of the Malayo-Polynesian family have been shown ever to have existed in South America, while they seem to be of very ancient lineage in Malaya; hence the people who speak these languages would seem to have spread eastward from there, and westward to Madagascar.

As indicated in the name, the family may be broken into two subgroups: (1) Malayan, in the Malacca peninsula itself and in Madagascar and the East Indies (including Malay, strictly so called; Atankara, Hova and Sakalava in Madagascar; many Philippine languages, including Tagalog, Visayan and Igorot; Javanese; the indigenous language of Formosa; and the languages of Borneo, the Celebes, Sumatra, and the Moluccas); and (2) Polynesian, comprising the languages of the Pacific islands except for New Guinea, Australia and Tasmania, and including such languages as Maori, Fiji, Yapese, Samoan, and Hawaiian.

The first of these subgroups—the languages more like Malay—

seem to lie structurally in the analytic column, with perhaps traces of an earlier inflective character. (Only in Javanese are there records of these languages older than a century or so.) Words are almost always disyllabic, and these two-syllable words appear to be derived from monosyllables. The phonemic system is fairly varied, and many true prefixes and suffixes are used, generally with a 1:1 morpheme-formant ratio; in the absence of these prefixes and suffixes the root, as in English or Chinese, is all message-material and not determined as to function, so that it is reported of these languages that they "do not distinguish the 'parts of speech' from one another." The existence of a system of classifiers (e.g., *buda dua orang* 'two children' = 'child-two-person,' *kuda dua ikor* 'two horses' = 'horse-two-tail') may be a further development of native analytical tendencies, or possibly due to Sino-Tibetan influence. (Influences on speakers of these languages may be thought of as from Sanskrit in regard to literature, from Arabic in regard to religion, and from Sino-Tibetan culturally.) Three Malay expressions have gained some general currency in English; *orang utan* which means 'man of the forest' or 'wild being'; *mata hari* which means 'eye of day' or 'sun'; and *salong,* a borrowing from the Mohammedan greeting *salaam,* which became (through British Army slang) our expression 'so long.'

The languages more like Maori, Tahitian or Hawaiian are distinguished by their very limited inventory of phonemes and syllable types—it may be said that, in general, a syllable can consist only of consonant + vowel. As there seems to be a tendency to dispense with most consonants, there are very many homonyms, and the languages have a very "liquid" sound, with many vowel sequences. Hawaiian is no doubt the most familiar to Americans, and certain words and phrases (e.g., *aloha oe,* "hail" or "farewell to you," *poi-poi* "to eat" or "food") are heard fairly often.

5. Other languages of Asia and the Pacific

Inclusive as the Malayo-Polynesian group is, it does not embrace all the languages spoken in the Pacific. An important exception is the native languages of Australia, of which there are more than a hundred, notably *Bushman.* They have been divided into a northern and a southern group, between which some see a relationship, others none. The fact is, however, that not enough is known about them to make any sensible or reasonable surmise about their genetic relationships or structure. The populations speaking these languages are excessively small and gradually declining into extinction, and they are located in almost totally inaccessible areas.

The same is true of certain other language groups which may be mentioned here. The indigenous languages of New Guinea, Halmahera, Bougainville and some of the Solomon Islands have been thought to be related, and the group has been named *Papuan*. All that is really known about these languages, however, is that they are neither Polynesian nor Indo-European. The native languages of Tasmania are now extinct, and therefore do not concern us here. In Indo-China, *Vietnamese* is neither Malayan nor Chinese nor Indian, but is usually thought of as belonging to a group (called *Mon-Khmer* or *Austroasiatic*) which also has representatives in eastern India (notably *Munda*) and elsewhere in the Malacca peninsula—in Burma, Tonkin, Cambodia, Annam, and Siam. Though profoundly influenced by Sino-Tibetan, these languages retain their own identity. They seem to have been originally agglutinating; but most have now become more or less analytic—no doubt under the influence just mentioned. Vietnamese is, of course, spoken by a large population.

The Nicobar and Andaman Islands in the Bay of Bengal have their own languages, though Nicobarese appears to be related to the Mon-Khmer languages. And Burushaski exists in solitary isolation in the northwest of India, quite surrounded by other languages none of which are related to it.

From this brief section it will be clear that any scholar whose tastes run to field work—who wishes to be among those who unearth the original data on which the whole structure of his science is built—has plenty of room in linguistics for this sort of original investigation. Indeed, the whole comparative branch of linguistics could undoubtedly stand rewriting, if the necessary data could be assembled.

6. The American Indian languages

Of all the languages in the world, probably none is structurally more different from the familiar languages of Europe than those of the American Indians. The Indian languages are therefore among the most valuable for the linguist to study—and it is not difficult to obtain abundant accurate information about them, for the majority are still living languages; nor need one even travel unduly far to come into personal contact with native speakers, since at least a few members of the race still live in almost every state of the Union.

Despite all this, however, and despite the fact that European races have been in contact with the Indians for five centuries, and many languages (even in North America) have been recorded in written documents for more than two hundred years—despite all this, the study of Indian languages made no impact on linguistic science until after the beginning of the twentieth century. This was due, probably, to two factors.

First was the assumption—so long unchallenged—that the "science of grammar" as left by Donatus was the ultimate truth about the nature of language and its operations, so that every newly encountered language was reported in the terms prescribed by traditional grammar, and wound up seeming to be substantially a dialect of Latin—this in turn being taken as further proof of the formula's universal truth. Second, the Indians were generally looked upon with the hatred and contempt which we reserve for those we really fear, so that anything unique about their language which could not be disguised could be dismissed as the result of their ignorance, stupidity and barbarism.

When linguists and anthropologists at last began to investigate the Indian languages thoroughly, the study at once greatly enlarged linguistic horizons. All the Indian languages are polysynthetic (a term which has already been explained[4]). Thus, they do not have word classes or "parts of speech"; most, in fact do not even have words, for every "word" is or can be a sentence. They do not have declensions and conjugations: the sentence is not made up of a "noun" in the "nominative," a "verb" in the "indicative," and a "noun" in the "accusative"—although prior to 1900 many of the learned would have assured us that no language could operate without these "essential" elements, and any expression that did not contain them was gibberish. (They would readily have agreed that Shoshone and Chippewa were in fact gibberish, expressing only as much sense as Indians were capable of.)

The Indian languages were at first regarded as a bewildering welter of unrelated idioms (as late as 1939 Gray could write "to give any general characterisation of them is quite impossible"[5]), and were categorized on a purely geographical basis. Within the last twenty years, however, great strides have been made in the study of Indian languages, and the picture has greatly changed.[6] The absence of records of older stages of these languages constituted one great obstacle,[7] but in 1928 Leonard Bloomfield made a pioneer demonstration of the application of the methods of comparative linguistics in such cases,[8] and now the North American languages, at least, have been seen to fall into less than a dozen families—perhaps fewer, when the study has progressed further.

It is, incidentally, conventional to describe the geographical distribution of American Indian languages more or less as of the time when Europeans first arrived on this continent (i.e., *ca.* 1500), since so many of them have since become extinct or have shifted to very distant regions,[9] and besides, as of today all are merely substrata to Indo-European languages—English, Spanish, Portuguese, and French.

On this basis it appears that in the seventeenth century, when the first English-speaking colonies were established in the New World, the entire northeastern quarter of the continent—with two exceptions to be mentioned presently—spoke languages belonging to one great family, the Algonkian. To this family belonged the languages of both Pocohontas and Samoset: such languages as Powhatan, Delaware, Mohegan, Massachusetts, Passamaquoddy, Penobscot, and Micmac. (The names suggest their approximate locations.) This vast family prevailed not only from northern Virginia to Labrador and Hudson's Bay, but westward as far as the Rockies, including such languages as Cree, Chippewa (called Ojibwa in Canada), Menomini, Potawotomi, Fox, Illinois, Shawnee, Arapaho, Blackfoot, and Cheyenne.

The domain of Algonkian was interrupted by two enclaves: Iroquoian, in New York State and adjacent areas; and Siouan, mainly located in the central Great Plains west of the Mississippi. Most of the Plains Indians were Siouan speakers: Sioux itself, Crow, and the languages spoken in what are now the Dakotas, Iowa, Missouri, Nebraska, Kansas, Arkansas, and northern Oklahoma, but with an enclave in the Southeast constituted by Catawba, Biloxi and Ofo.

The remainder of what are now the Southern states was dominated by the Natchez-Muskogean family, including the Chickasaw, Choctaw, Alabama, Creek, Natchez and Muskogee languages.

Algonkian is undoubtedly the first in importance of the Indian-language families, in the sense that it includes the greatest number of languages and covers the widest area. On that basis, Athabaskan would take second rank. This family embraces all the Indian languages of Alaska and Canada north and west of the Algonkian, with the exception of the Mosan languages of British Columbia and certain adjacent areas, and the belt of Eskimo-Aleut which stretches across the continent north of all the others and, for the most part, above the Arctic Circle.

But although Athabaskan belongs primarily to northwestern Canada, there is a remarkable enclave of this family in the Southwest (mainly Arizona and New Mexico, with parts of Oklahoma and Texas): the chief languages of this group are Apache and Navaho. This intrusive Athabaskan enclave is surrounded by languages akin to the Indian tongues of northern Mexico, which, with Hopi, Paiute, Shoshone and Comanche, form a large language family called Uto-Aztecan, dominating the Rocky Mountains and the Sierra Madre. Half of Arizona today is Indian country, and of that about half speaks Navaho, an Athabaskan language, and the other half Hopi, which is Uto-Aztecan. The Athabaskans were definitely felt as intruders in the Uto-Aztecan territory, which in part explains the bad reputation of the Apaches.

The Mexican members of the Uto-Aztecan family include Pima, Papago and—most illustrious of all—Nahuatl, the language of the Aztecs; many are not aware that this is still a living language, spoken in various parts of Mexico. Characteristic of the Aztec language was a lateralized dental appearing in words like *chocolatl, coyotl, Nahuatl,* and the common Mexican Spanish word *tlapalería,* "hardware store."

The Indian languages of the West Coast seem to fall into two families: Penutian in Oregon and California (including Chinook, once the basis of a trade language), and Hokan in the rest of California and Lower California, including Shasta, Yana, Yuma and, in Mexico and northern Nicaragua, Tlapanec and Jicaque.

For Mexico and Central and South America we cannot be nearly as detailed, since much less investigation has been carried on. Beyond the Mexican Indian languages already mentioned, we may cite Mayan, also still living in southern Mexico, Guatemala and Honduras. Of the many languages of the Mayan family, modern Yucatec is probably most like the language of the Mayan civilization at its height. Areas of Mexico and Central America not so far mentioned were, at the time of the Conquest, inhabited by speakers of languages about which little has as yet been ascertained—languages such as Zoque, Zapotec, Mixtec and Tarascan. However, more is being learned about these languages almost daily.[10]

In the southern hemisphere the picture is even sketchier. Besides the Indo-European Spanish and Portuguese, we have to note Quechua, the language of the Inca empire—also still living and spoken by several million people in Peru, Ecuador and Bolivia—and Guaraní of Paraguay and southern Brazil. The word "hurricane" is believed to be from Guaraní. Beyond this, little can be said; after all, of the few remaining unexplored areas in the world, several are in South America; and often where descriptions of language *are* available, little reliance can be placed on them (Grigorieff's grammar of Quechua,[11] for example, is essentially a translation into Quechua of the Royal Spanish Academy grammar of Spanish).

Still, enough evidence is at hand to support a surmise that the South American Indian languages are of a structure similar to that of the North American ones, and that there is a possibility of some day proving all of them to be related. Indian languages often operate with a very restricted inventory of phonemes, yet this does not lead to extensive homonymy, as in Sino-Tibetan or Polynesian, because while a limited number of phonemes and allowable clusters greatly restricts the number of possible *words* that can be formed, polysynthetic languages in effect form sentences directly out of formants; and since the formants may be less than a syllable, and any grouping is possible and may be combined in a "sentence word" with any other possible grouping, the possible number of such "sentence words" is quite large.

The student may well feel a little disappointed that, after listing as a topic "a survey of the languages of the world," linguistic science turns out to be able to give so little information about so many of them. This will serve to emphasize a fact we have not neglected to stress—that there is a tremendous amount of work to do in linguistics, and that the science would fill in the gaps faster if it could triple or quadruple the number of its recruits. All that a conscientious survey of the languages of the world can do at the present moment is to report the data available to date. No one will be happier than the writer to soon find that the outline given in these two chapters has become obsolete and needs complete revision.

Notes to Chapter VI

1. One of the differences between Hebrew and Aramaic was that the word for "son" was *ben* in Hebrew, but *bar* in Aramaic, as may be observed in the New Testament: cf. *Acts* xiii. 6, "Bar-Jesus." The name "Barnabas" is *bar-Nabbas* (e.g., *Acts* xiii. 1), and St. Peter's original name was Simon bar-Jonah (*John* i. 42).

2. The familiar speech sounds are produced while expelling air; "implosive" or "click" sounds are produced by sucking it in. See Chapter XIII, 3.

3. T. Heyerdahl, *American Indians in the Pacific,* New York, Rand McNally & Co., 1953, 621 ff.

4. See above, 76–80.

5. Gray, *Foundations of Language,* 407.

6. Cf. Hall, Robert A., Jr., "American Linguistics, 1925–50," *Archivum Linguisticum* III (1955), 101–25, IV (1952), 1–16; H. Hoijer, ed., *Native Structures of North America,* New York, 1951, *passim.*

7. For the same reason, as late as 1850 it was not realized that the Celtic languages belonged to the Indo-European family, until Zeuss' reconstructions showed that the common ancestor of Irish and Welsh was cognate to Latin, Germanic and Greek. There are records of a few Indian languages as much as four centuries ago; but this is still a rather short period for the comparative linguist.

8. Bloomfield, "A Note on Sound-Change," *Language* IV (1928), 99–100.

9. The Cherokees, for instance, moved all the way from North Carolina to Oklahoma, and the Seminoles, now in southern Florida, once lived in central Georgia.

10. Notably by researchers of the *Summer Institute of Linguistics,* whose headquarters is in Glendale, California, and which is affiliated with the Wycliffe Bible Translators of England and Australia.

11. S. Grigorieff, *Compendio del idioma quechua,* Buenos Aires, 1935.

Supplementary Readings to Chapter VI

Bloomfield, *Language,* 67–73.
Sapir, *Language,* 120–46.
Pei, *Languages of the World.*
E. A. W. Budge, *First Steps in Egyptian,* 1–48.
Greenberg, *Studies in African Linguistic Classification,* New Haven, 1955.

Chapter VII

Languages and Writing

It has been said that the two oldest and greatest inventions of man were the wheel and the art of controlling fire. This is probable enough: and if one wished to make a group of three, surely the development of writing must claim the third place. Without a system of writing, no matter how wise or sublime the thought, once uttered it is gone forever (in its original form, at least) as soon as its echoes have died away.

Indeed, it would seem that without a means of preserving wisdom and culture, civilization, which depends on the passing on of a heritage from generation to generation, could not develop. The facts, however, are otherwise: noteworthy civilizations *have* arisen and flourished without possession of any form of writing, usually by forming a class of society whose duty and profession it was to keep in memory what we write down in books (and, too often, subsequently forget). Even the average citizen in such a society took as a matter of course demands upon his memory which we today would consider beyond human capacity.

All the same, one may question whether a really complex civilization—one capable of governing large areas, for instance—could be supported by such a system. If there ever was one, we may be sure it has been grossly slighted by history—which, after all, depends almost entirely on written records. Who, for example, has ever heard the Gaulish version of Caesar's campaigns?

1. Ideographic "writing"

There seems to be no reason to doubt that the many systems of writing which have been developed at different times by various peoples

Figure 16   Prehistoric rock drawing

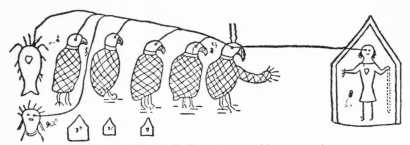

FIGURE 17   An Indian pictographic message*
This message of friendship was sent from an American Indian chief to the president of the United States—the figure in the White House. The chief, identified by the lines rising from his head, who is sending the message, and the four warriors behind him, belong to the eagle totem; the fifth warrior is of the catfish totem. The figure at lower left is evidently also a powerful chief. The lines joining the eyes indicate harmony, and the three houses indicate the willingness of the Indians to adopt white men's customs.

during mankind's long history all grew, by steps which we can and shall trace, out of man's ability to draw pictures.

Suppose you wish to preserve a record of your catching a twenty-pound trout, but happen to be illiterate. The obvious thing to do would be to draw and hang a picture of yourself catching the big fish. It was, apparently, an equally obvious thing to do some fifty thousand years ago, for the caves which yielded us the remains of the Cro-Magnon man first attracted attention because of their beautifully drawn pictures of a procession, perhaps a hunt, of animals (Fig. 16). We shall never know whether this was a mere decoration or a record.

Given the ability to draw well enough so that your representations of persons and objects can be readily recognized, it is, of course, not difficult to tell a complete story in one panoramic picture, or in a series of uncaptioned sketches. The range of information that can be conveyed in this way can be greatly extended if a few simple conventions are agreed upon between the artist and his prospective audience: the use of a totem-sign for a certain tribe; considering a prone man to be sick or wounded if his eyes are open, dead if they are closed, and so on. Several tribes of North American Indians made use of this kind of communication (Fig. 17).

* From Henry R. Schoolcraft, *Historical and Statistical Information Respecting the Indian Tribes of America*, I, 418.

In these circumstances, it will be noted, pictures act as a means for the communication of thought, and thus are somewhat like a language in themselves. Indeed, some authorities include this kind of communication among various forms of "language," but we have deliberately excluded it from our definition. It is common and conventional to call this kind of writing *ideographic writing,* and while the term is convenient, this is properly in no sense either language or writing, as we shall proceed to show.

Note, first, that the kind of communication achieved in Figure 16 is totally independent of the language or languages of the persons who make the drawing and of those who read it. The "text" may be correctly "read" in any language. It is not an effort to record the *language* in which the event is described, but, like language itself, to record the *original events*: we might even say it is a system alternative to language for symbolizing events. And therefore it is not strictly writing; for writing is always a *record or representation of language.*

Ideographic "writing" cannot be strictly language either, for it has two limitations which would make it unworkable as a system for expressing human thought. First, it is not within everyone's competence: some of us have no talent for drawing. This, however, could be offset by conventionalizing the characters to a few simple strokes, not immediately recognizable as the original picture except by previous knowledge of the convention (see Fig. 18).

But then the second, more serious objection still remains: even with such conventionalization, the system cannot adequately express the whole range of human thought; and to do so even partially will require thousands of characters and a system of such complexity that exceedingly few in the society could master it.

The Chinese people have an ancient and beautiful script which was originally, and still is largely, ideographic. The characters have been conventionalized, but it is still quite easy to recognize their origin, as was shown in Figure 18. Although there are many mutually unintelligible dialects of Chinese, the same written text can be read by any native (each in his own dialect), and the gist can even be made out by one who knows the principles of the system, but little of the language. Chinese writing is thus one of the strongest forces toward Chinese cultural unity, and for this reason the Chinese will probably never substitute another writing for it. But it is estimated that 70,000

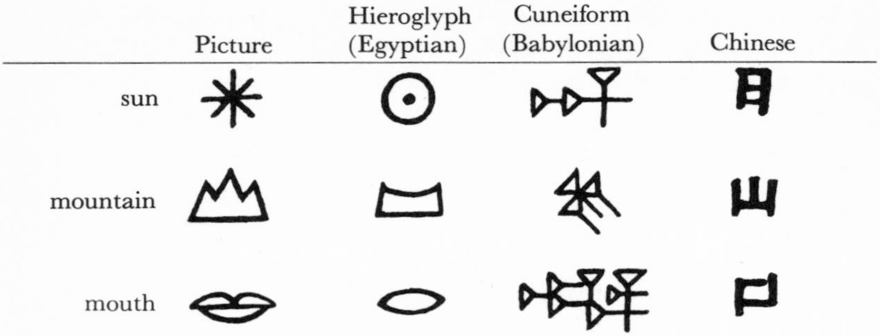

	Picture	Hieroglyph (Egyptian)	Cuneiform (Babylonian)	Chinese
sun				
mountain				
mouth				

FIGURE 18   Conventionalized symbols

to 125,000 characters exist (not all, of course, used with equal frequency), and it is said that a scholar takes seven years to learn to read and write Chinese if he already speaks it, while over 80 per cent of the native speakers of Chinese are illiterate in their own language.

Where there is considerable divergence between a language and its written representation, as in the case of Chinese or Italian, where many different dialects are written with the same spelling, or in French or English, where the language has changed considerably since the stage for which the writing was devised, a tendency may arise to consider the written language the "correct" language, of which the spoken language is a deformation which should be "corrected" to agree with the writing. This is particularly true when the writing either records, or once recorded, or is believed to record, the speech of a class of society which enjoys prestige, to which many native speakers would like to assimilate themselves.

This, however, always obscures things and puts the cart before the horse. Actually, the prestige class of any society probably least conforms its speech consciously to writing: sure of their status, its members do not worry about betraying an inferior origin in speech or behavior. It is said that if a man's table manners are absolutely disgusting, he is either a peasant or a duke. Writing is, in its essence, nothing but a means of recording language with some degree of efficiency. Whether one form or another of the language is "good" or "correct" is an entirely different question; a system of writing is good or bad according as it records, accurately or otherwise, whatever form of the language it is aiming to record.

However, because of the prestige of letters in largely illiterate populations (which is so great that *gramarye* has even been thought to have magic power), the opposite tendency to "correct" language according to written forms has been so strong as to lead to such things as the creation of a word like "misle" from a misreading of the word "misled."[1] Many similar examples could be given.

2. Pictographic writing

Any nation which finds occasion to use a form of ideographic writing with any regularity, even if all the writing is the job of one relatively small social group, will probably sooner or later take the simple and logical step to *pictographic writing*. In this case, the written sign, which in ideographic writing is the symbol for an *idea,* becomes the symbol of a *word.* For example, a device like ⌷ , which represents the floor-plan of a house, now becomes a sign for *per,* the Egyptian word for "house," or of *beyt',* the Hebrew word for "house." Another example: the picture 🐂 , conventionalized to Ɐ , which of course represented the snout of an ox, now becomes a sign for *alep,* the ancient Hebrew word for "ox."

The advantages of this step for the improvement of communication are evident. The written sign now symbolizes, not an idea, but a word, and a word is a far more precise symbol of a mental concept than any other which can be devised. With a sufficient stock of symbols of this new type, the writer can distinguish among a house, a stable, a barn, a shed, and a palace; whereas with ideographic writing he is pretty well limited to "house" vs. "big house" or "small house" (as there is no separate symbol for the adjective, the bigness or smallness cannot be specified and can range from "largish" to "enormous"). Much ambiguity is avoided: if you have tried to convey messages ideographically—or by "sign language," which is an acted-out version of the same thing—you know how easy it is for an intended message "the king is angry" to be interpreted "the old man is sick."

Pictographic writing is, moreover, true writing, since it is a means of recording language, not just an alternative way of expressing the concepts which language expresses.

All pictographic writing systems that we know have developed from ideographic systems, and show clear traces of this, notably in their tendency to preserve ideographic symbols among the pictographic. Thus, the ancient Egyptians had an ideograph for water, a representation of waves or ripples: 〰〰 . Eventually they derived from this a sign 〰〰 , standing for the word *mu*, which meant "water." But they often wrote the word *mu* as follows: 〰〰 〰〰 . And in writing of a river, the word for which was *átur*, 𓄿𓂧𓏤 they also added the water sign: *átur* was written 𓄿𓂧𓏤 〰〰 .

The purpose of these ideographic "determinants" was probably to help the reader who did not know the particular word or sign by giving an indication of its general connotation. Nouns denoting persons were usually given the "determinant" of a little man— 𓀀 — or a little woman— 𓁐 . For, despite the noteworthy increase in efficiency which pictographic writing represents, thousands of characters are still necessary; and one advantage of the ideographic system has been lost—the characters are no longer self-explanatory. (This is only a theoretical advantage on behalf of ideographic script, since, while the ideographic character for a bird should presumably be readily recognized as a bird, in practice the characters have to be conventionalized for the sake of those who do not draw well.)

A considerable number of pictographic writing systems have been developed at different times in different parts of the world, but, Sunday-supplement science to the contrary notwithstanding, quite independently of one another, so that we have no ground for talking about the "evolution" by man of the art of writing. There is no evidence whatever for a First Cave Man who sat with hammer and chisel and stone and figured out how to chisel the first message, after which man made improvement after improvement, until the peak (represented, of course, by English orthography of the present day) was reached. Actually, nations once literate have been known to lapse into illiteracy as a result of ruinous wars and social disorganization.

3. Syllabic writing, unlimited and limited

The step from pictographic to syllabic writing is an easy, logical and, it might very well seem, self-evident one; yet there have been several nations which developed the first without ever proceeding to the second. It would probably be safe to say, however, that a majority of those who came as far as pictographic writing took the step to syllabic script.

In pictographic writing it is, of course, as easy to develop a stock of thousands of characters as in ideographic; yet, strange as it might seem, there is still always a shortage. This shortage arises because it is either extremely difficult or impossible to represent some words in pictures. Take "velocity," for example. Is there any picture you could draw to express this that might not be read as, say, "the man is running"? Or, if you think you could picture "velocity," how would you handle "acceleration"? If you still think you could manage this one, what sort of picture, pray, would you draw for the word "the"?

The first step toward syllabic writing is taken when you permit yourself to cheat a little and take advantage of homophones. There is, let us say, a good pictograph for "the sea"; you use it to express the Holy "See," or "I see" (writing, perhaps, the characters for *eye* and *sea*).

When you have expressed the word "icy" by the characters for *eye* and *sea*, or *belief* by the characters for *bee* and *leaf,* you have turned the corner to syllabic writing. Any relationship whatever between the character and the *meaning* of the syllable it stands for is henceforth entirely irrelevant. The character expresses nothing but a sequence of sounds—the sounds making up one of the syllables of the language.

The first result of this is a gain of efficiency: a decrease in the number of possible characters (since more than one word or syllable can be written with the same syllabic character—in fact a great number can be written with varying sequences and combinations of a rather small number of characters). This gain is largely theoretical, however, for there will still be several thousand characters. The superiority of syllabic writing over pictographic from the point of view of efficiency will largely depend on the structure of syllables in the language using it. If syllables are generally or always simple in structure, a syllabic system of writing may work extremely well.

In every type of language, however, ambiguity and duplication are likely to be discovered in this kind of *unlimited syllabic* writing. It is often uncertain which of various homonymous readings is intended (e.g., does a character for "deep" joined to one for "end" mean "deep end" or "depend"?). And conversely, there are almost always two or more ways to say the same thing.

If the users of a syllabic system have a sense of logic, they will soon tend to adopt the practice of always writing the same syllable with the same character. The immediate result of this is for the first time to reduce the number of signs to manageable proportions: the sequence *baba* will always be expressed by signs expressing BA BA— never by signs for syllables such as BAB HA, BA ABA, 'B AB HA. Hence the number of signs is not so great as not to be within the capacity of the more or less average memory.

Since many languages have only one syllable-type—CV (i.e., consonant followed by vowel)—application of the principle above to the syllabic writing of such a language results in a very simple, logical and efficient system, next to alphabetic writing the most efficient writing possible.

The simplicity and efficiency are likely to prove elusive, however, when applied to languages of more complex syllabic structure. Even so, one almost inevitably arrives at the idea of having a series of signs representing syllables in which each consonant of the language is paired with each vowel: BA, BE, BI, BO, BU; DA, DE, DI, DO, DU; FA, FE, FI, FO, FU; and so on. A list of such signs is called a *syllabary*.

Some time after this stage of *limited syllabic writing* has been reached, the thought may occur that the inventory of signs can be further reduced by taking one form, without any specification, as the form for, say, BA; and then simply using diacritic marks to indicate the other possible syllable structures: something like the following:

△ BA	⃡ BI	⃤ BU
⃣ BE	⃥ BO	

This brings us very close to alphabetic writing. The last step in syllabic writing and the first in alphabetic writing might come about by accident; suppose a class of words ends in a syllable *-ba*, and in the course of time the vowel ceases to be pronounced. Now the syllabic sign △ stands for B alone, not BA; and some sign (in Sanskrit *virāma,* in Arabic *sukūn*) is invented to express this situation: e.g., △ will express BA, and △ will express B. By use of this sign the vowel of any syllabic sign can be suppressed, and any sign in the syllabary can be made alphabetic.

A situation like that just described is seen in the Semitic writing systems (Arabic, Hebrew), of which it is often said that they "write only the consonants." Actually, all the Arabic and Hebrew letters were originally syllabic signs, representing the consonant *and* a vowel (see Fig. 19).

4. Alphabetic writing

As will be clear by now, true alphabetic writing consists in having a sign for each *sound* (technically each phoneme) of the language, rather than one for each *word* or one for each *syllable.* This is the most efficient writing system possible, since a language will be found to have some thousands of words and at least a couple of hundred different syllables, but the words and syllables are made up of individual speech sounds which seldom exceed sixty to seventy in number, and sometimes number as few as a dozen. Hence an alphabetic writing system can, with the fewest possible units (a number easily within anyone's ability to master), record every possible utterance in the language.

It would seem that the different stages we have traced, from drawing pictures to ideographs, to pictographic and syllabic writing, so logically follow each other as inevitably to lead a nation or tribe from one to the next until ultimately an alphabetic writing would be achieved. But such is simply not the case. Many great nations, for example the Japanese, have come as far as syllabic writing, and never seemed to feel a need to go beyond it. Indeed, in all the history of mankind, alphabetic writing has been invented only once, and all the alphabets in the world that are truly so called are derived from that single original alphabet. It seems likely that but for a certain lucky linguistic accident, man would never have discovered the alphabetic principle of writing. Had that been the case, the history of mankind would certainly have been very, very different.

There is a strong probability that it was the ancient Egyptians who first hit on the alphabetic principle; but we cannot prove it, for we

Phoenician-Canaanite		Hebrew		Arabic	
'ā	𐤀	aleph	א	alif	ا
bā	𐤁	beth	ב	bā	ب
gā	𐤂	gimel	ג	jīm	ج
dā	𐤃	daleth	ד	dāl	د ḍād / dhāl
hē	𐤄	hē	ה	ḥā	ح
wā	𐤅	wau	ו	wāw	و
dzā	𐤆	zayin	ז	zai	ز
khā	𐤇	heth	ח ט teth	khā	خ
		yod	י	yā	ي
kā	𐤊	kaph	כ	kāf	ك
lā	𐤋	lamed	ל	lām	ل
mā	𐤌	mem	מ	mīm	م
nā	𐤍	nun	נ ס samek	nūn	ن
'ō	𐤏	'ayin	ע	'ain	ع ghain
pā	𐤐	pe	פ	fā	ف
tsā	𐤑	sade	צ	ṣad	ص
qā	𐤒	koph	ק	qāf	ق
rā	𐤓	resh	ר	rā	ر
sā	𐤔	sin, shīn	שׂ, שׁ	sīn, shīn	ش ,س
tā	𐤕	taw	ת	tā, thā	ت, ث

FIGURE 19   Semitic alphabets

Note: The names of the Old Semitic alphabet are surmises.
Letters in one alphabet which do not have correlatives in the others are set off to the side.
The traditional order of the Arabic letters has been modified slightly to stress parallels.

cannot show that all or even a majority of the characters which ultimately became the alphabet we know were used in Egyptian texts of any period (though an apparently sound pedigree can be made for a few of them).

Of course, the hieroglyphic writing had a stock of thousands of characters, and might well have included the ones we are looking for in texts which have disappeared or not yet been discovered. What is harder to explain, however, is that when the Egyptians wrote alphabetically, they gave alphabetic values to an entirely different set of characters (Fig. 20). Yet the Egyptians had been using a writing system for literally thousands of years, and had gone through all the stages. It does not seem likely that some other nation came along just as the Egyptians were on the point of discovering the alphabetic principle, snatched the discovery from under the Pharaohs' noses—and then taught *them* how to write alphabetically! There is certainly a mystery here which is still to be solved, and much fame (in learned circles) awaits him who solves it. If the Egyptians did indeed fail, after three thousand years, to discover the principle of alphabetic writing, it is striking evidence that man might never have had this art except for the lucky accident which we shall now proceed to describe.

Not being able to prove a connection between the alphabet and Egyptian writing, for the present we have to say that the oldest known genuine alphabet was the Old Semitic, ultimate ancestor of the scripts used today to write Arabic and Hebrew. This alphabet had, of course, been a syllabic script. How had it turned that all-important corner into alphabetic writing? It seems probable that it was prompted in this direction by the structure of the Semitic languages, as we shall show.

To us, the "root" of our verb *ask* is the syllable *ask,* to which various other syllables are prefixed or suffixed to make the various verbal forms, for example the past tense (*ask-ed*), the progressive present tense (*is ask-ing*), the third person singular present (*ask-s*), and so on.

With verbs like *drive* or *sing,* however, we might say that the root is a syllable *dr-ve* or *s-ng,* where the dash indicates some vowel, but not always the same vowel, since we have *drive, drove, driven, sing, sang, sung.* Something is expressed by the alternation of these vowels, to be sure (this alternation is technically called "Indo-European ablaut," see Chapter IV, 2), but the root of the verb is still a *syllable,* even with a variable vowel.

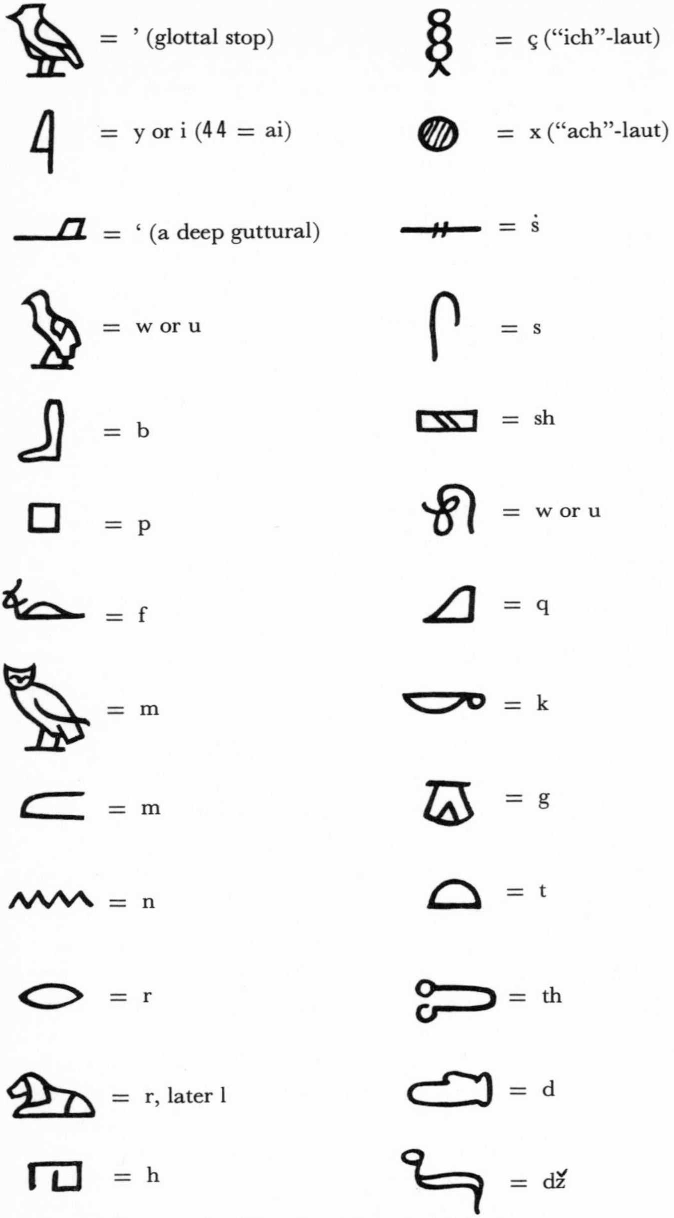

= ' (glottal stop)	= ç ("ich"-laut)
= y or i (𓇌 = ai)	= x ("ach"-laut)
= ' (a deep guttural)	= ṡ
= w or u	= s
= b	= sh
= p	= w or u
= f	= q
= m	= k
= m	= g
= n	= t
= r	= th
= r, later l	= d
= h	= dž

FIGURE 20   Egyptian alphabetic characters

128

It was probably some kind of ablaut system like this which led to the situation now characteristic of Semitic languages (which is really just a further step in this direction), whereby the meaning of "driving" would inhere in the consonants D-R-V, that of "asking" in '-S-K. In Semitic languages the "root" of a word is really a *sequence of consonants* (usually three), modifications of the root being effected by kaleidoscopic rearrangements of the vowels intervening.

Thus, anything to do with writing shows the consonants *K-T-B,* but "he wrote" = *KaTaBa,* "it is written" = *meKTūB,* "he got it written" = *KaTtaBa;* "scribes" = *KuTtaBūn,* and so on. Words which seem to us quite unrelated turn out to be, in this system, derived from each other, like *SaLāM,* "peace," *iSLām,* "the Mohammedan religion," *muSLiM,* "a Mohammedan." (From *salām* we get *'aslāma,* "he pacified, subjugated"; *islām* is "subjugation, submission" to God, and *muslim* is "one who has submitted.")

Obviously, no other type of language is better adapted to suggest to its speakers that there is a unit of word structure below the syllable; that BA is in turn composed of B- and -A. This is precisely what other nations might never have guessed. In Semitic, where BA alternates constantly with BI and BU, and sometimes with B- (the vowel being silenced), it is almost inevitable that every user of the language should develop a concept of the phoneme—a notion which is fundamental to the development of true alphabetic writing.

The structural nature of the Semitic languages is, therefore, in all probability the happy accident which became the key that unlocked for mankind, for the first and only time, the mystery of how to record speech by the method of maximum efficiency—one which does not have so many characters as to make learning it a complex art demanding years of training nor require a skill in drawing which few possess, nor consume large volumes of material for a relatively small amount of recorded message.

The consequences of this lucky accident are truly tremendous. If we did not have the alphabet, it would be impossible to hope for universal literacy, and therefore (if Thomas Jefferson's view was correct) for truly representative government. Writing could have been kept a secret art known only to a privileged few or to a particular social class which would thus have an undue advantage over the others. Information could not nearly so easily be conveyed from nation to nation, and the levels of civilization achieved by the Romans and ourselves might still be only goals to strive for. Truly, Prometheus did not do more for human progress than the unnamed scribe who first drew an alphabetic sign.

5. The wanderings of the alphabet

Let us here stress again that as far as can be ascertained from the available records, the principle of alphabetic writing has only been discovered once—hence, in the whole world *there is only one alphabet*. It follows that any people which writes in alphabetic signs has learned and adapted the use of the alphabet from another people who, in turn, had done the same. When the wanderings of this most potent cultural innovation are plotted, it makes an impressive odyssey. But the same would no doubt be true of every other discovery which has figured in an advance of civilization, if the same means existed for following its trail.

The earliest preserved inscriptions in alphabetic script date to about 1725 B.C. and were found in and around Byblos, in the country then known as Phoenicia (now Lebanon). It would seem that an alphabetic script which we might call Old Semitic was fairly familiar in that region at that time, though, as we have said, we cannot establish precisely where this script was invented, or by which Semitic tribe. It has been suggested that several Semitic peoples might have hit on the alphabetic principle at around the same time; but, if so, they seem to have soon adopted a common set of symbols.

This Old Semitic alphabet is of course the ancestor of the Hebrew, Phoenician, and Aramaic systems of writing. From these northern Semites, the knowledge of the alphabet appears to have passed, on the one hand, to the Greeks of Asia Minor, and on the other, to the Brahmans of ancient India, who developed from it their *devanagari*, the sacred script in which the religious rituals and hymns of the ancient Hindus were recorded (Fig. 21).

With this exception, it seems that the genealogy of every other alphabetic system of writing goes through the Greeks. And it was because of the structure of *their* language that the Greeks were responsible for the greatest single improvement in the system: the origination of signs for the vowels.

	a		ā
	i		ī
	u		ū
	ṛ		ṝ
	ḷ		ḹ
	e		ai
	o		au
	ḥ		

Written over a letter { ṅ
ṁ

क	k	ख	kh	ग	g	घ	gh	ङ	ñ
च	c	छ	ch	ज	j	झ	jh	ञ	ñ
ट	ṭ	ठ	ṭh	ड	ḍ	ढ	ḍh	ण	ṇ
त	t	थ	th	द	d	ध	dh	न	n
प	p	फ	ph	व	b	भ	bh	म	m

य	y	श	ç	ह	h
र	r	ष	ṣ		
ल	l	स	s		
व	v				

FIGURE 21   The Sanskrit alphabet

The Semitic dialects had certain sounds which did not exist in Greek. The symbols for some of these, such as *qoph* (Q), the sign for the velar guttural which had existed in Indo-European but had everywhere been replaced by *p* in Attic Greek, were simply discarded by the Greeks (except in their use as numbers, but that is a different story). In other cases, however, the Greeks kept and used the symbol for a syllable beginning with a non-Greek sound, but pronounced it *without the foreign consonant*—so that the symbol became a sign for the syllable's vowel.

Thus, the first sign in the alphabet originally stood for the syllable *'A,* where the sign ' represents the "glottal stop," a contraction and release of the vocal chords—not a phoneme in English, but used often enough as a separator between vowels (e.g., oh- 'oh), and you have heard it in Scottish dialect as a substitute for T: *bo'le* for *bottle, li'le* for *little.* Some dialects of Greek had this sound, and others did not. Those which did ultimately lost it, so that the sign ∀ (by now written in a different direction, A) everywhere became the sign, not for *'A,* but for the vowel *A.*

Other Semitic gutturals had had the tendency to influence adjacent vowels in the direction of O or U, and they accordingly, by the process just described, became the signs for those vowels.

A rather good illustration of what was going on is found in the sign H, standing for the syllable HE. In Ionic Greek, where the sound *h* was eventually eliminated, H became the sign for the vowel *e.* In Sicilian Greek, however, where syllables beginning with *h* still remained, the same H became the sign for *h*—which is our usage also, because we got the alphabet from the Romans, who got it from the Ionic Greeks, who followed the Sicilian tradition.

This fact explains deviations in *our* values for the alphabetic signs as compared with those of the standard (Attic) Greek alphabet (see Fig. 22). Since the alphabet had not been invented as a tool for writing Greek, each Greek dialect which adopted it had to modify it a little—to assign different values to some of the signs, and discard the excess signs or use them in new ways, according to the phonology of their own speech.

While practically all modern nations which have alphabetic writing got it directly or indirectly from the Romans, there are a few to whom the tradition passes directly from the Greeks, in some cases

Early Greek	Attic (East)	Sicilian (West)	Roman and Modern Equivalent
A	A	A	A
B	B	B	B
Γ	Λ	Γ	G and C
Δ	Δ	Δ	D
E	E	E	E
F	[F] (=[w])	F (=[w])	F
X	Y	Z	G
B	B (=[e])	H (=[h])	H
⊗	⊗	⊙	TH
{	I	I	I
K	K	K	K
L	Λ	ΛL	L
M	M	M	M
N	N	N	N
⊞	Ξ (=[ks])	—	—
O	O	O	O
)	Γ	Γ or Π	P
M	—	—	—
Φ	Q	Q	Q
9	P	R	R
3	S	S	S
T	T	T	T
	V	V	V (=[u])
	Φ	ΦΦ	PH
	X (=[x])	X or + (=[ks])	X
	↓	—	PS

FIGURE 22   Greek alphabets

Note changes in direction of writing and variation of values between Attica and Sicily   (after E. M. Thompson) concomitantly with direct northern Semitic influence. Between the third and fifth centuries A.D., the spread of Christianity occasioned the devising of the ornamental and highly efficient Armenian, and the intriguing, delicate Georgian alphabets. And when the feared Goths were marauding throughout Latin Christendom, Ulfilas, child of a Gothic father and a Greek mother, became the St. Patrick of the Goths, Christianizing them and translating the Bible into their language, writing it with an alphabet (Fig. 23) which, according to repute, he invented, basing it on Greek. Ulfilas' lucky bilingualism not only gave us our oldest extensive records of any Germanic language, but also, it is believed, served as the basis of the Scandinavian "runic" writing (Fig. 24), although some think it was the other way around.

Later, in the ninth century, when Christianity reached the Slavic peoples, two principal alphabets, the "glagolitic" and the "Cyrillic" (the latter named in honor of one of its reputed inventors, St. Cyril, who died 869 A.D.; the other inventor was his brother, St. Methodius, d. 885 A.D.), were devised to represent the then most generally used Slavic dialect. From these developed in the course of time the national alphabets of those Slavic peoples who were evangelized from Byzantium—the Russians, the Ukrainians, the Bulgarians, and the Serbs (Fig. 25). (In contemporary Russia the Cyrillic alphabet has in turn been adapted for writing many non-Indo-European languages of the Soviet Union.)

Slavs who got their religion from Rome had to struggle to put their complex Slavic phonology into the Latin alphabet, with what often seem (to English speakers) jaw-breaking results, as seen in names like Przmysl, Szczepiński and Wojcechowic. The name Vishinsky, as a rough transcription from the Cyrillic, is identical with the Polish name Wyszinski.

From the great Roman empire the art of alphabetic writing passed, by inheritance or adoption, to virtually all the peoples who know it today. They were responsible for many interesting and important innovations in the basic system which there is not space to detail here, but which may be found in any thorough and complete history of the alphabet. We shall just point out a few of the most significant ones.

The Romance-speaking peoples simply inherited their alphabet; in many cases, they did not realize that they were not still speaking, as

𐌰 = a	𐌹 = i	𐍂 = r
𐌱 = b	𐌺 = k	𐍃 = s
𐌲 = g	𐌻 = l	𐍄 = t
𐌳 = d	𐌼 = m	𐍅 = ü
𐌴 = e	𐌽 = n	𐍆 = f
𐌵 = q	𐌾 = j	𐍇 = ph
𐌶 = z	𐌽 = u	⊛ = hw
𐌷 = h	𐍀 = p	𐍉 = o
𐍈 = p	𐍑 = —, 90*	↑ = —, 900*

*did not represent a sound but were used as numbers

FIGURE 23   The Gothic alphabet

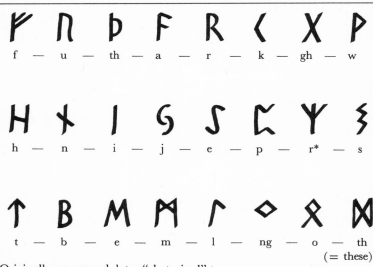

| 𐍆 | 𐌿 | þ | F | R | ᚲ | X | ᚹ |
| f | — u | — th | — a | — r | — k | — gh | — w |

| H | ᚾ | l | ᛃ | S | ᛈ | Y | ᛉ |
| h | — n | — i | — j | — e | — p | — r* | — s |

↑	B	M	ᛗ	ᛚ	◇	ᛟ	ᛞ
t	— b	— e	— m	— l	— ng	— o	— th
							(= these)

* Originally an s-sound, later "rhotacized" to r

FIGURE 24   The Runic alphabet

135

Cyrillic	Modern Russian	English Equivalent	Cyrillic	Modern Russian	English Equivalent
Ⰰ	а	a			
Б	б	b	Ȣ	у	u
В	в	v	Ф	ф	f
Т	г	g	Ѳ	ѳ*	f (originally th)
Д	д	d	Х	х	kh
Є	е	ye	Ѡ		ō
Ж	ж	zh	Ш	ш	sh
Ѕ		dz	Ꙗ	щ	shch
Ꙁ	з	z	Ч	ц	ts
Н	и	i	Ѵ	ч	ch
І	і*	i	Ъ	ъ*	"hard sign"
Ꙉ		d', t'	Ы	ы	ÿ
К	к	k	Ь	ь	"soft sign"
Ʌ	л	l	Ѣ	я	ya
М	м	m	Ю	ю	yu
N	н	n	Ѥ	ѣ*	ye
О	о	o	Ꙗ,Ѧ		ę, yę
П	п	p	Ѫ,Ѭ		ǫ, yǫ
Р	р	r	Ѯ		ks
С	с	s	Ѱ		ps
Т	т	t	Ѵ		ü

FIGURE 25 Slavic alphabets

(Some of the Modern Russian letters are given out of standard order for purposes of matching.)

* These letters were abolished in 1918.

well as writing, genuine but perhaps rather careless Latin. When they made an effort to write Latin more correctly, only then did they realize that theirs was actually a different language.

It was during the time when Latin was still spoken, however, that the first modifications had to be made in the alphabet—leading to the first diacritic signs. The sound *h* became silent in colloquial Latin in the first century B.C. and in standard Latin by the second century A.D. Thereafter the letter was a zero, expressing nothing, and hence could be used with other letters to express variations: TH for something like T that was not quite a T; GH for something like G that was not a G, and so on.

Another early diacritic, perhaps the earliest, was the letter G. Words like *signum* had shifted in pronunciation at a very early period from SIG-NUM to SING-NUM to, probably, [seɲo] (where the sign ɲ stands for what is technically a "palatalized n," as *gn* in French *mignon* or *ñ* in Spanish *cañón*). This made the G, in this particular position, another zero: and the idea logically arose that any sound could be distinguished from a palatalized correlative by prefixing G to the latter: N/GN; L/GL. Hence Romance languages blossomed with forms like *egli, Bologna, segno, Cagliari*. But Portuguese used the faithful H to express these sounds (*filho, senhor*), and Spanish, which had divested itself of doubled consonants, used a doubled letter (*castillo, suenno*), and later used an abbreviation for the doubled *n* (*sueño*)—for the Spanish *tilde* is nothing other than the well-known medieval Latin MS. abbreviation for an M or N (*tã, dōinū, ĩtētiōē*). Thus, the American who reads the Italian name *Castiglione* as *Cas-tig-li-o-ni* is murdering the harmonious genuine sound, since the spelling stands for *Ca-sti-lyo-ne*.

When the practice ceased of using as names of the letters the names of the objects they had pictured (or some meaningless derivative thereof, like *alpha, beta*), there arose the custom of naming a letter by giving (in the case of a vowel) its *sound,* or (in the case of a consonant), its sound *preceded or followed by [e].*[2] (In English this latter sound has uniformly shifted to [i], so we say the letters of the alphabet [e], [bi], [si], but Frenchmen say: [a], [be], [se].) In some exceptional cases, however, phonetic shift has eliminated the letter's sound from its name. Our name for R is [ar] (from earlier [er] by the same change which gives us *heart, hearth, sergeant*). In English pronuncia-

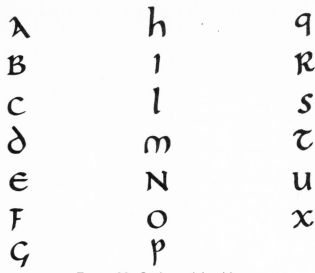

FIGURE 26   Latin uncial writing

tion, however, R is silent after a vowel, so the name of the letter R is *ah*—with no R in it.

Again, our name for *h* is *aitch,* a meaningless word in English but a preservation of French *la hache* "the hatchet"—suggested by the letter's appearance, to be sure (=h)—but originally containing its sound; no [h] has been pronounced in French, however, for over a century, so the name of this letter, too, fails to contain its sound.

In the course of time the Latin alphabet was written in various calligraphic styles: the *uncial,* for example, which happened to be popular in the fourth century A.D. (when Rome officially adopted Christianity) is still associated with ecclesiastical texts (see Fig. 26). By the time printing was invented, the so-called *Gothic* style was probably the most popular in northern and western Europe, and the earliest printed books used this character, which we now call *black letter.* There was even a handwriting based on black-letter type, which died out in the middle of the seventeenth century (see Fig. 27).

Our present letters J and W are known to have been invented in the sixteenth century. In Latin, since all W's had become V's by the second century A.D., the letter U, however written (V, U), expressed

138

	SMALL	CAPITAL		SMALL	CAPITAL
A			N		
B			O		
C			P		
D			Q		
E			R		
F			S		
G			T		
H			TH	p or ð, later	
I, J			U, V		
			W		
K			X		
L			Y		
M			Z		

(The letters varied somewhat in response to joining to preceding and following letters.)

FIGURE 27 Old English handwriting

that sound—the choice between the rounded and the angular form being purely a matter of calligraphy. The English language, however, had both the V sounds and the W sounds; so, to express the latter, English printers of the sixteenth century "doubled" the former, writing *vv* (or *uu*).

Latin also lacked any sound like English J; but this sound appeared in Old French in words where Latin had had *i*, either as *ee* or as *y* (*Januarius* > *janvier, iuvenis* > *jeune*), and printers traditionally used *i* for it. Medieval scribes often extended this letter downwards in an ornamental flourish at the end of a number (thus: xiiij), and no doubt it was this which suggested the adoption in English printing of this alternative form of *i* for the *j*-sound. For quite a while, however, many printers continued to regard i/j and u/w/v as interchangeable, and to print *Iohn, starres aboue, A VVinter's Tale, Jnterlude,* and so on.

We have been able to mention here only a few of the vicissitudes undergone by the alphabet—*the* alphabet, only one, always the same —in its long journey through space and time from the eastern shores of the Mediterranean to the far islands of the Pacific. There are, of course, many more details to the story, a genuinely fascinating one which the reader is urged to pursue in detail in some of the readings mentioned at the end of this chapter.

6. The "perfect" alphabet; the phonetic alphabet

From all that has been said, it should be quite easy to devise a criterion according to which one may judge whether the orthography of any nation is better than that of any other—to put it simply, whether French spelling, say, is "better" or "worse" than English.

The terms "good" and "bad" as applied to an instrument evidently mean nothing other than how well it does the job it was designed to do. An alphabet, like any system of writing, is designed to record a language. We have already shown that the alphabetic method is the most efficient for this task. The *best* alphabet, therefore, would be the one which is the most alphabetic—which most fully applies the basic principle of alphabetic writing in recording the language whose alphabet it is.

Now, the basic principle of alphabetic writing is to devise one separate sign, and only one, for each phoneme of the language. When there is a 1:1 correlation between the number of signs and the number of phonemes in the language; when a given sound is always expressed by the same letter and no other; when there are no digraphs (two letters to express one sound), nor cases of the same sound being expressed by different letters ("alternative spellings"); then you have the "perfect alphabet."

It can almost go without saying, of course, that no nation possesses a perfect alphabet, since each has adopted its alphabet from some other, and none has a system designed exclusively for itself. There would, of course, be nothing to prevent redesigning the system on the occasion of such an adoption; and to a large extent this was done when the Greek alphabet was made the basis for Slavic (Gothic, which we know only through its written records, we cannot judge). The spelling of Spanish, too, was extensively revised in the eighteenth century. Welsh and Manx were also respelled. The results were, just as might have been expected, that these orthographies serve their respective languages much more efficiently than most others, including English. But in no case so far has there been an orthographic commission with both the amount of scientific linguistic knowledge *and* authority or prestige to do a perfect job along these lines.

Because of the constant change and flux of language, too, it is unlikely that even a perfect alphabet would remain perfect for long. The effect of this is to put a penalty on eminence: the longer a language has had a recorded literature, the less efficient today, probably, is its spelling system—devised, no doubt, for the language as it was spoken centuries ago. Thus both French and English have an utterly preposterous system of spelling, which constitute a real obstacle to learning these languages, by native speakers as well as others. But even certain American Indian dialects, for which a spelling was first devised only a century ago, have now changed to the point where the spelling no longer adequately expresses the language.

Consider, too, that if the alphabet and rules of spelling (which is what the term *orthography* embodies) of a language like English were thoroughly revised by competent authorities and put on a basis of most perfect and rigorous efficiency, the language would become much easier to learn, and bad spelling would have been done away with. *But* within two or three generations from the date of adoption of the new system, everything ever written in the language prior to that date would be obsolete, and would either have to be reprinted in the new spelling or become, to 98 per cent of native speakers, as inaccessible as a medieval Latin MS. It is doubtful whether even the most uncompromising schoolteacher, once she fully realized the gigantic task involved here, would continue to maintain that it was not an excessive price to pay for good spelling on all her students' themes!

Hence it is probable that each language will have to get along with the spelling it has, however the same was adopted or inherited, and that its alphabet will never be much more perfect than it was at the beginning of its history.

The one attempt that has been seriously undertaken by adequately qualified people to devise an alphabet that would be, in a sense, "perfect"—for its own specific purpose, at any rate—is that first proposed by the International Phonetic Association. It is called the IPA or "phonetic" alphabet, and every serious student of languages should be thoroughly familiar with it and the science on which it is based (see Chapter XIII).

The aim of the IPA alphabet is to provide one sign, and only one, for each of the speech sounds that can be produced by the human vocal apparatus. (Naturally the number of such sounds varies with the sensitivity and discriminative power of the detecting instrument, up to infinity; so practical limits are adopted: one speaks of "broad" or "narrow" transcription, the latter being approximately the maximum average discriminative power of the human ear). To accomplish this aim, the Roman version of the alphabet is taken as a basis, and diacritics and varying letter styles are freely used.[2]

We must be quite clear on one point: the phonetic alphabet does not aim to be, and is not, the alphabet of any language—though it does aim to be an alphabet in which any language can be written. This apparent paradox will be clear after the student has read Chapter XIV. The ideal alphabet for a given language would provide *a single sign for each of its phonemes*. But what is a single *phoneme* in the structure of a given language may consist of two or more *sounds* perfectly distinct to the ear. In a particular language, P and F may be regarded as the same unit, so that the phonetic transcription [pifa] might be considered and spelled as /pipa/ by native speakers. With a little close observation, you can readily hear that the p of *pot* and the p of *spot* are not the same sound, yet they are treated as such in English.

The phonetic symbol is, therefore, essentially a formula expressing how the observed sound is produced by the vocal organs (or defining its acoustic characteristics). It tends to belong more to physics or physiology than to linguistics. But it is the means of recording the observed physical data on which every science must be based, and as such is indispensable to the linguist.

Let students be duly warned that it is impossible to do really distinguished work on any level in linguistics without being an accomplished phonetician. It is important to say this, because many of the younger students of linguistics nowadays seem to be hunting the short cut, the Northwest Passage to achievement without real work, in linguistics as in life.

Notes to Chapter VII

1. This is an extreme case of what is called "spelling pronunciation." More typical examples are the pronunciation, by Americans in England, of words like *twopence* and *halfpenny* as written.

2. For the phonetic symbols see Chapter XIII and Figure 30.

Supplementary Readings to Chapter VII

Fevrier, *Histoire de l'écriture,* 9–19, 112–71.
Bloomfield, *Language,* 281–96.
Sapir, *Language,* 19–20, 226–31.
Pei, *Story of Language,* 72–80.
Sturtevant, *Introduction to Linguistic Science,* 19–29.
De Saussure, *Cours de linguistique générale,* 44–54.
Ogg, *The 36 Letters, passim.*
Thompson, *Introduction to Greek and Latin Palaeography,* 9 and *passim.*

PART TWO

Chapter VIII

PREFACE TO THE
SCIENTIFIC DESCRIPTION OF LANGUAGE

At this point we begin what might be regarded as the more "advanced" part of this book: a description and explanation of the techniques used by professional linguists in the study and treatment of the phenomena of language. Although this part is designed primarily for those who wish to master these techniques with an idea of making professional use of them, this does not rule out the general reader, who might wish to learn something about the basic "tricks" of this trade. Most of these basic tricks are descriptive in orientation, since linguistic comparison can be soundly based only on accurate and thorough description.

The modern linguist, we have said, is one who applies the methods of science to the investigation of language. For him, therefore, the achievement of his ultimate objective would consist in being able to answer all questions that could be asked about language as a general concept, or about any particular language. In other words, he would be able to give a one-hundred-per-cent complete and accurate *description* of the topics mentioned—a description which would contain the material to answer any possible question. Hence, a large part of linguistic science is concerned with the scientific *description* of a language.

In what follows, therefore, it will be best and most efficient to present the material as a formula for the description of a language—as "traditional grammar" is commonly presented (unless, indeed, the presentation left us by the Romans was mistakenly taken as a formula for describing a language).

In the chapters to come, principles and procedures will be broadly outlined, and illustrations, when needed, will be given generally from English, occasionally from other languages likely to be familiar to the reader. It should be understood that no attempt is being made to give a really complete description of English or any other language, and that general principles and techniques might be applied differently in specific cases.

1.   The concept of "utterance"

The procedure of science is always to gather data, classify them, form hypotheses, test the hypotheses, and thus arrive at the basic principles governing the phenomena under study. The field of language is no different: we first collect specimens of the language, then attempt to discover the principles governing the phenomena. Thus, the linguist first makes a record or recording of as much of the language as possible—spoken, if at all possible, by native first speakers. This recording is then transcribed in phonetic symbols (see Chapter XIII).

With the phonetic text before him, the linguist now searches for a point of attack in seeking to elicit the structure of the text. He knows that the text is put together as an accumulation of structural units, but at this point he has no means of ascertaining the boundaries of such units. It is therefore necessary to set up an arbitrary provisional unit with which to begin work. This unit is the "utterance."

We may define the "utterance," after Fries, as *an amount of speech put forth by a single person before and after which there is maximum silence.* The term "maximum silence" is to be defined as any interruption of speech by a silence (on the speaker's part) which is either, for practical purposes, infinite, or at any rate longer than any of the other pauses observed during the course of speech.

When the text consists of a conversation between two or more people, utterances are easy to mark off: They evidently lie between places where one person ceases talking and another begins. (Obvious interruption of one speaker by another should be ruled out, of course, as Fries points out,[1] but this will very rarely meet the definition of "maximum silence"; indeed, interruption is more often characterized by overlapping.)

When only one person is speaking, however (telling a story, for instance), it will still be found that in the course of his speech he makes pauses of varying length; but they can be rated relative to each other, and those which are noticeably longer than the others can be identified as "maximum silences." (This does not, to be sure, eliminate a certain possibility of error, since maximum silence itself will probably vary in length, and it will probably turn out ultimately that a silence *x* milliseconds long *or longer* is maximum silence; as a result, some maximum silences will be identified as belonging among the pauses shorter than maximum silence. This margin of error has to be accepted at this point, however, and once the structural picture has begun to emerge, the error will stand out and be easy to correct.)

It will be noticed that the units occurring between maximum silences vary in length over a considerable range, but that the variation seems more erratic in conversation than in long, continuous speech, like public addresses or story-telling. The significance of this difference will be brought out later.

The definition here given does nothing, of course, to tell us what the structure of an utterance is, but at least it does two things: it gives us an experimentally observable unit with which to start; and we may also feel reasonably sure that expressions conforming to this definition contain all the structure necessary in the language for structural completeness—possibly more, but not less. Otherwise the listener would be bound to express his dissatisfaction or puzzlement in some way, before too long a silence.

2.   The parts of language

We have said that a language is a system of vocal symbols by which thought is conveyed from one human being to another. We now ask how this system is constructed, what are its parts.

A traditional approach assumes that the phenomena comprising any language can be classified in one or another of four categories, according as they concern:

(1) the sound-units making up the syllable,[2]
(2) the structural units making up the words,
(3) the syntactic units (words or word groups) making up the (simple, compound or complex) sentences, and
(4) the inventory of words in use in the language.

The traditional names for these categories are, respectively, Phonology, Morphology, Syntax, and Lexicon (or Dictionary). The first three are often treated together in one book called *the grammar,* and the last in a separate book called *the dictionary.* With grammar and dictionary, it was presumed, the student would have the aggregate of what was to be known about any given language.

As is so often the case, modern scientific linguistics has not invalidated this formula of description, but makes a few modifications. Within the last thirty or forty years, for instance, there has been an important change in point of view as to what should be the unit of description in phonology—from the "phone" to the "phoneme"—which we shall consider in more detail later (Chapter XIV).

It has always been hard to draw the line clearly between morphology and syntax, since so many languages use syllables not only to build up words but also to establish the structure of the sentence and the role of the word therein. More recently, we have come to know languages which really *do not have words*—that is, there is no level of structure between the syllable and the sentence, or, to put it in still another way, every word is a complete sentence and every sentence is but a single word. In the case of such languages, of course, there is no category of syntax, or at any rate syntax and morphology are identical, and the dictionary is something quite different from what we usually conceive under that term.

There are also languages in which no word is more than one syllable in length—in which, therefore, there is no morphology in the strictest sense, since whatever is accomplished by morphological means in other languages must in these be achieved by syntactic devices. And, finally, syntax tends to divide into two subgroups which might easily be distinct categories, according as we are dealing with the components of a single sentence structure, or with combinations of two or more sentence structures.

Despite these qualifications, the old formula is still serviceable and will be followed here in its main outlines. The order of procedure is equally logical starting from either end. Most texts begin with the simplest unit, therefore with the phonology; *we* shall follow the reverse order.[3]

3.   Formant and morpheme

We have already (Chapter I, 4) presented a theory of the word, under which it is regarded as a compound formed of two components, a physical element (the sequence of sounds of speech) and a semantic element (the amount of meaning expressed by that segment of speech). For the more profound student, however, this will not be a satisfactory unit in terms of which to describe language, because some languages do not have words, and because most words have more than one "semantic element."

We shall therefore use the more general terms *formant* and *morpheme* —"morpheme" for any amount of thought, any section of the chain of thought, which is distinct by virtue of the fact that a distinct sequence of sounds, or other physical feature of language, is assigned to express it. The *formant*, of course, is the actual physical expression of the morpheme.

Care must be taken not to equate the morpheme with the "concept" or any other psychological unit. A morpheme is simply a certain amount of thought, distinguishable only because it happens to have a linguistic expression in a certain language.

Some concrete illustrations may make the matter somewhat clearer. It would seem that we could properly see in the English word *book* a case of one morpheme expressed by one formant—the formant consisting of one syllable, a sequence of three phonemes. In the word *books,* however, we evidently have an additional formant (the final -*s*) expressing an additional morpheme (what might be called the "idea of plurality"). In this case, one of the two formants (*book-*) can occur by itself as a word, and is hence a *free form* in Bloomfield's terminology[4]; the other (-*s*) cannot occur independently as a word, but only within a word—only as part of a word; it is therefore, in Bloomfield's term, a *bound form.*

As is evident from this illustration, a formant is not necessarily a syllable. It is not even necessarily a phoneme. It may, for instance, be the use of one form instead of another: *him* instead of *he, I* instead of *me.* It may be the absence of a phoneme. In the case of verbs in English, for example, the absence of an -*s* where an -*s* could be present may be regarded as expressing plurality, since -*s* expresses the singular: *run* vs. *runs.* In such cases the term "zero formant" is sometimes useful. (Note that the "plurality" morpheme in the case of verbs evidently does not mean many of the *actions expressed by the verb*, but many *performers of the action*.)

The occurrence of one vowel instead of another within a word may be a formant: in *froze*, for example, the fact that the form is not *freeze* expresses a tense morpheme. The forms so far cited will also show that there is evidently no reason why the same formant (e.g., *-s*) cannot express more than one morpheme, either in different contexts (e.g., *book/s* = 'more than one book'; *book'/s* = 'belonging to a book'; *run/s* = 'one individual runs'), or even simultaneously: in Latin *servus*, for example, the formant *serv-* expresses the idea of "serving," while the *-us* formant expresses the morphemes (1) singular, (2) masculine, (3) nominative (subject of sentence)—all at once. The same morpheme can also be expressed by more than one formant: a language may have several different formants to express the plural of nouns. The ratio of formants to morphemes is different in different languages, even to the point of being characteristic of structure, so that it can be used as a norm in grouping and classifying languages (see Chapter V, 1).

A word in any language, then, is ordinarily to be analyzed as a series of formants expressing a series of morphemes, and may be visualized thus:

$$\text{word} = \frac{\text{morpheme} + \text{morpheme} + \text{morpheme}}{\text{formant} + \text{formant} + \text{formant} + \text{formant}}$$

Of course, as we have seen, the total of morphemes above the line is not necessarily equal to the total of formants below the line, since one formant may express more than one morpheme; also, any given formant below the line may quite possibly be found elsewhere expressing a different morpheme. A more accurate picture of the word's construction might, therefore, be something like this:

$$\text{word} = \frac{\overset{\displaystyle\text{morpheme}}{\overset{\displaystyle\text{morpheme}\quad\text{morpheme}}{\text{morpheme} + \text{morpheme} + \text{morpheme} + \text{morpheme}}}}{\text{formant} + \text{formant} + \text{formant} + \text{formant}}$$

There seems to be no definite limit to the number of formants that may occur in sequence, except such limits as an individual language may place on the length of the word.

4. Tools of analysis: commutation

A logical question at this point is: how do we ascertain the number of formants in a word and the boundaries of each? To this end we employ one of the basic tools of linguistics, *commutation*. Essentially, commutation is merely comparing words with each other, or, a little more precisely, comparing one item occurring in a given utterance with the same item as it occurs in another utterance. Thus we discover that individual syllables in a sequence of syllables can occur alone or in different sequences.

It was a principle of De Saussure's that language is *spoken* on a horizontal plane, but *constructed* on a vertical one. In other words, we pronounce the sounds and syllables of language one after another; but just before each syllable is uttered, the speaker's mind has chosen it from among all the syllables that *could* fit into the "chain of speech" at that point—all of which, presumably, are present to his mind, at least subconsciously. In considering any word or expression, it is most important to know what the alternatives were from which this particular one was chosen.

A good illustration of how commutation works may be cited from Sturtevant,[5] who once took his small grandchild to the doctor to have an infected ear irrigated. Later, when the child was suffering from a bad cold, he inquired whether he would have to be "nosigated." The little boy had evidently identified the word "ear" in the word "irrigate," and probably assumed that the remaining two syllables "-igate" were a formant expressing a morpheme "to flush with water or medicinal solution." The same child, after a formation of four airplanes had been pointed out to him, shortly afterward inquired if two planes flying together were a "twomation."

Evidently, we establish the boundaries of formants by *commuting* in this way until we arrive at a form no part of which occurs in any other combination. If this leaves some forms whose occurrence is extremely limited—say to only one word in the whole language—so that comparison or commutation does not enable us to ascertain very clearly the content of the morpheme, we are tempted to identify it as a variant of a more familiar formant. An example often cited is the Anglo-Saxon word *brȳdguma*, "a married man," cognate to German *Bräutigam* and containing two formants, *brȳde-* meaning "marriage" and -*guma* (cognate with Latin *homo*), meaning "man." This word should have descended to modern English as *bridegoom*; but, as the "meaning" of *goom* was unknown, the more familiar *groom* was substituted. There was at one time a tendency to call cucumbers "cowcumbers," and asparagus (formerly *sparagus*, Latin *sparagi*), "sparrowgrass."

Misidentification of formants creates many of the pitfalls in tracing etymologies. Because a final [-*z*] is a plural formant in English (*chair/chairs*, *tree/trees*), words borrowed from other languages containing final [-*z*] were often thought to be plural, and a singular which is historically a complete fraud became established as "correct" in English. Thus Latin and Greek *cerasus* becomes French *cerise* and English *cherries*, whence we form a singular, one "cherry." The wines made at Jérez de la Frontera in Spain—Jérez having formerly been pronounced [ʃeres] in Spanish—were known in England as "sherries," whence we take the false step of saying "Amontillado is a type of sherry." Forms like "Chinee" and "Portuguee" have circulated in spoken English, but never became thoroughly established.

Still more instructive, perhaps, is the "burger" series. This began with expressions in German such as *Hamburger Wurst, Frankfurter Wurst, Wiener Wurst*—Hamburg, Frankfurt or Vienna sausage. The word *Hamburger* in German has two formants: *Hamburg*, the name of a city, and -*er*, a suffix indicating a place of origin.[6] When these foods were brought to America, *Hamburger Wurst* was abbreviated to *hamburger*, which was probably (through commutation this time in English) identified as two entirely different formants, the familiar "ham" and a suffix "burger," presumably meaning "a piece of the previously mentioned food in a roll and served hot." Hence we now encounter *beefburgers, cheeseburgers, steakburgers, pizzaburgers, burger heaven* (an eating-place specializing in "burgers"), and so on ad libitum. Since *Bürger* in German means "resident of a small town" (French *bourgeois*), it must occasionally seem a little bizarre in Germany to read how much Americans love to eat burgers.

5. Message morphemes and structural morphemes

When we have broken up a word through commutation into its formants, we shall find that some of the formants express morphemes which are part of the information being conveyed by this utterance, while other morphemes serve merely to indicate the structure of the utterance. A word like *bookbindery* can be divided into *book/bind/er/y,* where all the morphemes are message morphemes: *-er* meaning "one who does it" (binding books), and *-y* meaning "place where such a person plies his trade." But a form *bookbinder's* contains a structural morpheme, since the formant *-s* is here meant to relate the word *bookbinder* to another word in a sentence; it does not add to the information conveyed, but only helps to clarify the construction of the sentence.

In many languages it is not infrequent to find a free form—an independent word—which expresses a structural, not a message morpheme; and sometimes the same formant expresses one structural and one message morpheme. A word like "the" in modern English is primarily structural, as a noun classifier—though its message function, indicating "the one previously mentioned," has not yet been forgotten.

The well-known "Jabberwocky" in Lewis Carroll's *Through the Looking Glass* gets its interesting effect by using, for all the message morphemes, formants which have no evident meaning to the average speaker of English.[7] If we in turn substitute blanks for these, we shall have a text which is almost all structure and practically no message:

'Twas _____ , and the _____ y _____ s
Did _____ and _____ in the _____ ;
All _____ y were the _____ s,
And the _____ _____ s out- _____ .

As Alice remarked of this passage, "It seems to fill my head with ideas —only I don't know exactly what they are!"

On the other hand, where the message is of paramount importance, or where the speaker has inadequate control of the structure of the language he is using, there is a tendency to drop out structural morphemes and present pure sequences of message morphemes, e.g., *him not know road Cheyenne.*

When one is learning a language, it should be possible to learn the structural morphemes and the formants which express them quite rapidly—if they are efficiently presented from this point of view. This leaves only one problem—mastery of more and more items of lexicon.

6. Immediate constituents

When we have divided a word into a series of formants, it is evident that the formants of the series are not all of the same chronological rank. For example, a word like *archery* presupposes a word *archer;* and the latter, in turn, presupposes a word *arch* (i.e., "bow"). Had this series started off with a Germanic root, we should have had *bow, bowman* and *bowmanship.*

We are interested, therefore, not only in the formants into which a word divides—in their number and nature—but in the *order in which they have been put together.* This can be represented for the case of *archery,* for instance, by the following arrangement:

$$\underline{\text{Order of discovery:}} \left\{ \begin{array}{ll} 1. \text{ archer-y} & 3. \\ 2. \text{ arch-er} & 2. \\ 3. \text{ arch} & 1. \end{array} \right\} \underline{\text{Order of origin}}$$

This could also be represented in another way:

$$\underline{\text{arch}| \ |\text{er}| \ |\text{y}}$$

It will be noted that, at each level of structure, the ultimate form at that level has been produced by adding a new element to the resultant of the preceding operation. For this reason it appears to hold true that *the immediate constituents at each level are never more than two.*

The second of the methods of graphic analysis illustrated above is probably preferable, since it shows at a single glance both the ultimate accretion and the order of formation. Analytic diagrams of this sort can sometimes become quite complicated; addition to a base form can take place at the beginning, middle or end, and the element added may itself be an accretion. For example:

$$\underline{\text{in}| \ |\text{toler}| \ |\text{abil}| \ |\text{ity}}$$

Nevertheless, the construction of most words is not very complicated, and the principle that the immediate constituents are always two seems still to hold true.

There is a strong feeling of chronology in the establishment of immediate constituents, since it seems a reasonable presumption that the layers of structure into which we dissect a word are those in which it was formed: hence, when we have broken the word down, we have presumably uncovered a portion of the process by which the language developed.[8]

If a language does not have a unit equivalent to the word, the occurrence and order of formants is either determined by a structural principle or not. In the former case, the structure of the utterance (i.e., the sentence structure) governs, there being no specific principle of word structure. We do not know of any authenticated example of a language which would belong to the latter type.

Notes to Chapter VIII

1. Fries, *Structure of English,* 23.
2. The terms "syllable" and "word" have not yet been defined, but see Chapter XII, 2, and Chapter XIII, 5.
3. Partly to avoid the difficulty mentioned by W. Haas in his review article "Linguistic Structures," *Word* XVI, 2 (August 1960), 259.
4. Bloomfield, *Language,* 160.
5. Sturtevant, *Introduction to Linguistic Science,* 97.
6. We say *two* formants with reference to the first stratum of immediate constituents (see pages 154–155). After dividing *Hamburger* into *Hamburg-* and *-er,* we can commute further and recognize *-burg,* "city," in *Hamburg.* Further investigation might establish a meaning for the remaining formant, *Ham* or *Hamm.*
7. This is also the basis of the old vaudevillian's and burlesque comedian's art of "double talk."
8. This, however, is not always the case. Sometimes the longer form precedes the shorter, as in "to sculpt" from "sculptor," by the process called *back formation.*

Supplementary Readings to Chapter VIII

Fries, *Structure of English,* 31–53, 256–58, 263–73.
Bloomfield, *Language,* 160–67.

Chapter IX

THE STRUCTURE OF TRANSFERRED UTTERANCES

At this point we must pause to reflect on the relationship of language to the situation in which it is used. In its relation to reality, language is a system of symbols. An important fact about language, however, is that it does not have to be used in the circumstances which it symbolizes, but may be used to re-create in imagination a situation which no longer exists in reality, or, indeed, never existed.

1. "Immediate" and "transferred" utterances

For an illustration, suppose that you seat yourself at table in a restaurant during your lunch hour, and a waiter asks you what you wish to eat, and you give your order. What is the situation? Your lunch. What is the topic of conversation? Your lunch. This is what we call an "immediate situation."

Suppose now that several hours later, back at your office, you mention your lunch to a friend, describing the restaurant and the waiter, what he said and what you said, and so on. What is the situation in which the speech is being uttered? Your office. What is the subject of your speech? Your lunch. You are using language to describe a situation (call this the *transferred situation*) other than that in which you are using the language (the *immediate situation*).

The importance of this distinction is that when language is used as a means of communication in an *immediate* situation, *not all the information communicated will necessarily be conveyed by language*. When you have sat down at a table in a restaurant, the circumstances express the message "I want to eat." The waiter does not have to ask you if you want food. If you *didn't* want to order a meal, you would have to tell the waiter so in language, since the *situation* carries an opposite implication.

Failure to take account of the difference between immediate and transferred situation has needlessly complicated the systems of syntactic analysis proposed by some linguists. If we take the trouble to separate utterances observed in transferred situations from others, we shall find that the structure of the latter is much less variable than that of the former, and that immediate utterances are often recognizable as fractions of transferred utterances.

In seeking to ascertain the structure of utterances, therefore, it is mandatory to begin with transferred utterances, since only in these can we feel confident that all the morphemes expressed in the message are represented by linguistic material in the accompanying utterance.

2. Establishing basic structural patterns

To say that a linguistic utterance has structure is to say that—as distinct from the case of a random series of words—some principle is determining the words which occur and the forms and order in which they occur. Think of a load of structural steel just after delivery to a building site as compared to the erected framework of the building. In the first case, any girder can be anywhere; in the second, each must stand as it does, and no other way, because it has a function in the structure which it would not fulfill if differently placed.

Or, suppose you are playing one of those games in which you draw cards from a pack, and each card has a word on it. The order in which the words come up is, of course, a chance one; yet you constantly endeavor to recognize in them meaningful combinations. To see meaning in one of these sequences of words, you would have to be able to see it as conforming to some standard pattern in the structure of your native language.

The total number of structural patterns comprising the syntax of a language cannot be very large or subtly organized, for the language must be used by all the people of a community, ranging from geniuses to morons; and experience shows that morons, and even idiots to a degree, can learn the language of their country adequately enough for communication. We may predict that when we have ascertained all the structural principles governing a given language, they will be few and simple, perhaps few enough and simple enough to be jotted down on the back of an envelope.

To ascertain the structural principles determining the form of utterances, it is logical to start by looking for the *shortest* (therefore least complex) utterance which, in the language under investigation, is found among those observed in transferred situations. (By restricting ourselves to the latter, it will be remembered, we make sure that all of the message which was conveyed on the occasion of the utterance under investigation is represented by linguistic forms in the utterance.) We choose the shortest utterance also on the reasonable assumption that it may turn out to be a nucleus from which longer utterances are built up.

In English and many European languages we shall find that this minimum utterance in transferred speech is a two-word unit:

(1)   John left.
                       We ate.
                       Time passed.
                       Morning came.

There are, of course, other two-word structures in these languages besides the type illustrated above; but they would not occur as complete utterances in transferred speech. (Questions and their answers, calls, and commands belong to immediate speech, and will be dealt with in the next chapter.)

Now, if the minimum complete statement (the minimum utterance) is two words, we may reasonably conclude that the fundamental structure pattern has two functions; and that each word—aside from its meaning as a word—discharges one of these functions. Let us symbolize the two functions by Roman numerals: I-II.[1]

Note that we shall use Roman numerals to symbolize *functions in the sentence.*It is very important, as remarked in Chapter VIII, 5, to distinguish the linguistic material which signals the *structure* of the message from that which signals its *content*—important, but not always easy, because frequently the signals for both are incorporated in the same word, even in the same syllable.

Let us assume, then, that, in the languages cited, I–II is a basic pattern for a sentence. To proceed from this point, let us use a very basic and always rewarding technique of linguistic analysis, what is called *commutation* (see Chapter VIII, 4): let us try to find out what we could substitute for either I or II without changing the structure.

To start by commuting I, we will quickly find that such expressions as the following can be used interchangeably:

(2)

	I	II
1.	John	left.
2.	The door	slammed.
3.	The great gate	closed.
4.	Bill's health	failed.

In other words, the expressions "John," "The door," "The great gate," "Bill's health"—all different items of information—are *structurally* identical; each functions as I, even though it may consist of two or more words.

To make the point still more strongly, let us alter the illustration to the following:

(3)

	I	II
1.	The door	closed.
2.	The great door	closed.
3.	Paula's door	closed.
4.	It	closed.

Here commutation has revealed four structures—four principles of organizing words—which will fulfill the I function in the I-II sentence. To highlight the structure, and abstract it as far as possible from the message information, we shall express them in special notation. (We shall explain later—see Section 3—the values of the symbols and how we arrive at them.)

1. the door . . . . d^1-I
2. the great door . . . . d^1-III-I
3. Paula's door . . . . I > I
4. It I

There are, of course, more than four structures which can fulfill the I function in the I-II sentence, but as our concern here is not to make a complete analysis of English but rather to suggest the method for making such an analysis of English or any other language, we shall not continue commutation until all are worked out. The total of such patterns, however, is not twenty, probably not fifteen.

It will be noticed that the pattern d¹-I falls into a rank of patterns subordinate to the pattern I-II. The latter is a *sentence structure,* while the former is a *sentence-component structure*—one which the native speaker does not consider complete, because it does not make a sentence, only a part of a sentence. We may use two terms originated by Bloomfield for these two types of word patterns: let us call sentence patterns *exocentric structures,* and sentence-component patterns *endocentric structures.*[2] It is evident that a tabulation of all the exocentric and endocentric structures in use in a language would be a complete description of the syntax of that language. This is the modern position superseding the traditional assumption that a listing of all the systems of inflectional endings (paradigms) completely describes a language's structure.

An entirely similar commutation can, of course, be performed with the other half of the I-II sentence structure:

(4)	I	II
	The door	closed.
		banged.
		squeaked.

That the two functions are really and totally distinct can easily be shown by demonstrating that nothing which will commute for II will commute for I, and *vice versa.* Expressions such as "banged closed" or "the door it" are not sentences or utterances; they have no structure; they are meaningless.

In the illustrations just given, note that we were keeping the *structure* completely identical, varying only the *content* of the message (by using different words in the II function). Compare, now, the following series:

(5)	I	II
	The door	closed.
		closes.
		will close.
		has closed.
		can close.

This gets very close to the border between structure-expression and content-expression. On the exocentric level, of course, these sentences are indistinguishable from those which preceded them. But on the endocentric level, this case seems more closely to resemble four alternative *structures* for II rather than four alternative *words* (all of them the same endocentric structure). Different words in the same structure normally express different messages. But here we are not dealing with completely different words, but with what appear to be modifications of the same word (the root "close")—sometimes by a variation in morphology (the structure of the word), sometimes by using it in conjunction with other words, sometimes by both devices.

As we have seen elsewhere (Chapter VIII, 3), where these differences are expressed by different endings on the same word, such endings are both structural and message-bearing, but the message morphemes expressed have almost become part of the structure, since the language so regularly expresses them; for example, in English, whatever information you want to convey, the language requires you also to determine and express the time and aspect of any actions mentioned: French requires you to determine and express "grammatical gender," and so on. While structural patterns have as their main purpose the organizing of word sequences into recognizable and predictable units, there is no reason why they cannot, secondarily, express content differences also. Naturally, it is precisely these which will be neglected by the speaker who "knows how to make himself understood" (i.e., convey the essentials of his message), though his command of the structure of the language is shaky. (Conversely, the student is generally trained to be very precise in this sort of thing, while remaining unable to express himself at all.)

Variations of the type *close/closed*, therefore, constitute a suborder of differentiation among endocentric structures which are identical from the point of view of sentence structure.

3. Structural word classes: "parts of speech"

So far, then, it appears that in English and several other well-known European languages, the simplest and minimum exocentric (sentence) structure is I–II—two words, of which one fulfills Function I, the other Function II. We have seen that there are a number of endocentric structures consisting of two, three or more words which can fulfill the I function, and, likewise, a number which can fulfill the II function.

An obvious question now is: When we hear a two-word utterance, how do we know that it is I–II and not something else, or, for that matter, which word is I in the structure and which is II (for, in a given language, might not the order II–I have a different meaning)? Clearly there must be signals to give us this information.

Position alone could do it if there were no other two-word patterns; in that case, "first of two" would be the signal for I, and "second of two" would be the signal identifying II. But, as we have said, there are other two-word structures, both exocentric and endocentric.

A second way for a language to identify the sentence-function of a word is simply to require the native speaker to know, as part of the grammatical data of the language, that a certain word always functions a certain way. The learner of the language, in other words, must learn a *list* of words which function as, say, I, even though they bear no sign to show this. In this case, the list for any given function is always a small one; for, if it taxed the memory of the native speaker, it would be unworkable. The words which are traditionally called "pronouns" are examples of such a list. Proper names are another: whatever is recognized as the name of an individual of a species is recognized as I without further specification.

A third device would be to affix a syllable to the word which is to function as I, a syllable which, whether or not it expresses anything else, carries the meaning "Functioning as I in the structure I–II." This was the method of a language like Latin. We say "slave," but Latin said *serv-us*—the extra syllable expressing the notions (technically the *morphemes*) of "nominative" (i.e., "functioning as I"), "singular," and "masculine" (see Chapter XII, 6). Even in English some use is made of this device: words ending in *-hood, -ness, -dom* normally function as I in sentences.

Another method would be to use a *word* to signal the I-function of the word immediately preceding or following. This is the method of English; a word functioning as I is normally preceded by the definite or indefinite article: $\left(\begin{smallmatrix}\text{the}\\\text{a}\end{smallmatrix}\right)$ *door/closed*. In this case, of course, the article is a word whose almost sole purpose is to convey information about structure, and which hardly conveys content-meaning at all.

We shall call such words determinants,[3] and mark them in our notation with a small letter; thus, the article (and certain similar words, such as the demonstrative pronouns and the numerals) is *Determinant Number 1,* or d¹. In English, the article serves to signal that the next word (or the next but one or two in certain other well-known structures) is I in the structure I–II. Any word, or even word group, to which d¹ is prefixed thereupon discharges Function I and can commute with anything else which does so; for example: "the *hunt* rode" (i.e., "the fox-hunt began"), vs. "we hunt"; "the *four-in-hand* is a dressy tie"; "a *run* occurred at the bank"; "three *men*"; "six *feet.*"

Words appearing in the function of II also have means of identifying themselves—through characteristic syllables (such as -*ed* and -*en*) which are seldom or never added to nouns; through characteristic combinations of words ("will speak," "have spoken"), which do not occur among the structures functioning as I; through non-use of the article.

This marking of words to indicate actual or potential function in a sentence structure naturally creates *word classes,* i.e., groups of words marked in the same way. These are what traditional grammar called "the parts of speech." All words marked to function as I naturally fall into a class by themselves—a class which, in English, includes what are traditionally called "nouns," but also pronouns, numbers, and a certain number of expressions consisting of more than one word (*multiverbal endocentric structures*). Thus, a word belonging to our word category I should not be called "a noun" for it is not entirely equivalent to the traditional concept of a noun; we prefer to call it "a nominal," and members of category II, "verbals" rather than "verbs."

Are there other word categories and determinants besides those so far mentioned? There are, if there are in English other exocentric structures besides I–II, and if at least some English words are distinctively marked to give them a function therein.

4. Exocentric and endocentric structures

Though a great many English sentences can be reduced to the I–II formula—especially if all multiverbal endocentric structures equivalent to either element are taken into account—there are, indeed, several other basic sentence patterns in English. What has been said so far will suggest the method by which additional basic patterns are established. (The first new step, for example, would be to isolate three-word sentences in transferred speech which cannot be reduced to I–II.) The principal basic sentence patterns of English, to which at least 95 per cent of English sentences containing only one S_1 (see Chapter X) can be reduced, are as follows:

Exocentric Structures[3]

1.	I–II	Time passed.
2.	I–II–I[a][4]	Madison was President; I am he.
3.	I–II–I[c][4]	We chose him. Tom ate dinner.
4.	I–II–III	I am cold. (III = "adjectivals")
5.	I–II–IV	He is here. (IV = "adverbials")

A single utterance may, of course, include the elements of two or more basic sentences; e.g., I–II–III–IV (*he/rode/tall/in the saddle*), I–II–I[c]–IV (*he/ate/the apple/slowly*). Elements may also be repeated, e.g., I–II–IV–IV (*she/wept/very/quietly*).

We now turn to endocentric structures, considering first those commutable with I.

Endocentric Structures Equivalent to I

1.	d¹–I	The house
2.	III–I	Old men
3.	d¹–III–I	The big house
4.	d¹–III–III–I	The big old house
5.	I = I	Robert Smith; Dr. Jones; Hancock Street
6.	I > I	Smith's house
7.	I < I	Man of Aran
8.	I–d³–I	Jack and Jill
9.	I–IV	Men in motion

This list may not be complete, but structures other than the above are rare. Note the introduction of d³ for a determinant indicating that the next word has the same function as the preceding one (traditional term "conjunction"). Note, also, that any commutation of I can be used in its place, even in the structures just cited: e.g., I = d¹–I (*Jones, the barber*). This can lead to sentences apparently very complex; also, d^1 can label almost *any* following structure as I: It/contained/a *je ne sais quoi.* $\left(\begin{array}{c} \text{I–II–I}^c \dots \\ d^1 - I \end{array} \right)$

Endocentric Structures Equivalent to II

1.	II	went
2a.	$II^a \ II^b$	has gone, will go, tore up, am told, is going, was broken, can come
2b.	$II^a \dots II^b$	tore (it) up, was (totally) ruined

Endocentric Structures Equivalent to III

Equivalents to III, which we name "adjectival expressions" or *adjectivals*, are in English and other Germanic languages almost always established by position. In these languages, the structures III–I (*cold winters*) and d^1–III–I (*the big house*) are so familiar that anything in the III position in this pattern can be recognized as III: *up-to-date news; under-the-counter transactions; the I-don't-care girl: a down-to-earth individual; the now-you-see-it-now-you-don't method.* Still, there are some adjectival suffixes, such as, for instance, *-like,* cf. *child/childlike;* a contemporary speaker of English would probably say "monkeylike" rather than "simian."

Note that traces of the Romance structure, I–III, can be found in English, usually (but not always) outside ordinary usage, for instance, *court-martial, lieutenant-general, body politic; fee simple; the Swiss family Robinson* (a bad translation for "a Swiss Robinson family"); *Goody Two-Shoes* (normal Germanic structure would be "Two-Shoes Goody").

Endocentric Structures Equivalent to IV

1.	IV–IV	very well; long ago
2.	IV–IV–IV	most exceptionally well[9]
3.	d^2–III–I	in great haste (the traditional "adverbial phrase")
4.	d^1–I–IV	a year ago; thirty years ago
(5.	I–II–IV–I^c)	(I gave *him* some)

Note that we classify what many languages call "the dative case" as structurally equivalent to an adverb or adverbial phrase. This is based on commutation: "I gave *him* the book" is the equivalent of "I gave the book *to him.*"

Insofar as a dative exists in English, it is expressed only by structure, as indicated in Number 5 above, where the position of IV in the exocentric structure is the signal of its function: I–II–I–I is normally interpreted as Subject-Verb-Indirect Object-Direct Object. If something were substituted for the second I, the sequence would probably become ambiguous (the first I being taken as I^c); cf. Shakespeare's "Knock me at the gate" (II–I^c–IV or II–IV–IV), Johnson's "Call me a cab" (II–IV–I^c interpreted as II–I^c–I^c). Where this dative survives and is clear ("I spoke him fair," "I told him so") it is because the verbs in the sentence belong to a list of verbs which "take the dative."

We are now in a position to list the structural words we have called "determinants."

Determinants

d^1 = determinant of I (article, numbers, demonstratives)

d^2 = determinant of IV (usually a preposition)

d^3 = (1) determinant of equal function: signals that the next endocentric structure functions as did the last;

(2) connective between independent exocentric structures (in traditional terms, "co-ordinating conjunction")

Note, also, the use of either the symbol $<$ or $>$ to indicate the morpheme "of," whether expressed by that word or by part of another word: "the top of the hill" (d^1–I $<$ d^1–I), "Bill's house" (I $>$ I), "mother mine" (I $<$ I). This special symbol is needed because, while we might postulate a d^4 corresponding to "of," the function is frequently (even in English) indicated by an ending on a word, which would require a different symbol, and we want to avoid having two symbols for the same morpheme. The purpose of $<$ is to indicate that the preceding (or following, according as it faces) I-structure is subordinated to the other one in such a way that the two together function as I (the "genitive relation"), not as I + I (*Jack and Jill*).

It has not, of course, been our purpose in this chapter to develop a complete grammatical analysis of English or any other language, but only to suggest how such an analysis would be worked out. Nevertheless, the principles and notation presented here will enable the reader, should he care to try, to work out the structure of a great majority of utterances in English.

To summarize the method (which has been developed from the work of Charles C. Fries, although there has been considerable adaptation, especially of the notation), one first seeks to establish the basic sentence patterns of the language, those to which all actual utterances (in transferred speech) can be reduced; that is, to determine all the distinct functions in the sentence, in terms of which any possible sentence can be analyzed. These functions will always be revealed in signals[5]—the exact nature of which will, of course, vary with the type of structure of the language—which tell the native speaker the functions of words in the sentence. These signals can be discovered by analysis and commutation of utterances.

The basic sentence patterns of a language are its *exocentric structures.* The next step is to investigate the level of structure just below this— the *endocentric structures,* or patterns of word groups—multiverbal structures which discharge a basic function in the sentence just as a single word would do.

A complete list of all the exocentric and endocentric structures of a language, plus a presentation of the signals used by the language to identify to the user of the language the functions of words and other structural elements (the "paradigms" of Latin and Greek grammar, which were taken as the complete analysis of structure for all languages, were roughly this kind of presentation), would be a complete statement of the syntactic structure of any language. On one condition, of course: that "immediate" speech, which we have ruled out of consideration until now, is not differently structured. This question we shall now proceed to examine.

Notes to Chapter IX

1. We here deviate from Fries, who prefers to designate sentence functions by Arabic numbers: see *Structure of English,* 68–72, 76 ff.

2. Bloomfield, *Language,* 194–96.

3. See Fries, *Structure of English,* 89.

4. We distinguish I[a] from I[c] on the basis of the form-difference *he/him, she/her*; it is, of course, true that the majority of nominals show no difference of form in subject or object usage.

5. Except in the case of words which are part of a limited list (see page 162).

Supplementary Readings to Chapter IX

Langer, 53–63.
Fries, *Structure of English,* 25 ff.
Bloomfield, *Language,* 170–83.
Sapir, *Language,* 62–66.
Gray, *Foundations of Language,* 228 ff.

Chapter X

THE STRUCTURE OF IMMEDIATE UTTERANCES

To resume at the outset an important basic definition, we designate as "immediate" speech that speech whose subject—whatever the language discusses—is present to both speaker and hearer at the time the speech is produced. This is, of course, in contrast to "transferred" speech, whose subject is *not* present to either the speaker or hearer at the time the speech is produced, and therefore cannot be known by the hearer, through any means other than language.

The importance of this distinction is that immediate utterances may require less language than transferred utterances to communicate the information which the speaker wishes to convey to the hearer, since the hearer can gather certain information by observation and by reasoning from observation. This is a cardinal principle underlying the whole argument of the present chapter.

1. Incomplete utterances

It has been shown in Chapter IX that an utterance in transferred speech normally has a definite structure, and that this structure is always one or a combination of a few basic patterns provided by each language for the purpose; these were discussed, and a technique for describing them was outlined. This structure (traditionally called the "sentence") is so well established and so well understood by native speakers of the language that such speakers are immediately aware whenever they hear an utterance in which an essential element of the pattern is lacking. This awareness is shown in the hearer's behavior and speech. If you turn to a friend and say, "My brother, yesterday," he, after a second, says impatiently, "Yes, yes, go on," or "Your brother *what*?" or "Well, well, what about your brother?" or any of a number of similar expressions.

Perhaps the principal complaint of teachers of English in the grammar grades is that their pupils write "incomplete sentences." This is a significant problem, though less simple than it seems. Unless interrupted or physically unable to pronounce all the words,[1] native speakers never speak in "incomplete sentences," even when their minds are subnormal or psychotic.

Upon closer investigation it appears that the pupils *speak* complete sentences, but *write* sentences which, if read according to their own punctuation, are incomplete. The trouble generally turns out to be that they do not understand *punctuation,* and write, for instance, a comma where they should put (and in speech do put) a period. (The school textbooks, however, generally try to explain punctuation in terms of "grammar," and, while adjuring the pupil to put a period at the end of a complete sentence, usually leave him with no realistic criterion of what a complete sentence is except that it has a period at the end of it.)[2]

This teaching problem stands apart from our concern here, but it helps to establish the fact that native speakers are keenly aware when the structure of an utterance is "incomplete"—in transferred speech, that is. Immediate speech is a different matter altogether.

2. The fractional nature of incomplete utterances

If the utterances which occur in immediate situations were collected and studied, it is the contention of this book that—with a few exceptions to be mentioned specifically—they would always be found to be *fractions of complete sentences*. Although space is not available to give a really thorough demonstration, the general line of reasoning can be indicated. A number of utterances occurring in "immediate" or contact situations are listed below in the first column.[3] In the second column is an analysis of the structure of these utterances, according to the formulae developed in Chapter IX; and in the last column are possible sentences in which each utterance could occur, showing how each structure fits as a fraction into the larger structure. (In many cases, this sentence is the one from which the fraction is known historically to have been abbreviated.)[4]

Good morning	III—I	(I wish you a) good morning.
See you	II—1^c	(I will) see you (later).
Say	II	(I) say.
Indeed?	IV	(Is it so) indeed?
Indeed!	IV	(It is so) indeed!
Thanks	I^c	(I give you) thanks.
What?	I	What (is it)? What (do you want)?
Very well	IV—IV	(That is) very well.
Sure	IV	(That's for) sure.
Of course!	IV	(That happens) of course.
Good!	III	(That is) good!
Please!	II	(If it) please (you)!
Pardon	I or II	(I beg your) pardon. Pardon (me).

These examples are from telephone conversations, which do not, perhaps, constitute the typical "contact" situation. Examples of another type can be found in *titles and signs,* which are usually structure I—that is, a nominal expression, possibly quite complex on the next level or levels of structure but always adding up to something that would function as I in a complete sentence pattern, such as: *the house of the old woodcutter,* I . . . . ,

$$(d^1—I<d^1—III—I)$$

or *the man with the pack on his back,* I . . . .

$$\left(\begin{array}{l} d^1—I \begin{cases} IV \\ d^2—d^1—I \begin{cases} IV \\ d^2—III—I \end{cases} \end{cases} \end{array} \right)$$

Take, for example, signs on buildings: "Graybar Building," "Doylestown Hospital," "Odd Fellows Hall," "Masonic Temple," and so on; or paintings in a gallery: "Venetian Sunset," "Cos Cob, Connecticut, in 1831," and the like. All of these probably imply sentences like "(This is the) Odd Fellows Hall," or something similar— the linguistic demonstrative formula "This is (the) . . ." being quite unnecessary when you are standing in front of the object to which it would call your attention.

Slightly different structures may be observed in "No Parking Here," "No Parking This Side," "Left Turn Only," "By Authority," where the implication is "No parking (is permitted) on this side," "(This regulation is promulgated) by authority (of the police)."

Note, too, that many expressions which occur most often, if not exclusively, in immediate situations are actually complete sentence patterns; for example:

I see.	Excuse me.
I know.	You know.
Tell me.	

The two categories of utterances used in immediate situations which have so far been mentioned are identifiable as either complete sentence patterns or fragments of complete sentence patterns and also do not present a very great range of variety. Moreover, they are recognizable as appropriate to one side of a conversation—so much so that they can sometimes be used without regard to what the other speaker has just said.[5] A relatively short list would include over 90 per cent of those encountered.

The remaining category, however, comprises expressions which, though still identifiable as sentences or sentence fragments, occur altogether unpredictably and with limitless variety. These expressions, besides, are altogether meaningless standing by themselves. Examples of the expressions now in question are:

> I'm sorry, he isn't.
> Yes, completely.
> Oh, any time tomorrow.
> Very well indeed, thanks.
> Do you?
> And yourself?
> Between ten and eleven.
> Oh, work.[6]

These expressions lose most of their peculiarities, however, and in fact become quite easy to classify, if we make one simple assumption: that for purposes of classification, *we may count as part of an immediate utterance anything in the utterance just made by the previous speaker.* In other words, since the utterances in question are always *responses to other utterances,* it is hardly illogical to suppose that the second speaker saves himself time and trouble by not repeating words just uttered by his interlocutor.

Viewed in this way, the mysterious, incomprehensible fragments listed above become perfectly clear and simple when taken as fragments repeated from some preceding patterns and word groups. To illustrate, here are the citations with the utterances which, in the contact situation, immediately preceded them:

Is Mr. B. in?	I'm sorry, he isn't (in).
Was the factory destroyed by the fire?	Yes, (it was) completely (destroyed by the fire).
When shall I call on you?	Oh, (you may call on me) any time tomorrow.
How does your wife feel?	(She feels) very well indeed, thanks.
I prefer tea.	Do you (prefer tea)?
My wife is fine, thank you.	And (how do you feel) yourself?
When may I phone?	(You may telephone) between ten and eleven.
What do you intend to do there?	Oh, (I intend to) work.

Lest it should be thought that we are making an unwarranted postulate in claiming that "Thanks!" implies, and is possibly abbreviated from, a sentence such as "I give you thanks," we may cite examples in languages other than English, where surviving case forms clearly prove the point. Latin says *gratiās*; why accusative plural? Because it stands for the sentence *grātiās ago,* which also occurs. German says *danke schön;* the *schön* does not agree with *danke,* and the expression certainly does not mean "fine thanks," but evidently is short for either (*ich*) *danke* (*Ihnen*) *schön* or (*ich gebe Ihnen*) *Danke schön.* In German, also, "good morning" is *guten Morgen,* where the accusative form of the adjective clearly implies an expression like (*ich wünsche Ihnen einen*) *guten Morgen.*

The principle operating here is also seen in cases where a linguistic pattern or formula of more than minimum length occurs so frequently, or in such self-explanatory contexts, that a part of it can easily fulfill the function of the whole—for example, in the case of numbers, where "nineteen hundred and sixty" regularly becomes "nineteen sixty," sometimes "nineteen and sixty"; "four dollars and twenty-five cents" becomes "four twenty-five"; "two shillings and six pence" becomes "two and six,"[7] and so on.

The fact of abbreviation in these circumstances probably does not require demonstration. Significant, however, is the implication that the short, terse expressions used in everyday contact situations appear to be *always abbreviated from the fullest and most complete structures in the language.* This is, of course, just the reverse of what has generally been assumed, that complex structures were "gradually built up from the grunts of primitive man." It is on this assumption, in turn, that teachers of languages have proceeded in using the abbreviated expressions of conversation with which to begin courses in a language. It would seem that the reverse procedure might be pedagogically superior.

3. Monomorphemic structures: imperative and vocative

A story is told that when a tourist in Moscow inquired of his guide how it happened that certain Soviet citizens had cars with chauffeurs while most did not, he was told that "in the classless society, all citizens are equal, but some are more equal than others." In the same way it could be said that, while all speech situations meeting the definition given above (Chapter IX, 1) are immediate or contact situations, some of them are more immediate than others. The contact situations par excellence are those involving questions, calls and commands. Many languages have special structures for utterances falling into these categories.

In English and related languages we encounter in these cases a characteristic structure which, in its most elemental form, is restricted to a single morpheme,[8] as in calls—"John!"; "Captain!"; "Doctor!"— or in commands—"Run!"; "Speak!"; "Listen!" The structure here is evidently /I/ in the first case, /II/ in the second; in other words, a single-morpheme structure is a call if the single morpheme is a nominal, a command if the single morpheme is a verbal. Where the form used is not structurally marked or more common in one function than the other ("speak" is rarely a nominal), there is ambiguity: "fire" may mean "fire your gun" or "there is a fire." But the situation determines the choice.

These structures are, of course, like other sentence patterns, capable of expansion: "Mr. Smith!" or "Captain of the Guard!" or "You in the brown coat" are multiverbal structures equal to I (the first is I . . . ., the second I . . . ., the third I . . . . .); "come here!" or

$$(I = I) \qquad\qquad (I < d^2 - d^1 - I) \qquad\qquad (I - IV)$$

"Go quickly!" are easily analyzed as II—IV.

In languages similar to ours, therefore, we may say that a "complete" utterance must include at least I and II in transferred speech, but may be restricted to either I or II in immediate speech. The absence of I in an utterance, therefore, will signal to the hearer that the utterance is immediate speech, and is either a command (e.g., "come to the fair") or to be completed from the preceding utterance (e.g., ". . . [and] came to the fair").[9]

A special intonation is often given to calls and commands, and may be counted as a structural formant expressing the call or command situation; but it is not essential to the situation, as may be seen from the fact that the nature of the utterance is usually perfectly clear in a written document, even if the latter be wrongly punctuated and read aloud with the wrong intonation.

In other languages the call-and-command structure may not be so different from the structures of other utterances. In Latin, for instance, every word had to have endings—structural formants—which defined its function in the sentence or in sentence-component structures. If the word was part of a call, it had the "vocative" ending: *servus* = "slave, subject"; *servum* = "slave, object"; *serve* = "slave, called to." (In time, of course, the vocative "ending" became identical with the nominative; but this was part of the breakdown of the original system.) A command had an "imperative" ending (in the plural: *valē-te, vocā-te*; in the singular, it was usually a zero formant, and the whole form often became identical with the stem: *dic, vocā*).

If one should here cite two-morpheme "imperatives" like German *bleiben Sie*, these will turn out to be the exceptions that prove the rule: for these are not imperatives, but "hortatory" subjunctives. The essence of any subjunctive is that it is a form which puts the hearer on notice that the verb so marked does not necessarily state a fact, or what the speaker believes to be a fact—which is always the implication of the ("indicative") forms normally used in speech. Because of this significance, subjunctive forms are naturally used in the expression of hopes, wishes, opinions, doubts, conditional statements, and so on. (Compare the toast, "Long live the Queen!"—we don't know whether she will or not—with what the Prince of Wales might have said in the fiftieth year of Victoria's reign: "Long *lives* the Queen!")

The subjunctive therefore comes to substitute for a command when there is a feeling that the normal form for a command is too peremptory and a polite hope should be expressed instead. To a servant, one may say, "Open the door!" But to a social superior, one feels that one should rather say, "I hope it may please His Excellency that he should open the door." In the liturgy of the Mass, the few occasions when the priest says to the congregation, *orāte!* ("pray!") probably date farther back than *orēmus!* ("let us pray!")—although, in the later Roman Empire, the meaning was probably practically identical.

4. Quasi-imperatives and interjections

We have seen that a basic characteristic of immediate speech situations is a tendency to take advantage of the nature of such situations to limit linguistic expression as much as possible: wherever a part of the information constituting the message to be transmitted can safely be assumed to be evident from the situation—including words that have just been uttered—the linguistic forms required for their expression are regularly suppressed, even though, it appears, the complete structure required in transferred speech is always *first* conceived and *virtually* present.

It is in the light of this principle that some of the most irregular and perplexing utterances met with can be satisfactorily explained. If a certain expression, however it originates, comes to be standard in a certain situation, any part of the expression, it seems, may assume the function of the whole. As a result, we not infrequently encounter words used in a way quite different from their original or ostensible function; but the expression will be perfectly comprehensible as soon as we discover the steps which have led to its present use, or the circumstances in which it is normally used.

This occurs most commonly in commands, which frequently have the structure II—IV, and are abbreviated to IV: "Hence!"; "Out!"; "Quickly!"; "Down!"—a verb like "go" or "get" having originally been a part of all these utterances. A IV—IV structure is less common: "Under the bed, quickly!" The pattern I^c—IV, or, IV—I^c is seen in military commands, e.g., "Eyes . . . right!" and "Right shoulder . . . arms!"—evidently for "(Turn your) eyes (to the) right," "(On the) right shoulder (put your) arms."

Military commands, in fact, have often been deliberately conformed to the formula "command of information" and "command of execution": in other words, it is necessary to make clear to the soldiers, first, what it is they are to do, and second, the precise moment when they are to do it. For this reason, perfectly regular structures like "Face to the left!" and "March to the rear!" became "Left . . . face!" and "To the rear . . . march!"

On the other hand, sometimes a two-word command in the structure II—IV becomes so familiar in a typical situation as to be reduced to one word. Thus, for some reason, "Come!" does not seem strong enough in contemporary American English, and one usually says instead "Come here!" or "Come on!"—but these are pronounced as one word, *C'mere, C'mon*: the fairly common situation of starting with two formants to express two morphemes, then the coalescing of the formants, leaving one formant expressing two morphemes. (Another example is Latin *ad illum* > Old French *al* > Modern French *au*, once pronounced [au], and therefore still just possibly analyzable as two formants, but now pronounced [o].)

This, perhaps, suggests how a great many, if not all interjections originated. Two contemporary speakers of American English meet, and one says to the other, "Hi!" This ejaculation has developed phonetically from "how are you?" = [hawɑja] > [hɑːjə] > [hɑj], and the origin is still fairly well remembered, for the person addressed may reply, "And how are *you?*" The older expression "hello" is probably related to *hail, hale* and *health*, and might have originated in a phrase like "be hale, O!" (Romans said *salue,* "be well," and the ancient Irish said *slán leat,* "[let there be] health to you.") The fact that interjections are different in different languages, and follow the phonetic development of their respective languages (e.g., Germanic *ach* becoming *och* in Scottish and *oh* in English), suggests that they were not always in a class by themselves.

5. The structure of questions and negatives

In many languages, questions have a highly characteristic structure, quite divergent from any of the other utterance-patterns, even including those used for immediate situations. In some ways, as will be shown, the treatment of questions seems to run parallel to the treatment of negatives. Questions are normally used in immediate situations, in the sense that (with the rare exception of rhetorical questions, which are clearly an artificial stylistic device) a hearer who is expected to answer is always present. However, the subject matter of the question may be something not present to speaker and hearer. Questions, therefore, are not pure immediate speech.

It might be supposed *a priori* that the logical way to structure a question would be to have a formant expressing the question morpheme and to introduce it into the sentence in any convenient position, so that the question corresponding to the statement, "He is a doctor," would be, in literal translation, "Question he is a doctor," and in idiomatic translation, "Is he a doctor?"

The formant or particle might have two possible positions, one making a question of the whole utterance (as in the illustration just given), the other calling into question only an individual term, e.g., "He is a question doctor" = "Is it a *doctor* he is?" (Note the similarity here to the behavior of negatives.) Some languages do just this, for example Russian with its particle *li*.

Another relatively simple, though linguistically somewhat more sophisticated method of handling the question situation would be to adopt an intonation formant—a characteristic intonation pattern which can turn a statement into a question with or without any other structural device. Russian, again, uses this method, and so does English in sentences like: "He's a doctor?" Languages which make no other use of intonation patterns may be found using one unique tone-formant for this purpose.

Interrogative and negative structures eventually get intertwined with each other, because questions, like statements, may be positive or negative: the negative question equivalent to "He is a doctor?" would be "(Is it true that) he is not a doctor?" Here, however, other factors generally become involved to complicate the situation. There may be an impingement of the immediate situation (see Chapter XI, 5), and structures may be diverted from their logical meaning to express the speaker's emotional attitude or the answer expected. Combination of a negative question with a positive one often expresses the speaker's impatience, as if to say, "Is it so—or not? Give me an answer one way or the other; don't leave me in suspense!"

In English the simplest negative interrogatives now primarily suggest the answer expected. Compare the following:

Question	Expected Answer
Is he a doctor?	Yes or no.
Isn't he a doctor?	Yes.
He *is* a doctor, isn't he?	Yes.
He isn't a doctor, is he?	No.

The last is the real negative question, but note that "no" in answer to a negative question is equivalent to "yes"—that is, it indicates agreement; by the same token "yes" would mean "no!"[10]

Latin had a similar system for suggesting the expected answer:

esne Quintus?	Are you Quintus?
nonne Quintus es?	You're Q., aren't you?
num Q. es?	Surely you aren't Q., are you?

It has been suggested that both a negative particle and an interrogative particle represent a fairly high degree of abstraction, and that probably in the early stages of the history of language (again permitting ourselves to speculate where we have no evidence) it was more probable that there were parallel conjugations of positive, negative and interrogative verbs, rather than one verbal form for all three, shifted from one to another by a negative or interrogative particle; the latter is a more efficient system, but requires longer to develop. To corroborate this hypothesis, a certain number of parallel positive-and-negative verbs can be cited: Latin *dicere,* "to speak," *tacere,* "not to speak" ("to be silent"); *scire,* "to know," *ignōrāre,* "not to know"; *adesse,* "to be present," *abesse,* "to be absent"; German *sprechen/schweigen,* and so on.

When we find in Celtic a more or less regular process along these lines, where a verb shifts to a different form when it is negative or interrogative, so that *chonnaic mé* means "I saw," but *ní fhaca mé* means "I did not see"; *tá mé* means "I am," but *bhfuil mé* means "am I?", we are tempted to think we have uncovered a great linguistic principle. In sober fact, however, the evidence does not justify this hypothesis. Careful investigation reveals that, insofar as these alternations tend to form a system, it is a system in process of development rather than the breakdown of one formerly general. The parallel forms that can be listed are, for one thing, always an infinitesimal minority of the negatives and interrogatives in the language; and what is more, it can often be shown that the "negative verb" was derived from the positive one at some remote period, either by a negative particle or some other prefix: *gno-sk-ō > Latin gnosco, *ṇ-gnō-s-ō > Latin ignōrō; *con-icc > chonnaic, *fo-icc > fhaca.

One other question-structure which accounts for the form of questions in a considerable number of languages is the switching of position of I and II ("You are . . ." becomes "Are you . . . ?"), which seems to pervade all the Germanic tongues. It never was at home in Romance languages, and French, after struggling with it for centuries, is at last eliminating it via such formulae as est-ce-que, and étais-je? is now rare or literary. This latter device has also developed in English since the eighteenth century: we no longer say "he likes it not" and "go you?" but rather "he doesn't like it," "do you go?"(or "are you going?"). The interrogative formula, of course, can become equivalent to our first device—a formant expressing a question morpheme.

Another factor that complicates the structure of questions is that in many languages the normal forms of speech imply that the speaker is stating what he at least believes to be a fact, and that if he has any reason to doubt its factual nature, the hearer must be alerted to this by special forms (subjunctives or optatives).[11] Questions and negatives, naturally, almost always call for these special forms.

Classical Greek, for instance, had one negative particle (οὐ) that was used to deny that something which could have been real was so in fact (e.g., "he is not here"), and a different one (μή) to deny that something considered a mere possibility would become real (e.g., "that it might not rain"). Thus Ulysses told Polyphemus (Odyssey ix. 366) that his name was Outis, not Metis, so that later when the giant cried, "Outis blinded me," it would be a negative statement of fact, understood as "I was not blinded by anyone." Had he used Metis in his cries, the meaning would have been "May no one hurt me."[12]

Oddly enough, the words which speakers of Indo-European languages think of as "interrogative" words par excellence are not directly related to questions in the sense in which we have been discussing them—namely, utterances specially patterned to elicit from the hearer confirmation or denial of a statement. The "interrogative" words of Indo-European bear the same relation to words used in that type of utterance as a word negating one item only bears to a word negating the whole statement: in other words, the "interrogative pronouns" and their ilk, while making the sentence in which they occur interrogative, question only one item in it—nor do they question its *existence,* they merely ask whether this particular one is the object of choice.

The interrogative words—apparently all marked in Indo-European by an initial Q-sound—are correlative with the demonstratives, the system apparently being:

> this—that—which?
> here—there—where?
> thus—in that way—how? (= In what way?)
> I—you—who?

While this is the underlying system, the primary use of these correlatives seems to have been in question-and-answer situations:

> What?   That.
> Which?   This.
> Where?   Here.
> How?   So.
> When?   Now.

Since the closest relation of these words is to the demonstrative, we may analyze them as formants expressing a demonstrative morpheme plus a question morpheme; "What?—That" could be paraphrased as "Query, that—confirm, that"—and so with the others illustrated. Since a query is expressed, the sentence becomes interrogative; still, the query is not about the truth or falsehood of the proposition expressed by the sentence, but only as to the choice actually made between two or more alternatives, or as to the precise nature of the alternative chosen. What is clear is that these words were not meant to be, and are not, the primary device by which sentences in Indo-European languages are given an interrogative form.

We have written at some length about questions, yet as will be evident, the last word has by no means been said. A vast field of investigation in the area of interrogation, both in regard to its mechanics and its semantics, still awaits the researcher. The purpose of these remarks has been mainly to indicate potentially profitable lines of investigation suggested by modern linguistics, in contrast to the totally sterile approach of traditional "grammar."

Notes to Chapter X

1. For example, when drunk, drugged, or lapsing into unconsciousness. Cf. Wilkie Collins' *The Moonstone,* Chapter IX.

2. See Fries, *Structure of English,* 10–11.

3. These are of the type described by Fries, *Structure of English,* 42–43; see *ibid.,* 3.

4. See page 31.

5. It has been humorously observed that one might gain the reputation of speaking fluent and elegant German by simply learning to say correctly a few expressions like, *ach so? wie Schade! Ja, ja, natürlich,* and *ausgezeichnet,* and at every pause throwing in whichever one seems most appropriate.

6. These are of the type treated by Fries in *Structure of English,* 45.

7. Not "two, six" because there are other units in the system, and "two, six" might be "two pounds, six shillings." The latter actually becomes "two pounds six."

8. This might be analyzed as one message morpheme, plus a structural morpheme expressed by a zero formant.

9. The presumption at this point is, of course, that we do not have more than one complete sentence-structure in the utterance. Cf. page 184.

10. Compare the song of yesteryear which featured the refrain, "*Yes,* we have *no* bananas."

11. Perhaps this is linguistic proof that the ethical precept against lying is founded on a sentiment quite general among mankind. Would it follow that, where a language does not require special forms in this situation, its speakers are less averse to lying?

12. Of course the verb would also have been different—subjunctive or optative.

Supplementary Readings to Chapter X

Whitney, 1–6.
Sapir, 82 ff.
Gray, 38–41.
Pei, *Story of Language,* 26 ff.
Fries, *Structure of English,* 165–72.
Roberts, *Patterns of English,* 272–85.

Chapter XI

COMPLEX SYNTACTIC STRUCTURES

Thus far we have been studying the *minimum* structure required by utterances of various types, if they are not to be identified by the native speaker as incomplete, as failing to communicate anything to him and leaving him bewildered—as his behavior would show. This minimum structure, we have seen, is what is commonly called the *sentence*; and each language has certain basic sentence patterns to which the most complex simple utterances can be reduced. And we have presented a technique and a notation for describing and analyzing this structure of the sentence and its components in any language.

But, of course, there is no reason at all why a given utterance should consist of one sentence and no more; there is nothing whatever to prevent a basic pattern from being repeated two or more times within an utterance.

If we had to deal with mere repetition of sentence patterns, the end of one and the beginning of the next would no doubt be marked by a distinct juncture, and no special treatment would be required. But there exists here an opportunity, of which languages take advantage in varying degrees, to organize repeated sentence structures within an utterance into a higher level of structure. It is this level of structure that we have now to examine.

1. The sentence structure as a unit of higher forms

Let us designate a sentence structure as S, which will therefore become the symbol for any of the half-dozen basic sentence structures constituting the fundamental grammatical structure of any given language. Supposing, then, that we have an utterance like: "He's badly hurt. Get a doctor!" The formula of analysis for such an utterance will be

$$S_1 \quad \| \quad S_2$$

where the double bar indicates a boundary or juncture. Now, S_1 here can be analyzed as I–II–IV–III, and S_2 as II–I^c; but we are no longer concerned with the analytical structure at the sentence-level: we take this for granted, since we are taking sentences as units.

Should our utterance be of the type: "He went out into the street and hailed a taxicab," the analytical formula will be only slightly different:

$$S_1 - d^3 - S_2$$

and it will be noted that we count S_2 as complete although I is not expressed in it, in accordance with the principle already established (see Chapter X, 2), that anything just said in one utterance can be counted as part of the one immediately following. As a result, the difference between this utterance and one like "He called to them | and | they came" would not appear on this level of analysis (both would be $S_1 - d^3 - S_2$), but would, of course, appear on the basic-pattern level, where S_2 would in the first case be (I)–II–IV, while in the second it would be I–II.

At the present level of analysis our concern is to investigate the manner in which $S_1, S_2, S_3 \ldots S_n$ are connected with each other in utterances including more than one; to establish the patterns of such complexes—if there is a definite, limited number—and to determine the nature of the words or formants to be identified as d^3.

2. Connective and substitution signals

It is evident that the words to which traditional grammar gave the name *conjunctions*—co-ordinating or subordinating—are, in general, identical with the words which we mark as d^3, and thus the symbol d^3 will be given to words which could substitute for "and" in the sentences given above. Such words as *but, so, for, yet, or,* and *nor* will fall into this category.[1] These words express mostly a structural morpheme—they indicate that the next structure (whether endocentric or exocentric, whether a sentence component or a complete sentence pattern) fits into the over-all structure at that level in the same function as the preceding structure. There is, of course, a subordinate message morpheme, accounting for the use of different words with the same structural function. Thus, d^3 can be used either within a sentence or between sentence structures.

A question that arises here is whether it is necessary or worth while in English to distinguish between "subordinating" and "co-ordinating" conjunctions. One wonders whether this is a distinction perpetuated by tradition from languages like Latin and German, where the "subordinating" conjunction was followed by a special mood or structure in the following clause. (Incidentally, the traditional observation that "subordinate clauses are incomplete, while co-ordinate clauses are complete" is specious, for in applying the rule, the "co-ordinating" conjunction is eliminated from the clause following it, while the "subordinating" one is not. If we judged both on the same basis, a clause like "for it was raining" is no more complete than "if I had money.")

Close investigation fails to substantiate any solid ground for the division into co-ordinating and subordinating conjunctions in English. Possible grounds for distinguishing two types of d^3, however, do appear. Two sentence patterns are often connected by a word like "therefore" or "however,"[2] whose position in the clause it introduces is flexible: it may stand at the beginning or end, or in the middle; whereas "and," "but" or "for" may stand only between clauses. Also, words of the "therefore" type may connect only complete sentence patterns, never parts or components of sentence patterns. They seem always to come at a distinct juncture, never to substitute for a juncture. In the case of a pattern like "I have married a wife, therefore I cannot come" (Luke xiv. 20), however, there is a juncture between S_1 and S_2, and it is possible to analyze the utterance as $S_1 \parallel S_2$, not identifying the "however" or "therefore" as d^3, but simply as IV within one or the other clause. Since these words are normally bounded by junctures, we might also classify them as interruption structures (page 189).

As a matter of fact, in Indo-European languages, all or almost all connectors between S_1 and S_2 seem to have had some other purpose originally, and to have been adapted to use as conjunctions relatively late in the history of their respective languages.[3] It seems probable that Indo-European did not, until late in its history, develop structural organization on the level we are here considering: in other words, normally each utterance contained only one sentence pattern, or at most a repetition of two or more divided by junctures. Greek, Latin and Russian often use participles where modern languages would use subordinate clauses. This impression appears to be confirmed by the style of works in Indo-European languages—such as those of the Greek Gnomic poets, or the Irish "Red-Branch" legends —about which there is reason to believe that they might have been first composed at a very remote period.

We arrive, therefore, at the conclusion that when S_1 and S_2 occur in sequence, connection between them is made either by juncture— simply marking a boundary between S_1 and S_2—or by a class of connective words which we shall call d^3 (those which pattern like "and," "but," "if," "when," and so on), or by a combination of both, that is, a juncture followed by a connective word. (In the written language the last is the normal situation, for a comma is usually put between clauses, but in the spoken language, as observation will testify, the juncture is frequently omitted.)

3. Infixation of one S in another

If structures are to be made with complete sentence patterns as a unit, the simplest and most logical process is accumulation—simply putting one S after another, either with a boundary between the S structures, or with a formant that will either substitute for or supplement the juncture or boundary sign. When there is a boundary, we hardly have what could be called a deliberate *structure* at all.[4]

There is a second type of structure, however, which is very common in languages derived from Indo-European: the interruption of one S to present a different S, after which the structure of the first S is concluded—a situation which gives the following analytical picture: $S_{1a} \parallel S_2 \parallel S_{1b}$ ("This man—I shall call him Smith—was a criminal"), or, $S_{1a}-d^3-S_2-\parallel-S_{1b}$ ("This man, whom I shall call Smith, was a criminal"; "The person whom you met at the door was my father").

Here again, the first sentence is scarcely to be considered a deliberate structure; only when the connective word substitutes for a juncture should it be so classified, otherwise the S_2 may be regarded as a mere interruption. In the case of $S_{1a}—d^3—S_2—S_{1b}$, however, we begin to have a distinctive pattern, suitable for cases where S_2 gives additional information about ("modifies") a particular word in S_1, and it is desirable to place it immediately adjacent to that word. The structure becomes even more distinctive when, as frequently in modern English, the d^3 is left out: "The course the captain steered." Here the sequence I-I-II alerts the hearer to the construction, which can only be S_{1a}—S_2,[5] since this particular sequence never occurs as a single sentence pattern—although the only possible alternatives, I-II-I and II-I-I ("Is/your brother/a doctor?") make single sentences.

It will be evident that the "infixed" clauses are those traditionally labeled "relative clauses." In Indo-European languages it is very easy to demonstrate that the "relative pronoun" is a late development. In many cases it is almost identical with one of the demonstrative pronouns. The development apparently was somewhat as follows:

1. I know a man. He is a carpenter.
2. I know a man. That (man) is a carpenter.
3. I know a man / that is a carpenter.
4. The man / that is a carpenter / will step forward.

When the juncture represented by the period at the end of the first clause in Number 1 and Number 2 is omitted, the demonstrative has assumed the function of the connective.

With this kind of construction, S_2 can be made to serve most of the functions of I in S_1: subject—"*That it is true,* is pity"; genitive—"We are made aware *of the fact that* . . ."; dative—"I direct your attention *to the fact that* . . . ." Accusative is handled differently, by the "reduced sentence" structure.

4. The "reduced sentence" structure

The reader may have noticed that we have been taking up the distinctive patterns that weave several distinct sentence patterns into one complex sentence in what may have been the order in which they developed. The construction now to be taken up would seem to be the latest and newest; on the other hand, it may have developed independently, and conceivably be the oldest of all.

This structure differs somewhat in different languages, but in general it provides a form in which the elements of a sentence can be put *without constituting an independent sentence,* so that this "virtual" sentence can be enclosed in another sentence as an endocentric construction.

Since the functions I-II will make a sentence, it is only necessary to develop a structure that will suggest both I and II and not be a sentence.

An ancient example of this structure is the verbal noun or adjective—the *participle,* and the constructions in which it figures. In Greek, Latin and Russian these are frequently found where English would have to use a clause:

σύ εἰ ὁ ἐρχόμενος;	Are you the one/who is coming?
morituri tē salūtāmus	As we go to our death, we greet you.
на слéдующий день.	(He returned) on the day/which followed.

There is one limitation to use of the participle, however: it will attach a II-morpheme to one of the words in a sentence, but the I-morpheme of the implied S_2 has to be one of the components of S_1. We do not, therefore, consider a participial construction a "reduced sentence" in the fullest sense, that is, the reduction of a complete sentence. It is rather a modulation, a case of taking due advantage of an occasion when two structures partly overlap.

The genuine reduced sentence is most generally formed with the infinitive, in English marked by the word *to,* which we shall figure as d^4 in this usage. A simple and common example of the construction is the sentence of the type "I want to go" (I-II-I^c), patterning like d^4-II "I want money," and expressed in some languages by two clauses: "I want it, that I should go." In this instance, however, the I-function is still taken from S_1. When it is different from the I in S_1, we get a sentence of the type "I want/him to go," which is equivalent to "I want that *he* should go." Note that while "I will go" is I-II$_a$-II$_b$, "I want to go" is I-II-d^4-II. The d^4 is used wherever the first verbal form cannot be classified as an auxiliary.

It is evident that the general strategy of the structure of complex sentences is to take one S as the main one, and work in the direction of giving other S's some function in the structure of this main clause, or a relationship to some particular word in this main clause. Thus, the structure of complex sentences tends to evolve into patterns similar to those of simple sentences, except that complete sentence patterns, instead of intra-sentence functions (and words discharging these functions), are the units.

Within the scope of the present chapter, it is impossible to be much more specific than this, since the precise patterns of organization at this level of structure are different in different languages, and their detailed description belongs to the specific description of each language. We have used English for illustration, but have not gone into detail even with that language.

5. The structure of interruptions and exclamations

When a speaker, after beginning an utterance, is interrupted by another speaker, no particular structural problems result insofar as the first speaker is concerned. When the interruption is over, he usually completes the structure he has begun, sometimes repeating the words already uttered, perhaps adding a formula like "As I was saying." Occasionally, of course, the conversation takes another turn, and the half-finished grammatical structure is forgotten and never completed.

The utterance of the speaker who interrupts, however, is by no means always a complete structure. Its structure is, in fact, more often than not irregular; but this irregularity is understandable in the light of its purpose. Such an utterance is not usually intended to convey information to the first speaker; if this were the speaker's intention, it would be more efficient for him to wait until the first speaker had finished, and then speak in a complete structure.

The purpose of the interruption, however, is generally to express agreement or disagreement (hearty or violent, as the case might be) with what the first speaker is saying, to correct the first speaker, to assure him of the second speaker's continued attention—in short, to express the *second speaker's attitude* toward what the first speaker is saying.

For this, complete grammatical structures may not be necessary. Certain words, such as "Oh!," "No!," "Yes," "Uh-huh," may be confined to such use and may be therefore part of a short, easily mastered list. Certain single adverbials or sentence components, such as "good"; "too bad"; may become conventionalized for such contexts.

The correction-interruption merely offers one word or structure in place of another, which is either accepted or rejected by the first speaker; for example:

> "So I'll see you at two o'clock——"
> "Three o'clock."
> "Oh, yes, (I'll see you at) three o'clock, in the . . ." etc.

Or else:

> "Now, that was in 1932, and——"
> "Thirty-three."
> "No, thirty-two—in 1932, and . . ." etc.

The interruption aimed at reassuring the first speaker of his hearer's attention generally consists of such words as "Yes," "Fine," "I know," "I see," "M-hm," "Oh?," "You don't say," "Indeed?," "My word," "What do you know,"[6] "That's right," "Of course," and others which the reader can easily add, or ascertain by observation. The list would, of course, be quite different for different languages. In French, for example, we might have "Comment?," "Ah?," "C'est ça"; in German, "Ach so?," "Wunderbar!," "Ja ja," "Natürlich"—but the purpose is the same. (Frequently noncomparable and dissimilar formants, as between one language and another, express equivalent morphemes in this use, making strict "translation" impossible. French *Mon Dieu* does not "mean" 'My God!' in English; it means something like 'By George' or 'Darn!' The descriptive linguist does not do his job completely if he merely describes the formants without gaining insight into their functions—to know which is to penetrate to the heart of the linguistic system under description.)

Sometimes the listener's close attention is signaled by a repetition of the last word or two just spoken by the other speaker, thus:

> "So I went to the railway station——"
> "The railway station——"
> "And bought a first-class ticket——"
> "Ticket."

Just as a speaker in a conversation expects and receives periodical signals assuring him of his listener's continued attention, so he, by a reverse of the same coin, from time to time signals his awareness of the other speaker. This is done by the use of expressions which seem conventional, but which have undergone a semantic shift in order to fulfill this purpose. The message morpheme is totally suppressed in favor of the structural morpheme, to the extent that the formant may be used in a way quite opposite to what it ordinarily means: in these contexts "now" does not mean "at this time," "then" does not mean "at that time," and so on.

This may be regarded as the impingement of the immediate situation on whatever is the subject of the conversation, even when that is something else. When the subject of the conversation is the same as the situation in which it is uttered, there tends to be less impingement. For example:

> "Pardon me, sir, but can you tell me the way to City Hall?"
> "Straight ahead two blocks and turn left."
> "Thank you very much."

On the other hand, impingement formants turn up quite regularly in transferred speech. Let us imagine the above exchange as related later to someone else:

> *"Well,* I was walking along Main Street, *you see,* and it didn't look like the City Hall was anywhere around there, so I decided to ask somebody. But it was sure a tough neighborhood, *yes sir,* and *I'm telling you,* I didn't like to stop and talk to anybody, *you know?* But along came this fellow, *see,* and he looked a little more sober than the others, so I decided to take a chance. *Well,* I asked him politely where City Hall was. *Now then,* here's the strangest part of the story. This fellow, *you see* . . ."

In the same category can be put exclamatory interruptions like: "My! How pretty," "It was, Oh! So sad," "Ah, so pure," "Mm! That's good," and so on. These are all designed to signify to a listener the emotional attitude of the speaker, whether or not it is directed toward or occasioned by the subject of his speech. This is probably why exclamations are normally structured as interruptions, and of all the material of language, frequently cannot be shown to have been derived from fuller forms. (This may yet be accomplished, however: exclamations vary with language—and are therefore evidently learned behavior, not universal human reactions; as Kipling pointed out long ago,[7] even the syllables we use for sobbing or laughing are different in different cultures—and sometimes seem to follow the development of a language;[8] yet, on the other hand, they often use sounds which are not phonemes in the speaker's language.)

Traditional grammar, of course, made no distinction between immediate and transferred speech, and treated practically none of the topics discussed in this chapter. This is why a student who has learned a language by the traditional method sounds so artificial when he tries to talk it, and—until the methods of linguistic description are improved —can acquire real ease and *Sprachgefühl* only after more or less prolonged contact with the native-speaking community.

Notes to Chapter XI

1. *Nor* inverts I and II in the S_2 it introduces, if I is expressed in that S_2; cf. Byron: "My hair is grey, but not with years, / Nor grew it white / In a single night" (*Prisoner of Chillon*). This holds equally true with an auxiliary or periphrasis: "nor has it . . . ." "nor does it . . . ." Cf. Roberts, *Patterns of English,* 208.

2. Roberts (218 ff.) calls these words, and others which pattern like them, "sentence connectors."

3. Old Irish, for example, really has no subordinate clauses at all.

4. Under these conditions, the structural difference between a complex utterance and a sequence of simple ones—even by varying speakers—is either imperceptible or negligible.

5. Bear in mind that if the first I is a "relative pronoun" it is a figured as d^3.

6. An abbreviation of "what do you know about that?" It is perfectly obvious that this expression is not intended to ask the speaker what he knows.

7. See Kipling's short story, "The Man Who Came Back," in which the Englishman is recognized by the fact that he does not sob on the syllable Afghans use for sobbing. In many languages one does not laugh "ha-ha"; Russian, in fact, has no /h/-phoneme, and one who observes closely will notice that a native speaker of standard Russian really laughs *kha-kha.* (It would not surprise the writer if someone some day demonstrated that this syllable was derived from the root meaning "to laugh.")

8. As remarked earlier (page 177), the relation between German (and probably earlier Germanic) *ach,* Scottish *och,* and English *oh,* seems to parallel the relation between German *brachte* and the Scottish and English pronunciations of *brought.* There may possibly be an etymological connection between German *weh!,* English *woe!* and Latin *vae.*

Supplementary Readings to Chapter XI

Roberts, 201–222, 265–285.
Gleason, 92–110.

Twaddell, *The English Verb Auxiliaries.*

E. Alarcos Llorach, *Gramática estructural de la lengua española,* 72–75.

Nida, *Morphophonemics.*

Hockett, "Two Models of Grammatical Description," *Word* X, 2–3 (1947), 210–34.

Jespersen, Otto, *The Science of Grammar.*

Nida, *Outline of Descriptive Syntax.*

Chapter XII

THE STRUCTURE OF WORDS (MORPHOLOGY)

Etymologically, the word *morphology* means "the science of forms" (the German equivalent is *Formenlehre*), and it has not infrequently been used to mean the description of all the phenomena of a language other than (1) the order of words in a sentence or clause, and of clauses in a sentence, (2) the inventory of words in the language (the *lexicon*). This point of view arose at a time when the only languages thoroughly studied by philologists were of the Indo-European family and were structured similarly to Latin and Greek: they definitely had word-units, and a majority of the grammatical structure was included in the composition of the word. Modern linguistics must necessarily restrict this definition to narrower limits and for the most part exclude those devices—whether formants, patterns of order, or intonation curves—which give structure and meaning to utterances; in other words, we wish to treat grammatical structure of the language (what corresponds to the traditional term "grammar") as an independent category (as we have done in Chapters VIII to XI). This leaves morphology concerned only with the principles of structure of word-units.[1]

In traditional grammar, morphology had become largely a listing of inflectional formants in logical groupings or "paradigms." We are less concerned with devising groupings for "endings" than with ascertaining how the word-unit is made up. We shall divide words into formants, see if the formants fall into notable categories, and endeavor to find out the principles governing the selection and order of formants within the word.

1. Why we have words

It once was thought that all languages have words, that "words" and "language" were synonymous terms. But with the growth of our acquaintance with languages which do not have words (in the sense that in these languages, every distinct group of syllables is as much a sentence as a word) have come the questions, why do languages have words? Which is suggestive of a higher stage of linguistic evolution, to have words or not to have them?

Though an *a posteriori* proof is out of the question, we can make a confident surmise as to why languages have words. If we dictate to a group of persons who are asked to write down exactly what they hear a single meaningless syllable of possible occurrence in their native language, all or nearly all will produce an exact transcription of what was dictated. Approximately the same thing will occur with two or three syllables, though individual phonemes may (in the absence of meaning) be misidentified by various individuals in the group. But with four or more syllables it will become evident that our subjects not only cannot record the syllables accurately, but cannot even be sure how many there were.

Now, if at this point the matter of dictation be shifted to words meaningful in the language of the listeners, we shall find that four, five, even seven or eight syllables can be accurately transcribed; and in fact, if the person conducting the experiment purposely makes small errors—saying, for instance, "fackpory" instead of "factory"—the listeners will copy down what the word *should* have been, and insist that that is what they heard. Evidently, the existence of unit boundaries and a principle of organization, and of a semantic reference for each component, is a great aid to the memory.

This is no doubt why we have words. The more there is to express in an utterance, the more formants, naturally, are required. If these become numerous and result in a very long string of syllables, it may become difficult for the hearer to keep track of them. Hence, it would appear that the development of a structural unit which may be called a "word" would suggest a later rather than an earlier stage in the development of language from its beginnings, though many disagree.

The difficulty of remembering a long string of syllables, even with the help of words organized according to well-known principles, especially for the ignorant mind, still has its influence: it will be found that in most languages there is a distinct tendency for the *spoken* language and the *argot* to confine their vocabulary to small words, "words of one syllable"—three or four at most; while the language of the learned is proverbially polysyllabic.

2. The identity of the word

The spelling systems of most modern languages call for the separation, in writing or printing, of words from each other by the use of spaces between them. It is perfectly obvious, however, that we make no such division in the spoken language. To the keen inquirer, therefore, the question might occur: since in actual speech we utter formants in a continuous sequence without division, do we really have words at all?

The question is a good one insofar as it springs from a disposition to be realistic about language—an understanding that the spoken syllables are the language, not an imperfect and possibly "corrupted" reproduction of the written forms. But actually, although apparently pauses are used only for syntactic boundaries, and although there might be argument about whether a given formant or sequence of formants is "free" in the sense of being a word, there is ample objective ground for our conviction that most languages have word-units. For one thing, an accent, always occurring on the first, or last, or next-to-last syllable of the word, may fix the word's boundaries (this is probably the original reason for word accent). Sequences of phonemes inadmissible between syllables of a word will often be admitted between words. In languages where the structure of the word is "root + endings," it is easy to recognize a new word when a new root appears. Of course, here and there a word boundary may become obscured, as in such cases as *orange, apron, adder*.[2]

It might be mentioned that while a word must be at least one formant, and a formant is normally at least one syllable, there are such things as nonsyllabic words (the formant being only one or two phonemes). Many of the Slavic languages have prepositions which consist of a single consonant, and are, of course, pronounced as part of the next word: *v* means 'in,' *vMoskvé* means 'in Moscow.' (Nonsyllabic words are necessarily "enclitic" or "proclitic": an *enclitic* is pronounced as part of the preceding word, a *proclitic* as part of the following word. Even words of one or more syllables may sometimes be enclitic or proclitic; Latin, for example, had an enclitic word for "and," -*que*, seen in *senatus populusque Romanus,* instead of *senatus et populus Romanus.*) Surprisingly enough, even English provides examples of enclitic words: such words as *would* and *am* are often eroded in conversation to *d* and *m*: *I'd like to know; I'm not going; my brother'd come.*

Problems that are much less easily disposed of concern whether a given sequence of formants, used sometimes with one semantic reference and sometimes with a different one, is one word or a pair of homophones, or whether a given word and one differing from it only slightly, the difference expressing only syntactic function (e.g., *servus* vs. *servum, book* vs. *books*) are to be considered as one word or two. But these problems belong to the special field of lexicography (see Chapter 14).

3. Patterns of word structure: compounds

We may venture the speculation that, when the word-unit was first discovered, its organization was planless and purely accidental: a limit may have been arbitrarily placed after every third or fourth formant. In languages as we know them today, however, the formants making up a word are never placed by chance, but always according to definite patterns. These patterns differ somewhat according to the structural type to which the language belongs, but many agree in a general way in placing formants which express message morphemes first, followed by formants expressing structural morphemes.

The order of formants in polysynthetic languages is, of course, outside the scope of morphology, since the principles to which it responds are those of sentence construction, and the patterns formed are essentially sentence patterns. In the case of the other three types of languages, we can often justly regard the first two or three formants— as many as express message information—as the *root.* The formants that follow, expressing operational instructions, or modifications of the basic information, may be called, in the agglutinative languages, *postpositions*; in the inflecting and analytic languages, *suffixes.* In the case of analytic languages, we shall expect to see fewer endings, more words containing a root only, and more "structural words"—independent words expressing little or no message information, but serving almost exclusively as operation indicators.

The principle of organization of a word tends to be identical with
the history of its development, as far as this latter can be surmised: a
word like *undisciplined* presupposes *disciplined*, which in turn presupposes *discipline*—and, to take a step into history, Latin *disciplina* presupposes *disco* and *doceo*. If words are analyzed with due regard to the
layers of accretion of immediate constituents (see Chapter VIII, 6),
principles of morphological structure will more readily appear.

Going somewhat contrary to Bloomfield,[3] we do not assert that the
root of a word in a given language must be a free form *in that language* (we need only cite legitimate English words like *bellicose*),[4] although presumably it must have at some time been a word in *some*
language, and it would appear probable that, if it has been borrowed
en bloc from another language, the root is not likely to be productive,
in the sense that other derivatives will be made from it. (In etymology—see Section 7—this is often a clue that the history of a word
cannot be traced in the language where it is first encountered.) It is
best, it would seem, to define "the root" as those formants which carry
the message information of the word. Often a word which, like *bellicose,* or *retain, detain, conceive,* can be divided into formants in another
language or on a historical and etymological basis, must count as a
single root from the point of view of the language under study.[5]

It seems likely that at some stage of the development of language,
the root and the word are identical—the word contains nothing that
is not part of the root—as is still the case in languages of certain structural types. Even in languages where this is the prevailing situation,
however, this is rarely true in all cases.

It will often appear from commutation that the root consists of two
or more elements which can occur as independent words. In this case
we say that the word is *compound.* Compounding is one of the chief
means at the disposal of a language to increase its stock of words, and
in the inflecting and analytic languages—where the structure of the
word is relatively inflexible, and one is expected to meet the expres-
sive requirements of a given situation by using established words, not
by creating an *ad hoc* agglomeration of formants—new vocabulary is
always being formed while the language remains living.

Long ago the Hindu grammarians made a very thorough classification of compound words in Sanskrit,[6] and most of the categories
which they established can be identified in most other languages,

though forming different systems. In English, a series of words like *animal tamer, snub-nosed, hearthstone* and *gooseberry* demonstrate the three stages of the formation of a compound word: the group of words regularly used together; the hyphenated group, 'or group written and accented as one word; lastly, the compound formed so long ago that, though it is recognized as a compound, one element of it has become meaningless. Compounds in all the stages may be found in the English of any given period, since the process is constantly going on.

It appears that almost any grammatical structure can be taken as a word and as the compound root of derived words: witness expressions like "the take-it-or-leave-it attitude," where position changes a whole sentence into III, or "It has a *je ne sais quoi* about it," in which a sentence *in another language* is made I. We have noun compounds developed from III–I (*blackbird, bluejay, hothouse, electric shaver*), from IV–I (*dishpan*, i.e., *pan for dishes; homework*, i.e., *work at home; baby buggy*, i.e., *buggy for a baby*); from I–I representing a sentence nucleus, I^c–II (*animal tamer*, i.e., *tamer of animals, [one who] tames animals; office seeker*, i.e., *seeker of office, [one who] seeks office*); from II$_a$ II$_b$ taken as I (*take-off, markup, blowout, count-down*), and so on. Needless to say, *a black bird* is entirely distinct from a *blackbird*—and *a hot house* is not necessarily a *hothouse*. A *baby buggy* may be a small buggy (just as a baby grand piano is a small piano) as well as a buggy for babies.

The most common compounding pattern in the Indo-European languages, however, is the simple juxtaposition of two nouns, the first modifying the second: *a doghouse* is a kind of house, not a kind of dog.

Compound adjectives are also frequent, e.g., *flap-eared, three-cornered* (representing III–I plus the participial suffix *-ed* giving adjectival function), *stone-ground* (representing IV–III, "ground by stone"), to name only a few. Moreover, any compound word may in turn become one of the constituents of another compound, yielding almost limitless possibilities: cf. *back-seat driver, home loan office;* here determination of the immediate constituents is of the utmost importance, since evidently a "back‖ seat │driver" is not "a driver of seats who is in back" (back│ │seat│ │driver), and a "home│ │loan│ │office" is "an office for home loans," not "a loan office at home." Some languages pursue the possibilities in this direction a good deal further than English; the celebrated propensity of German for compounding[7] is often partly a spelling convention (German would write *office seeker* as one word), but something like *Kriegsgefangenenentschädigungsgesetz,* "a law for the indemnification of war prisoners," proves that the reputation is not altogether undeserved.

4. Derived words

After we have separated out, in a word under analysis, those formants which convey message morphemes and, among the latter, those formants or sequences of formants which also appear as independent words, the remaining formants, all bound forms, will fall into two categories: derivative prefixes, infixes or suffixes; and inflectional "endings." The former are still part of the message information, but are clearly secondary: they are mainly intended to effect slight modifications in the information conveyed by the root, and thereby to elicit new words from a word already formed. The inflectional formants, on the other hand, are intended to give the word a role in a grammatical pattern and to fit it in with other words. Of course, these two purposes not infrequently overlap in a given formant.

To illustrate, in English the word *book* has only one formant, which is the root. The form *books* contains an additional formant *-s,* which is both derivative and inflectional: it adds the information that we are speaking about more than one book, but also serves to tie this word with other words—with plural verbs, adjectives, and so on. A word like *bookbinder* is a compound word (immediate constituents book| |binder, containing another derived word, *bind-er*) of the type I–I for Iᶜ–II (see above, Section 3). Finally, a word like *bookbindery* is a derivative of *bookbinder;* the *-y* formant expresses the note of "place where a trade is carried on," hence, *the bookbinder's shop* (in these last three words we have expressed by an independent word, "shop," what the derivative suffix *-y* expresses in *bookbindery*). Many who recite Longfellow's *The Village Blacksmith* do not realize that the "smithy" is not the smith, but the place where he works.

In a phrase like *the bookbindery's machinery,* we have another formant *-s,* which is inflectional; it does not modify the meaning of *bookbindery,* as *-y* alters that of *bookbindery* and *machinery*. This is a typical inflectional suffix. Naturally, these are less frequent in the analytical languages.

Derivative formants may be included in a word anywhere, but to put them before the root undermines the identity of the word; never-theless, it is done by a great many languages. In Indo-European there appears to have been a time when the word always began with the root and was accented on the first syllable. Then, particularly among verbs, new words were derived by prefixed formants (which, it seems, originally just happened to precede the verb in the sentence): *stand, withstand, understand; capio, incipio, recipio*. Immediately the problem arose: should the word-accent be moved to the first syllable—which would take it off the root and possibly cause elimination, through con-traction, of that vital syllable—or should the accent remain on the root, which would keep the compounding process clear but would re-move a useful indication of the beginning of the word? Germanic ap-pears to have at first followed the latter practice (giving the insepa-rable-prefix verbs), then, more recently, the former (whence the sepa-rable-prefix verbs). Latin appears to have stuck with initial accent at first (whence the vowel reduction in the root *-cap-* seen in *incipio*), then shifted to the other practice. Celtic compromised: it would pre-fix one formant without shifting the accent from the root, but would shift the accent if two or more were prefixed—which led to many "ir-regular" forms in which the original root was altogether lost.

What may be called "infixes" were much less used, yet one or two illustrations can be found in many languages. Some Greek roots (e.g., λαβ, 'take') infix an *-m-* in the present tense (λαμβ-αν-ω). Latin (also Greek) has several examples of an infixed *-sc-*: *ignosco vs. ignotus*, etc. Infixes may not be intentional; in some cases, they arise when part of the original root drops out in certain forms because of pho-netic developments.

5. Root, stem and ending

When we have analyzed a word into formants and determined the succession of immediate constituents, we ultimately come to a form which is not further divisible (from a contemporary point of view, at least),[8] and appears to be the original base from which accretion be-gan. This may be viewed, according to an ancient metaphor, as the *root*, to which forms are added either at the beginning or at the end: e.g., if "drive" is our root, "overdrive" is an example of adding at the beginning, while "drive/s," "driv/ing," "driv/er," "driv/er/s" are examples of addition at the end. Besides these, "drove" is an example of an internal-change formant; and "drive-in," "drive home," examples of a discontinuous formant (i.e., two formants, expressing one morpheme, which do not occur together within a word, but as two at least potentially independent words, which may have other words in between). The root is frequently a word in its own right, but not necessarily. Underlying *legal, legality, illegal,* is a root *-leg-* which is not in use because we already have the word *law.*

The term "prefix" is generally suitable for formants attached at the beginning of the root, and "suffix" for those added after; but not all formants preceding or following the root can properly be called by those names. Only if the subordination of these formants to the root-formant is very evident—as, for example, when they express mainly or exclusively structural morphemes—are the traditional terms applicable in their fullest sense. In a word like "car-wash," the formant *wash* is not a suffix; but in "washer," *-er* is a suffix.

When endings are added to a root, analysis may reveal a formant which seems to express little except to vary the form of the root for combination. In a word like "political," we have clearly two formants, one of which is also seen in "politic/s," "impolitic," and similar forms. But in *"politico-legal,"* the root form has been expanded by a syllable to "politico-," apparently solely for the sake of combination.

Again, the infinitives of Latin verbs fall into four types, as shown in the forms *vocāre, habēre, dīcĕre,* and *venīre.* In these forms we can clearly distinguish *-re* as the sign of the infinitive, and the roots *voc-, hab-, dīc-* and *ven-* (seen in such other words as *vox, hābilis, dīxit, convēntiō*). But what about the vowel between the root and the various endings? Have we four types of infinitive (four "conjugations": -āre, -ēre, -ĕre and -īre), or one infinitive ending *-re,* and four stems, *vocā-, habē-, dīcĕ-,* and *venī-?* The latter is the more efficient statement of the facts. (Needless to say, the traditional one is the former.)

It is conventional to describe the evident facts in a language like Latin to say that inflectional endings are normally added to the *stem,* which is derived from the *root.* Actually, it is probably more correct to say that because of various accidents in a language's historical development, the commutation process can be carried further in some words than in others—giving alternative forms of the root, one longer (the stem) and one shorter (the root). There is use for the concept of a "stem," i.e., the root plus a formant which adds nothing to the message and little to the structure, but puts the root into a form suitable for combination. The value of abstraction of the "stem vowel" as a separate entity may, however, be questionable: beloved of grammarians, it makes for neat paradigms, but it is doubtful whether it reflects actual relationships in the language.

6. Inflections, "agreement" and correlative words

From what has already been said, the nature of the type of formants traditionally called "inflectional endings" will be clear. They are those whose chief, if not only purpose is to fit the word in which they occur into the grammatical structure of the language. Thus, they indicate whether the word is I, II, III or IV, whether it is subject or object in the sentence in which it occurs, whether it is part of an endocentric structure in which it is subordinate to a word of the same class. Naturally, inflectional formants are most numerous and most complex in the "inflecting" languages.

There are certain message morphemes which are usually expressed by these formants simultaneously with their structural meaning. Thus, having identified a word as I, they may also indicate that more than one item of the species named by the word is under discussion. Having identified it as II, they indicate the time of occurrence or character of the action designated by the word.

Finally, there are certain structural functions of inflectional formants, not necessary for the grammatical structure, not adding anything to the message, often of apparently accidental origin, yet persistent and stable to a high degree. Grammatical gender, for example, appears to have arisen simply because pronouns, with forms for different sorts of referents, were used to avoid repetition of nouns. (A classification into animate and inanimate beings might be logical, and indeed seems to peek through here and there in the Indo-European system; but it is, we trust, obvious that *actual* gender has nothing whatever to do with grammatical "gender," which often arbitrarily makes inanimate objects male or female, and sometimes makes obviously feminine beings neuter.[9]) So-called "plural" forms of verbs by no means indicate any notion of plurality in the action named by the verb, but rather in the *subject* of the verb.

It appears that the functions which these features must discharge in those languages which use them must be *to tie together,* to mark as belonging together *the words belonging to certain important exocentric or en-docentric constructions.* If the terminal syllables of the verb—even after its verbal character, its aspect and its tense have been signaled—vary in response to the terminal syllables of the noun which is its subject, this certainly constitutes an additional mark for the I–II structure, and very clearly singles out among nouns in the nominative case which one is I for the structure. If the adjective in III–I varies certain syllables according to the "gender" of I, it helps to mark off the words constituting the III–I structure.

This "agreement" feature—or, as we prefer to call it, "bonding"—apparently grew up by accident in the Indo-European languages at a time when they were highly inflectional, and probably because of the habit of such languages of expressing two or three morphemes by the same formant. In an analytic or agglutinating language, if it was thought necessary to indicate that the subject of the verb was female, this morpheme could be indicated by a formant included in the subject-word; but this morpheme probably would not be expressed again in the verb. In an inflecting language, however, the "gender" morpheme would be included in one formant with others which it was necessary for the verb to have. Though not absolutely necessary, "bonding" was found useful for the reasons given above, and it often was preserved for a long time.

It is because of this high morpheme-formant ratio that inflecting languages are particularly subject to crystallization of inflectional formants into rigid systems, the "declensions" and "conjugations" so well known in traditional grammar. It is, or should be, plain upon very cursory inspection that these are very tautological and uneconomical, and therefore highly inefficient. One syllable is used to express the dative in the singular, a different one to express the dative in the plural, two more to express the same distinction in "feminine gender," and an additional quartet of endings for each of three or four "declensions." (Most "paradigms" could be greatly abridged, to be sure, by recognizing *syncretism* in tabulation, rather than listing the same form under four or five different headings, thereby asserting a distinction which does not actually exist; but a good deal of inefficiency would still remain.) A language more sparing of effort and more economical of resources would—short of the limit set by the possibility of ambiguity—express a given morpheme only once or twice, always by the same formant. It is, therefore, no accident that inflectional languages develop in the direction of analytic.

Noting that rigid systems of xM:f and xf:M* are more or less confined to one language type, and are pretty inefficient even there, it seems quite amazing that for such a long period it was thought that these alone were the tools of grammatical structure: that to give a language's declensions and conjugations was to give its "grammar," and conversely, if one had to admit with embarrassment that one could not set these up for a language, the language was obviously barbarous and had no coherent structure.

Similar to "bonding" formants are *correlative words,* which occur as members of pairs, so that the occurrence of one of the pair alerts the listener for the appearance of the other. In this manner two words, two endocentric structures, or two full sentence structures (clauses) may be balanced or related to each other. In English, well-known examples are:

> *as* soon *as* possible
> *either* one *or* the other
> *the* more *the* merrier
> *such* items *as* bread, milk, cheese, etc.
> It was *so* cold *that* the rivers froze

The correlation effect is not in the grammatical function of these words (all can be classified in categories containing other words not correlative), nor is it signaled by any special formant. The correlation resides in the fact that the native speaker has simply memorized the fact about each that it is correlative, and the word that is correlative to it. This morpheme, in other words, is an example of a structural morpheme not formally expressed, the words involved being part of a limited list (see VIII, 5).

7. The history of the word (etymology)

One of the most fascinating branches of linguistic science is *etymology,* whose task is to ascertain the origin and history of the words used in any language. The etymologist is a linguistic detective: he seeks to discover, if he can, when and how each word came into being, and

---

* The formulae mean "many morphemes to one formant" and "many formants to one morpheme."

how it came to have the form and meaning which it has today. The course of this investigation often turns up a veritable treasure-trove of unrecorded history, forgotten trades and traditions, the ways and conditions of life of other days, and choice archeological finds.

Thus, etymology tells us that *copper* was supplied to the ancient world principally from the island of Cyprus, and probably at least as early as 800 B.C. (Cyprus was called *Kupros* in very early Latin, and copper was simply "the Cyprian metal," *cuprum aes*). From etymology we learn that the Gauls whom Caesar fought wore clan tartans, as do their modern descendants: Caesar refers to them as *braccatae gentes,* i.e., people who wore trousers (since the Romans did not, they considered the practice barbarous), and *braccae*—whence Scots *breeks,* English *breeches* and French *braies*—was a Celtic word, evidently identical with Old Irish *brecc,* "varicolored," and modern Scottish *breacán,* "the kilt." The words *calico* and *damask* tell us that these types of cloth originated in Calcutta and Damascus respectively.

One aspect of the etymologist's work is historical. Ideally, he would like to find out exactly when a given word was first coined and everything that has happened to it since then. This is possible with only a minority of words, since a language inherits the bulk of its word-stock from earlier stages of itself and ultimately from a parent language, and somewhere along that route the trail is lost for lack of evidence. Some words, indeed, might have an unbroken lineage back to the beginning of speech, if only we had the evidence to trace it. On the other hand, we know almost the precise moment of the birth of the word *gerrymander*[10] and the approximate time of origin of such words as *okay, shyster, to pan out, bedlam.*

Much of the flavor of the style of, say, Addison, comes from the absence in his writing of words which came into English after his time. It is surprising that scholars have not taken this into account in their criticism of such authors; but those trained in the *literature* of any language seem generally to have little or no interest in the language itself.

The importance of historical research in serious etymology cannot be too highly stressed. The very first thing that must be done, before attempting to theorize on the origin of a word, is to secure all available information on the changes of form and usage it has undergone since its first known appearance. Thus, if we were seeking the etymology of the word *savage,* we might go off on the wrong track altogether if we did not observe that the contemporary French form *sauvage* suggests an *l* in the word. In the sixteenth century, we find, it was actually written *selvage* in English. Italian *selvaggio* then confirms our suspicion that we may postulate a Late Latin form **silvāticus* (from *silvā*) meaning "one who lives in the forest." Similarly, the word *aisle* would present an insoluble problem until we discovered that the *s* was introduced into the spelling by analogy with the homophone *isle* (where the *s* was not pronounced either): then we realize that *aile* was a simple borrowing from French—retaining in English, however, the Old French pronunciation—and meaning "a wing" (on either side of the "nave"). The absence of the documents, and of facilities for easy access to them, required for this kind of investigation resulted in the fact that really scientific etymology was impossible until the nineteenth century.

If we cannot trace a word back to its origin, at what point can we consider an etymology complete? On this, policy is not clearly defined. Judging by the practice of most etymologists, if the word is ultimately from Indo-European, one likes to develop if possible a plausible reconstruction of the Indo-European root; otherwise one tries to trace the word at least as far back as the point where it entered the language under investigation. To do this often requires, not only a mastery of several languages, but a fairly intimate knowledge of the linguistic history of each, in order to be able to decide how to account for the changes of form recorded for the word, and what sort of original root can be judiciously postulated. It is here the philological side of etymology comes to the fore.

Like linguistic science as a whole, etymology requires arduous training and compendious knowledge if its results are to be more than mere ingenious, or even learned guesswork. When pursued by scholars adequately qualified, however, etymology makes rich and often spectacular additions to the store of man's knowledge about the languages which serve both to unite and to divide us.

Notes to Chapter XII

1. This definition is equivalent to that more subtly expressed by Bloomfield (*Language,* 207), "by the *morphology* . . . we mean the constructions in which bound forms appear among the constituents . . . the constructions of words and parts of words."

2. Formerly *norange, napron, nadder*: the *n* became attached to a preceding indefinite article. This also explains nicknames like *Ned* and *Nan*. Cf. O. Jespersen, *Modern English Grammar*, I, 2.426. By overcorrection, forms such as *nown* and *nuncle* had brief circulation.

3. Cf. Bloomfield, *Language*, 242.

4. Although it might be argued that account should be taken of levels of usage: a word like *bellicose* would probably not even belong to the vocabulary of a non-learned user of English. There is no reason why an unlettered native speaker might not use a word borrowed for a certain purpose whose root had no analogy in the language; but if this became a really common word, it is probable that analogies, even if fanciful, would be found—cf. the mis-identification of *ham* in *Hamburger* (see page 152).

5. There are, of course, words—free forms—which do not have a "root" in this sense—that is, completely structural words, which may have no message information (although the great majority probably contain *some* message information). This is a case in which a formant which would be part of a word in one language would be a free form in another.

6. For some of the Sanskrit categories of compounds, see Bloomfield, *Language*, 235.

7. Cf. Mark Twain's "Beauties of the German Language" in *Mark Twain's Autobiography*, with introduction by A. B. Paine, N.Y., Harper, 1924, 164–65 (Vienna, Feb. 3, 1898).

8. This function appears still to have validity. It is correct to write "Department of Modern Languages," but it pains us to hear the organization referred to as "Modern Languages Department"—why? Because *modern-language-*, though written as separate words, is really the first element of a compound (compare Note 7), seen also in *Modern Language Journal, Modern Language Association*, and the like. The distinction is clearer in German, where *in der Altstadt* is something altogether different from *in der alten Stadt*. In Irish, *bean sean agus bhocht* is "a poor old woman," but *seanbhean bocht* is "a poor crone."

9. Thus, in German, the hand and fist are "feminine," but the finger and arm are masculine, the eye is neuter but the nose is feminine, and in the sentence, "the little girl sat on a log and cried bitter tears," the tears are feminine, the log is masculine, but the little girl is neuter.

10. It was in the year 1812, when Elbridge Gerry was governor of Massachusetts. Looking at a map of voting districts, someone remarked that the northeastern district looked like a salamander, and someone else said,

"Don't you mean a *gerrymander?*" (Cf. *Dictionary of American English.*) The word *shyster* pretty certainly originated in New York City about 1840, but the precise circumstances have not yet been discovered (cf. Mencken, *The American Language,* 158, 231; *Supplement One,* 314).

Supplementary Readings to Chapter XII

Bloomfield, 207–26, 227–46.
Gray, 144–78, 179–223.
Gleason, 51–91.
Skeat, *The Science of Etymology, passim.*
Pei, *Story of Language,* 95–99.

Chapter XIII

THE PHYSICAL ELEMENT
IN LANGUAGE (PHONETICS)

The "compleat linguist" (to paraphrase Izaak Walton) must study and master all that properly belongs to linguistics in the realm of observable physical phenomena, and, indeed, he should know enough about the physical sciences upon which linguistics impinges to take advantage of discoveries made and machines invented by acoustical engineers. (For a description of the basic division of the phenomena embraced by the study of language see Chapter I, 4, and Figure 5.) Although these topics come within the scope of the science of *phonetics,* which has an identity of its own, certain branches of it may be considered as branches of linguistic science, and we venture the proposal that every student who hopes to win a worthy place in the professional field of linguistics must be an accomplished phonetician.

1. Outline of the history of phonetics

At the end of the nineteenth century the study of the sounds of which speech is made up—a study at one time full of the most preposterous notions and the wildest stupidities—finally adopted scientific method and soon emerged as a recognized physical science. The first real phonetician was probably Wolfgang von Kempelen (1734–1804); but he was far ahead of his time, and his adventure with a "chess-playing machine" which turned out to be a hoax discredited all of his perfectly sound work, as had happened more than a century before to Father Athanasius Kircher.[1] Nevertheless, Von Kempelen's *Mechanismus der menschlichen Sprache* (1791) is the first really serious and responsible attempt to describe the sounds of speech. Almost half a century after Von Kempelen, J. Müller's *Hand-*

buch der Physiologie (2 v., Coblenz, 1834–40), not intended for the study of language, nevertheless gave attention to the physiology of the speech process, thus laying some of the groundwork for the soon-to-be-born science. A mid-nineteenth-century effort toward attempting to improve traditional orthography—which, of course, amounted to a search for a phonetic alphabet—also served to prepare the way: a noteworthy text is R. Lepsius' *A Standard Alphabet* (London, 1863).

The first serious work in what we now call phonetics, however, was E. Brücke's *Grundzüge der Physiologie und Systematik der Sprachlaute* (Vienna, 1856). Brücke was a physiologist, but in this work he established the limits of scope of the new field. He was followed by Eduard Sievers, whose *Grundzüge der Lautphysiologie* went through several editions.

In this branch of linguistics, however, the French took the lead around the turn of the century, and the names of the abbé Rousselot (*Principes de phonétique expérimentale,* Paris, 1897–1909), Paul Passy, founder of the International Phonetic Association, and a little later, Maurice Grammont (*Traité de phonétique,* Paris, 1933), are all still well known. The influence of their work is seen in American and English grammars of French, which for several decades were alone among foreign-language grammars in starting the elementary textbook with a short course in phonetics. It was believed that this would greatly help the American or British student to master the very unfamiliar sounds and intonations of French; and so it would have done, had it not generally doubled the student's hatred for a subject which required him to break his head on phonetics *in addition to* the foreign language.

The early twentieth-century French work in phonetics awakened similar interest in the subject in England. George Bernard Shaw's character in *Pygmalion,* Professor Higgins, was probably suggested by Henry Sweet (1849–1912); and Sweet's best-known follower was Daniel Jones, author of many of the most distinguished works on phonetics in English.

2. The two branches of phonetics

Until well into the twentieth century phonetics continued to be most nearly allied to physiology, and the sounds of speech were described and named according to the organs producing them and the position of these organs in relation to surrounding structures. The terminology devised to designate the sounds of speech reflects this stage, and it is still largely physiological. From the point of view of teaching, it was taken for granted that an accurate description of the sound's articulation would enable the student to reproduce it most accurately.

With the development of physics, however, and especially of acoustics, it became possible to describe sounds with great discrimination from the physicist's point of view—that is, as a wave motion. As usual in science, the analytic process was followed by synthesis: physicists found themselves able to produce speech sounds by machines and by electric currents—sounds which, if not entirely identical with those produced by human organs, could be identified and transcribed as such.[2] It was also demonstrated that even the human organs of speech could produce the sound-units of a given language from positions other than those customarily adopted, as long as the acoustic effect—i.e., the shape of the resulting sound waves—was the same.

As a result of the developments in physics, therefore, we have now two different techniques with which to study the sounds used in human speech, according as we wish to describe them from one point of view or the other. Each technique is entirely valid, and each leads to certain discoveries that the other might never suggest. Even implications for teaching are found in both: it has been suggested that, utilizing principles of acoustic phonetics, machines could be constructed to analyze the model acoustically and also the student's imitation, compare the two, and advise the student by a light or buzz whether his imitation is close enough to be acceptable.

Obviously, the thoroughly trained linguist must understand and be able to manipulate both techniques. We shall, therefore, proceed to give an outline, first, of the articulatory or physiological approach to the description of speech sounds, and second, of the acoustic phonetician's view of the same matter.

3. A sketch of articulatory phonetics

It has often been pointed out that man does not, in the strictest sense, have "organs of speech," since all the organs used by man in

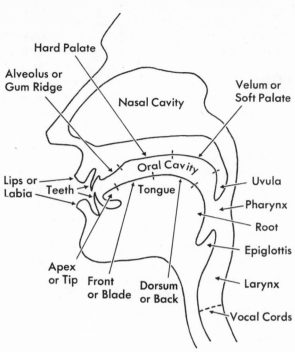

FIGURE 28   The organs of speech

speaking have at least one other function which seems more fundamental, such as breathing and eating. Thus, the act of speech begins
with inhalation (often the drawing in of breath by a person is a signal that he is about to speak; as stories put it, "he took a deep breath
and launched into a tirade of abuse," etc.). The stock of air thus accumulated is expelled through the *trachea,* or windpipe, and the
larynx which is at the top of it (Fig. 28).

Thus far breathing is not different from speaking. The distinction
lies mainly in what happens to the air when it reaches the larynx. If
it is allowed to pass through without interference we have breathing
or "respiration." Any interference with the passage of the air is
likely to produce noise; and that noise is probably a speech sound
in some language.

It is the tensile vocal cords in the larynx which in the first instance determine the amount and type of interference with the air stream, and thus modulate it for speech. If they are left completely relaxed, the air passes through without producing a sound. If they are somewhat tensed, a friction sound is produced (whispering), and if they are tensed still further, their vibration produces a musical tone which is the individual's *voice*. Either voice or whisper is modulated, in ways to be described, into discriminate units making up the sound system of the language.

Before going into detail in this direction, however, we may mention that the voice as produced in the larynx would not be audible enough for practical speech unless reinforced by several resonance chambers, chiefly the mouth, the nasal passage, and the sinuses— just as the tones of a violin string would be inaudible without the box to reinforce it. (Thus, it is literally true that one could not carry on speech without the help of the "holes in his head.") The particular shape and acoustic properties of these cavities (which can be studied as phenomena of physics) determine the precise quality of each person's voice,[3] which generally sounds higher to its owner than to others, because he hears it partially by conduction through the head bones, while others miss these frequencies.

The vocal cords can be completely closed to stop off momentarily all air from the lungs; and the sound heard immediately after the release of this stoppage is called in phonetics the *glottal stop*. It is not infrequently used—for one purpose or another—in languages of whose sound system it is not a member (cf. English, in some dialects of which it substitutes for *t*, e.g., *boᵓle*, for 'bottle,' *baᵓle, liᵓl,* and in which it is often used for separation, e.g., *Peᵓ-orᵓ-iᵓ-a*); and it is a regular unit in the sound systems of many languages, notably those in the Semitic family.[4]

The whisper sound, too, is also used as a phoneme in many languages—it is familiar in English as the sound of *h*—and also occurs in languages in which it is not a phoneme: Italian, for instance, like other Romance languages, has no *h*, yet it is possible for a native speaker of Italian to say [ho].

There is a third "glottal" sound (the term is used to designate sounds produced in the larynx, generally by adjustments of the vocal cords), the so-called "voiced *h*"—which has been a subject of controversy inasmuch as it would seem *a priori* impossible that [h] (breathing) and voice could be produced simultaneously; nevertheless, some languages have a phoneme which it seems difficult to describe otherwise. We shall not go into the matter here. Note that it is customary to write phonetic transcriptions, or sounds which have been analyzed phonetically, within square brackets, [ ].

Some languages have sounds produced by contractions of the *pharynx,* the area between the larynx and the root of the tongue: for examples, we may cite Arabic *'ain* and its voiced counterpart—usually written ' and *gh* in transcriptions, but frequently unsounded in many contemporary Semitic dialects, including Palestinian Hebrew. What the "laryngeal theory" (see Chapter IV, Note 15) refers to as "laryngeals" may have been pharyngeals, if they ever existed as actual speech sounds.

The majority of sounds used in the languages of the world, however, are either *oral* or *nasal*—that is, they are produced by interference with the stream of air by organs within either the mouth or the nasal passage—the cavity which extends behind the nose and connects with the pharynx. The pharynx can be closed off at will from the nasal cavity by the *velum,* or "soft palate," and normally is; but when the velum is lowered, the resonance of the nasal passage is added to that produced in the mouth, and so we can have *nasalized* as well as *nasal* sounds.

Among the oral sounds (and, in a sense, among the nasal ones also; we shall see the qualification presently) a basic distinction is between *vowels* and *consonants.* The distinction is essentially a matter of duration and sonority; the sounds we classify as "vowels" are louder, contain much more energy, and last many times longer than those which fall into the "consonant" classification.

The most characteristically consonantal sounds are what we call "stops"—those produced by a momentary stoppage of air, either by the lips (*labial stops*), by the tip of the tongue (*dental stops*), or by the base of the tongue (*velar stops*). These are, evidently, incapable of having more than momentary duration. The most characteristically vocal sounds are the well-known "cardinal vowels," *a, e, i, o, u,* produced by different positions of the tongue within the mouth—in no case, however, effecting much interference with the passage of air.

The vowels are of literally hundreds of times longer duration than most of the consonantal sounds.

Midway between the two extremes, however, the line between vowels and consonants becomes much harder to draw; certain sounds are regarded as consonants in one language, as vowels in another. It seems, in fact, that a vowel cannot be defined in relation to consonants in terms of absolute duration; the distinction between them becomes a phonemic matter (see the next chapter).

Within the realm of consonants, there is a certain basic pattern that includes the most important consonants of a majority of languages—simply because it pretty well covers the possibilities of distinct articulations. This basic pattern takes the following shape:

	Labial	*Dental*	*Velar*
Voiceless	p	t	k
Voiced	b	d	g
Nasal	m	n	ng (as in si*ng*)

FIGURE 29   Basic consonants

We have already seen that stoppage of air can be effected in three maximally distinct locations: by the lips, by the tip of the tongue, and by the elevated back of the tongue. In each of these positions there can be effected a simple stoppage, a stoppage accompanied by voice, and a stoppage accompanied by voice and lowering of the velum, which last, of course, causes the resonance to come wholly from the nasal passage. The uninitiated do not suspect the close relationship existing among the sounds in the vertical columns of Figure 29, but the reader may try reading aloud a passage containing many *m*'s, *n*'s and *ng*'s while holding his nose as if it were "stuffed up," and see if they do not all come out *b*'s, *d*'s and *g*'s ("I thigk I'be sufferig frob a cold id the dose"). Theoretically, in whispered speech there should be no difference between *p*'s and *b*'s, and in unfamiliar words they probably would be confused; but in ordinary whispered conversation, we use means—too complicated to detail here—for preserving the distinction.

The various directions in which this basic rectangle of consonants can be expanded may be left for a fuller outline or for more advanced study in phonetics. Suffice it to say that such distinctions as variation in point of articulation (*t/t*),[5] aspiration (*p/p*[h], etc.),[6] palatalization (k/k', etc.)[7] and affrication (t/t[s])[8] may be introduced to elicit up to approximately twenty phonemes from this basic set of modes and locations of articulation.

The consonants in Figure 29 are all stop consonants. For all but the nasal ones, a *spirant* articulation is also possible. We have spirant articulation when the contact of organs (e.g., tongue and roof of mouth) which, when complete, produces a stop, is not quite complete. Because a small opening is left between the articulators, the air used in speaking is forced through under pressure, producing a sort of hissing or hushing sound; the spirant corresponds to the stop which would have been produced if the stoppage had been made. Thus, the *ch* sound of German (or of Scottish *och aye!*) is the spirant of the sound represented in English by the letter *k*.

Besides those corresponding to stops, quite a few other spirant articulations are possible. The shape of the slit or groove through which the air passes here assumes considerable importance, giving acoustic character to the sounds produced. Thus, *groove* spirants are [s] or [ʃ] sounds, lateral fricatives are [l] sounds.[9] Most of the spirants, like the stops, may be either voiceless or voiced.[10]

Sometimes a language does not make use of an articulatory possibility because it is relatively hard to hear. Thus, the spirant [ɸ], corresponding to the stop [p], is the sound one makes when blowing out a match. In many languages the /f/ phoneme has this articulation, as, for example, Japanese *Fujiyama*.[11] But in English and other languages a spirant comprising voiceless friction—not between the lips, but between upper teeth and lower lip—has been substituted, because it is much more audible. Consonants so articulated are called *labiodentals*; English [f] and [v] belong to this class.

A final type of consonant articulation is the *trill*. In this case we have a rapidly repeated articulation, or an extremely rapid alternation of two similar articulations. The most noteworthy is the *r* of most European languages, which is actually a rapidly repeated *d*.[12] It is used in the Scottish dialect of English, and is often called "the Scots burr." (The *r* used by most Americans is quite a different sound, however, which might well be considered a vowel.) Other examples of trills are the French *r,* for which the uvula is rapidly vibrated, and the so-called "Bronx cheer," which is essentially a labial trill—a rapidly repeated [p].

All the articulations mentioned so far modulate air proceeding from the lungs and being *expelled from* the mouth and/or nose (explosive articulation). As in playing the harmonica, it is also possible to produce at least some distinct sounds by drawing air *into* the mouth (implosive articulation). This is the mode of articulation of the exotic *clicks* of Hottentot and other rare languages. (Oddly enough, however, all the Hottentot clicks are used in English, though as exclamations, not sounds of speech: the one corresponding to *l* is used to speed up horses; that corresponding to *t* as a sign of disapproval, often written *tck-tck, tsk-tsk, tch-tch,* and so on. Finally, the labial implosive is nothing other than a *kiss!* Naturally, in countries where this is a sound of speech, it cannot be used for a sign of affection—and in those countries, the gesture of affection is nose-rubbing.)

It is hoped that, with what has been said—brief as it is—the reader will be able to understand the organization of the chart of phonetic symbols set forth in Figure 30, and that the chart will suggest to him the articulations of sounds not dealt with at all, or not in detail. The references at the end of this chapter provide a wealth of material for the student who wishes to acquire real competence in the science of phonetics.

We have seen that the articulation of vowels is characterized by offering practically no resistance to the passage of air through the mouth, so that the acoustic character of vocalic sounds is determined by the shape of the resonance chamber formed by particular positions of the tongue and jaws. An important result is, as has also been mentioned, that vocalic sounds are much longer and louder than consonantal ones.

The mouth is open for all vowel sounds, but slightly more so for some than others, which is responsible for the traditional terms "close" and "open" in the phonetic description of vowels. The really significant articulator, however, is the tongue; the relative elevation of either its tip or its base (and sometimes intermediate positions) gives us a basic set of vowels and a basic pattern of classification, in relation to which almost all the vowels used in most languages can be quite precisely located from an articulatory point of view. In Figure 31 we locate what

THE INTERNATIONAL PHONETIC ALPHABET.

(Revised to 1951.)

		Bi-labial	Labio-dental	Dental and Alveolar	Retroflex	Palato-alveolar	Alveolo-palatal	Palatal	Velar	Uvular	Pharyngal	Glottal
CONSONANTS	Plosive	p b		t d	ʈ ɖ			c ɟ	k g	q ɢ		ʔ
	Nasal	m	ɱ	n	ɳ			ɲ	ŋ	ɴ		
	Lateral Fricative			ɬ ɮ								
	Lateral Non-fricative			l	ɭ			ʎ				
	Rolled			r						ʀ		
	Flapped			ɾ	ɽ					ʀ		
	Fricative	ɸ β	f v	θ ð / s z / ɹ	ʂ ʐ	ʃ ʒ	ɕ ʑ	ç ʝ	x ɣ	χ ʁ	ħ ʕ	h ɦ
	Frictionless Continuants and Semi-vowels	w / ɥ	ʋ	ɹ				j (ɥ)	(w)	ʁ		
VOWELS								Front Central	Back			
	Close	(y ʉ u)						i y ɨ ʉ	ɯ u			
	Half-close	(ø o)						e ø ɵ	ɤ o			
	Half-open	(œ ɔ)						ɛ œ æ ɐ	ʌ ɔ			
	Open	(ɒ)						a	ɑ ɒ			

(Secondary articulations are shown by symbols in brackets.)

Other Sounds.—Palatalized consonants: ƫ, ᶑ, etc.; palatalized ʃ, ʒ: ʆ, ʓ. Velarized or pharyngalized consonants: ɫ, ᵭ, ᵴ, etc. Ejective consonants (with simultaneous glottal stop): p', t', etc. Implosive voiced consonants: ɓ, ɗ, etc. ɼ fricative trill. σ, ƍ (labialized θ, ð, or s, z). ʅ, ʒ (labialized ʃ, ʒ). ʇ, ʗ, ʖ (clicks, Zulu *c*, *q*, *x*). ɺ (a sound between r and l). ɴ Japanese syllabic nasal. ɧ (combination of x and ʃ). ʍ (voiceless w). ɪ, ʏ, ω (lowered varieties of i, y, u). ɜ (a variety of ə). ɵ (a vowel between ø and o).

Affricates are normally represented by groups of two consonants (ts, tʃ, dʒ, etc.), but, when necessary, ligatures are used (ʦ, ʧ, ʤ, etc.), or the marks ͡ or ‿ (t͡s or t‿s, etc.). ͡ ‿ also denote synchronic articulation (m͡ŋ = simultaneous m and ŋ). c, ɟ may occasionally be used in place of tʃ, dʒ, and ƫ, ȡ for ts, dz. Aspirated plosives: ph, th, etc. r-coloured vowels: eɹ, aɹ, ɔɹ, etc., or eʴ, aʴ, ɔʴ, etc., or ɚ, a˞, ɔ˞, etc.; r-coloured ə: əɹ or əʴ or ɹ or ə˞ or ɚ.

Length, Stress, Pitch.—ː (full length). ˑ (half length). ˈ (stress, placed at beginning of the stressed syllable). ˌ (secondary stress). ˉ (high level pitch); ˍ (low level); ˊ (high rising); ˏ (low rising); ˋ (high falling); ˎ (low falling); ˆ (rise-fall); ˇ (fall-rise).

Modifiers.—˜ nasality. ̥ breath (l̥ = breathed l). ̬ voice (s̬ = z). ʻ slight aspiration following p, t, etc. ̫ labialization (n̫ = labialized n). ̪ dental articulation (t̪ = dental t). ˙ palatalization (ż = ʑ). ̣ specially close vowel (ẹ = a very close e). ̨ specially open vowel (ę = a rather open e). ˔ tongue raised (e˔ or e̝ = ẹ). ˕ tongue lowered (e˕ or e̞ = ę). ˖ tongue advanced (u˖ or u̟ = an advanced u, t̟ = t̪). ˗ or ˍ tongue retracted (i˗ or i̠ = ɨ˖, t̠ = alveolar t). ˒ lips more rounded. ˓ lips more spread. Central vowels: ï (= ɨ), ü (= ʉ), ë (= ə˔), ö (= ɵ), ɛ̈, ɔ̈. ̩ (e.g. n̩) syllabic consonant. ̆ consonantal vowel. ʃˢ variety of ʃ resembling s, etc.

Figure 30

(Courtesy Association Phonetique Internationale)

	Front	Mid	Back
High	i		u
Mid	e	ə	o
Low		a	

FIGURE 31   Basic vowels

are traditionally known in phonetics as the "cardinal vowels" (more or less equivalent to the vowels of Italian or Spanish), adding the English "schwa" (represented by *a* in *sofa, comma;* phonetic symbol [ə]), as a typical example of a "middle vowel."

If close investigation is made of the actual mouth and tongue positions in the pronunciation of the vowels of a particular language, say English, these positions will be found to assume a trapezoidal or triangular shape (Fig. 32), which has become familiar to students as "the vowel triangle." In Figure 32, note the symbols [æ] for the sound of *a* in *hat, back,* and [ɔ] for the sound of *a* in *fall, Walter.*

By referring to this pattern of classification and to the "cardinal vowels" or those of a particular language, it is possible to define a vowel in terms of its articulation so that one proficient in phonetics can produce it with reasonable accuracy, even without having heard it before. Thus, we may describe a vowel as "a high front vowel, more open than the [i] of English *machine*," and a phonetician would probably identify the [ɪ] of English *hit*. We can describe German *ü* as "approximately the [i] of English *machine,* pronounced with the lips rounded," and a student can come close enough to the sound produced by a native speaker of German to be understandable to the latter.

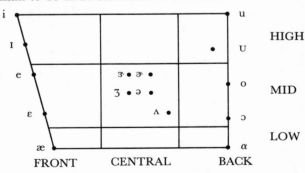

ʌ = u in *but*
ə = a in *sofa*
ɝ = ir in *first*

FIGURE 32   The vowel triangle

But when it comes to extremely fine points, phonetic description on the articulatory basis is hopelessly hampered—first by the fact that it is extremely difficult, if not impossible, to make sufficiently close observations of articulating organs in operation; second, by the fact that fine points in phonetics invariably shade off into phonemics (see the next chapter), since the investigator discovers that the actual sound produced on a given occasion is highly variable, provided it fulfills the norms for the phoneme it represents.

4. Outline of acoustic phonetics

Articulatory phonetics studies and classifies the sounds of speech according to the way in which they are produced. Acoustic phonetics is a subdivision of that branch of physics which studies sound: it therefore studies speech sounds according to their characteristics as sounds, however produced.

Sound is, as physics tells us, a wave motion in air, very much like the wave motion created in a body of water when we drop a stone into it. A cross section of the resulting ripples, or waves, is illustrated in Figure 33.

In air, a sound-wave is propagated from its source in all directions; but viewed in section in any single plane, a wave may be correctly represented by the familiar "wavy" line.

Three characteristics of any sound are *pitch, loudness* (or volume) and *timbre:* the first refers to whether it is a "high" or "low" sound, the last, to those characteristics which enable us to tell a note (pitch) played on a piano from the same note played on a violin.

Pitch is determined by *frequency* (in fact, the two words are equivalent terms, one in music, one in physics). Suppose, at the seashore, you take a stopwatch and count the number of waves that break on the beach within a minute: you are measuring the frequency of that particular wave motion (presumably it would be higher in a storm). But audible sound is not produced until we have 20 or 30 pulses per *second,* and even this would be a very low sound; most familiar sounds result from vibrations, or cycles, of several hundred per second. The note A (above middle C) to which orchestras tune, has a frequency of 440 *cycles per second.*

The *loudness* of a sound is determined by the amplitude of the waves.

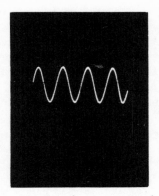

FIGURE 33   Sound as a wave motion

The pitch 440 cps (cycles per second)—the A above middle C to which the symphony orchestra tunes—as represented by an oscilloscope. (Courtesy Professor Thomas N. Dodd)

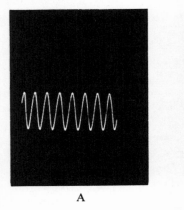
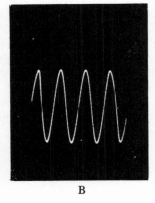

A   B

FIGURE 34   Pitch and loudness

A. Oscilloscope representation of the pitch 880 cps, i.e., the note A one octave higher than that in Fig. 33. Note that there are twice as many waves in the same space.

B. Oscilloscope representation of the pitch 440 cps, played considerably louder than that in Fig. 33. Note that there are the same number of waves in the time interval as in Fig. 33, but the waves are taller from top to bottom, i.e., they have more "amplitude." (Courtesy Professor Thomas N. Dodd)

In Figure 34, it will be noted that the *frequency* of the motion (2.5 waves per centimeter) is the same for A and B, but B is a much more ample wave than A: the height (or depth) of each wave in B (measured by the line *b*) is three times that of A. The sound represented by B would, therefore, be a much louder sound—exactly three times as loud.

The *timbre* of a sound is somewhat more complicated. Actually most of the things that produce tone do not produce only one tone, but a cluster of tones at once, one of which is dominant (called the *fundamental*); the remainder (the *harmonics*) are in harmony with it. To be audible for practical purposes, the sound must be reinforced by resonance chambers or resonators; and these inevitably reinforce some of the harmonics more than others. From this fact arises the character of the tone—the difference between one man's voice and another's, or between a piano and a tuba producing the same bass note.

Sounds may be divided into *musical sounds* and *noises*. In musical sounds, as just described, there is either one pure tone (uniform vibration at the same frequency), or a cluster of tones with varying loudness at various frequencies—but all such frequencies are in mathematical proportions; that is, if the fundamental has a frequency of 110 cycles per second, the harmonics will have frequencies of 220, 330, 440, 550, 660, and so on up to about 25,000 cycles per second, above which sounds are inaudible to the human ear.

If, on the other hand, the loudness of a sound is scattered at random over the whole range of frequencies, a listener would call the sound *noise*. In language, vowels are closest to musical notes, and most consonants are noise.

It will be evident that we are working toward an alternative way of describing a speech sound: not according to how it is produced, but according to its physical characteristics as a sound. This description can be given in terms of *amplitude, frequency,* and *timbre*. The last, however, is most usually neglected, because it involves a highly technical procedure known as Fourier analysis, whereby one complex wave is resolved into several simple waves. The process formerly required a formidable number of man-hours for each sound so analyzed; but with today's mechanical computers, quite a good amount of analysis can be done in a reasonable time.

Various mechanical devices have been developed that can convert sound into some visual form which can thus be more readily studied

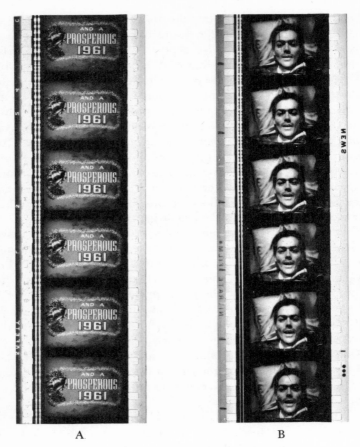

A   B

FIGURE 35   Sound on film

Music at left (A), speech at right (B). Variable-area method: sound is converted into electricity, whose fluctuations are represented by variations in the area of light and dark on the sound track. The recording is stereophonic (note the two tracks). Note that silence is two straight lines (bottom frames of B). Width of the track represents loudness; patterns represent the character of the sound, and repetitions of these within a time unit establish pitch. If you rotate this page so as to make the sound tracks horizontal, you will see that they are very much like what an oscillogram would be if pushed very close together and much reduced. Each film segment shown (6 frames) represents a time duration of a quarter of a second.

and, perhaps, permanently recorded. Familiar for a long time and part of the equipment of every radio station is the *oscilloscope,* which analyzes the sound fed into it in a continuous wavy line. When broadcasting equipment is turned on but not operating, the oscilloscope pictures the radio wave which is the station's frequency. When something is broadcast, this tone is "modulated" by varying its frequency (FM = frequency modulation) or its amplitude (AM). A pure tone appears on the oscilloscope almost exactly as it is drawn theoretically, but a speech or a full orchestra naturally create much more complex patterns. A greatly enlarged tracing of the groove of an LP record would, in different proportions, look almost exactly like an oscillogram of the same sounds.

The "sound track" of a sound film (Fig. 35) is another way of converting sound into a visual image; when "scanned" by a photo-electric cell, this strip will be converted back into, for example, dialogue with a musical score behind it. But the machine which is of most use to linguists and most used by them is the *sound spectrograph,* which does more or less the same thing as the sound film, but with more precision.

The sound spectrograph produces a vertical band in which the amount of energy (amplitude) in a given range of frequencies is measured and recorded by lighter or darker shadings in each frequency range. Figure 36a illustrates a spectrogram. The vertical axis represents the frequencies within the range of human hearing. The horizontal, left-right dimension is time; the spectrograph does not really analyze continuously, but new readings at intervals of a few seconds can be set side by side, and thus produce a sort of continuity. The blackness or grayness of the bands reflects amplitude—more sensitively than a sound film, since it is on a larger scale. Figure 36 represents a continuous-type spectrogram.

The lowest frequency range at which energy is shown is the fundamental note, those above it the overtones. It will immediately be seen that usually one or more of the overtones is stronger than the fundamental: this is why we hear a man singing [a] on the note C, instead of hearing just the note C. It appears that certain of these strong overtones—three, or perhaps only two—determine the acoustic character of the vowel, to the extent that black marks can be *drawn* on a tape at the levels corresponding to the appropriate frequencies, the tape

These days a chicken leg is a rare dish.

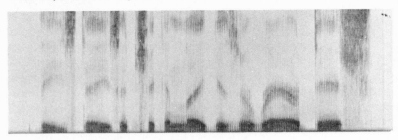

It's easy to tell the depth of a well.

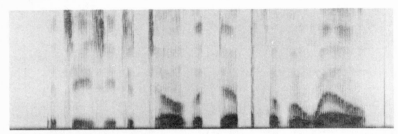

Four hours of steady work faced us.

A large size in stockings is hard to sell.

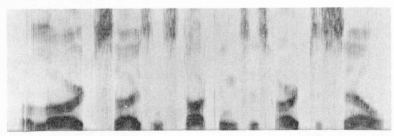

FIGURE 36a   Sound spectrograms: natural (Courtesy Haskins Laboratories)

These days a chicken leg is a rare dish.

It's easy to tell the depth of a well.

Four hours of steady work faced us.

A large size in stockings is hard to sell.

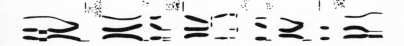

FIGURE 36b   Sound Spectrograms: artificial (Courtesy Haskins Laboratories)

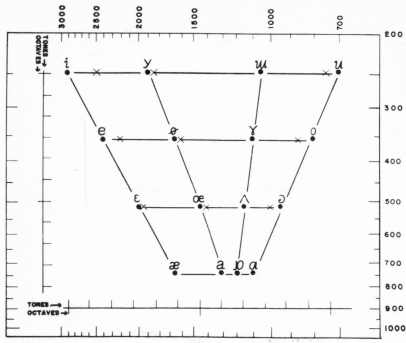

FIGURE 37   The vowel triangle plotted acoustically

This is the figure which results from plotting the "cardinal vowels" according to the frequency positions of the first and second acoustic "formants."
The frequency of the first formant is the vertical co-ordinate at extreme
left, and that of the second formant is the horizontal co-ordinate at the bottom. The inner co-ordinates are in cycles per second. The vowels are the
synthetic, standardized vowels called "cardinal vowels"; the crosses indicate
where the actual vowels of French would fall in this figure. From Delattre,
Liberman, Cooper, and Gerstman, in *Word,* VIII, 3 (Dec. 1952), p. 200.

passed through a playback, and a distinct, if inhuman voice clearly
pronouncing a series of sounds (Fig. 36b) can be obtained.[13] (The thou-
sand-and-one other details on an actual spectogram pertain, therefore,
to the individual voice, the regional accent, the sex of the speaker, and
so on.) These characteristic frequencies are called "formants."[14] With
respect to consonants the spectrogram is more complicated, but the
situation is essentially similar.

Curiously, and yet not, perhaps, surprisingly, if we graph the principal vowels in such a way that their position becomes a function of the frequency of their two principal formants, we get a figure quite similar to the "vowel triangle" of physiological phonetics (see Fig. 37). This is probably no accident, since the reinforcement of a given formant is doubtless due to resonance from a particular area of the system.

The data recorded by a spectrogram contain a tremendous, perhaps infinite amount of information, not all of which has even yet been elicited. What is clear is that between the two approaches—physiological and phonetic—we have much more ample and accurate information about the sounds of which speech is made up than ever before.

5. The nature of syllables

Although sixth-grade students are supposed to know what a syllable is (since certain rules of punctuation are based on the separation of syllables from each other), the definitions offered by most English grammars and the older dictionaries are so hopelessly inadequate as to be almost laughable. What, for instance, is "a single or articulated vocal sound"?[15] What is "separate and complete enunciation"?[16]

And yet, as is so often the case in language, the humble, unpretentious native speaker, so often condemned and "corrected" by the grammarian, subconsciously knows infinitely more about his language than any scholarly book has yet described: for the average person, without the help of any definition or the ability to make one, can almost always tell how many syllables there are in a word; and the aphasiac, even after he has lost the power to pronounce recognizable words, can mutter the right number of syllables for the word he is trying to say.[17]

Just as it is difficult always to distinguish clearly between vowels and consonants, so it is difficult to account for the fact that certain sounds, normally not syllabic, form syllables under certain circumstances, or do so in some languages and not in others. But it is not as hard to draw the line between syllabic and nonsyllabic sounds as between vowels and consonants, even though syllabic sounds are generally vowels and nonsyllabic ones, consonants.

A syllable is simply a *peak of sonority* with certain sounds grouped around it. Normally, a vowel is the nucleus of a syllable, and a word has as many syllables as it has vowels. If we graph the loudness of a sequence of sounds making up a word, we naturally find that some are louder than others: but we find also that some (the vowels) are hundreds of times louder (Fig. 38a). The user of a language will hear as many syllables as there are peaks in such a graph. Now, as we know, certain consonant sounds approach the sonority of vowels, and this can create ambiguity: when the spread between the loudest sounds and the next loudest is great, there is no doubt how many peaks there are; but when the next loudest sounds are very close to the loudest, it may be possible to decide only on a phonemic basis whether two adjacent loud sounds make one syllable or two (Fig. 38b). Conversely, if all the sounds in a sequence are of relatively low sonority, one or more of them may function as vowels in this particular sequence, and we would say that it had become "syllabic" (Fig. 38c).

This helps us to an accurate understanding of what are tradition- ally called *semivowels*. The sonority of the vowels [i] and [u] can be reduced by drastically abbreviating their duration, to the point where, adjacent to other vowels in a sequence, they may function as con- sonants. This produces the phenomenon noted as a *diphthong*, which may be defined as a succession of two (or, in the case of *triphthongs*, three) vowels in a sequence, which nevertheless make only one syl- lable. When this is the case, it is because one or two of the vowels in the sequence is acting as a consonant. Diphthongs are spoken of as *rising* if the semivowel precedes the vowel, and *falling* if the reverse is true.

It can truthfully be said, then, that the nucleus of a syllable is al- ways a vowel, if it be borne in mind that sounds not ordinarily thought of as vowels may behave as such under certain circumstances. The arrangements of consonants and semivowels which go together with this nucleus to form a syllable may, of course, range from the very simple to the very complex—from the syllable type CV (consonant + vowel) to the type CCCVCCC (e.g., English *scrounged*)—but it will generally be found that any given language admits only a limited number of the possible types and combinations, and different ones at the beginning of the syllable than after the nucleus.

Usually, the farther one goes from the nucleus, the fewer are the phonemes acceptable in that position; and there is often a trend to increase sonority from the beginning to the nucleus, and decrease it from there to the end of the syllable; for example, *tn-* (or any combi-

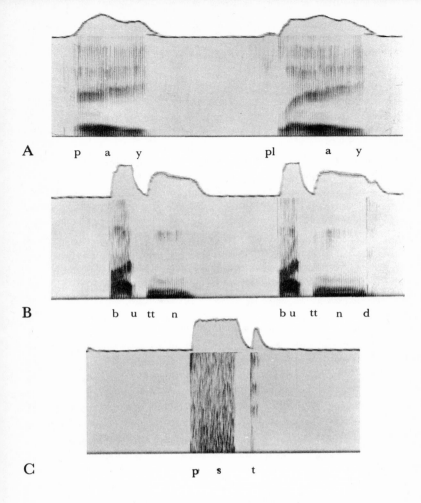

A p a y pl a y

B b u tt n b u tt n d

C p' s t

FIGURE 38 Consonantal vowels and syllabic consonants

In each section of this figure, the top line is a recording of the *loudness* of each successive speech sound (as indicated at the bottom), and under it is a spectrogram of the utterance similar to those in Figure 36. In (A), note that of the three sounds in the word *pay* (phonetically [peⁱ]), the [p] has relatively little volume, but the [i] is almost as loud as the [e]: hence [ei] can count as one syllable (a diphthong), but if *i* were made more prominent by stressing and lengthening it, it could become a syllable, as in *payee*. In (B), the *n* functions as a vowel because of its sonority (not as great as that of *u*, but much greater than that of *b* and *d*). In (C), *s* functions as a vowel because, while ordinarily not sonorous enough to do so, it is much more sonorous than *p* or *t*. (Courtesy Haskins Laboratories) nation of voiceless stop and "liquid") might be acceptable only at the beginning and not at the end of a syllable, while the reverse would hold true for combinations of the type -*nt*.[18]

Some languages permit no consonants whatever to occur after the nucleus, and in such a language all syllables are said to be *open;* conversely, when one or more consonants occur at the end of a syllable, that syllable is called *closed*. In many languages there is a tendency to avoid sequences consisting of repetitions of the same consonant (called *doubling* or *gemination*) or of the same vowel (called *hiatus*), or of sequences of vowels which do not form diphthongs. It should be regarded as an indispensable part of any scientifically complete description of a language to ascertain and report on all these facts. (Traditional grammars, of course, ignore syllable structure completely.)

Where does one syllable end and the next begin? Is there any observable boundary between syllables? On the whole, these questions still await final answers from the experiments of acoustic phoneticians. There seems to be sufficient objectivity in the concept of the syllable so that several scholars, asked to divide a given word in a given language into its constituent syllables, would probably arrive at the same results, and these might vary with the language: *general* in English consists of the syllables *gen-er-al,* but in French the syllables are *gé-né-ral.* But one suspects that the criterion applied is analogy: one assumes that sequences of sounds which can occur at the beginning of a word can occur at the beginning of a syllable, and that those which can occur finally in a word can occur finally within the syllable. (To say that one divides the word into fractions each of which can be pronounced by itself is to say essentially the same thing.) It would seem that syllables are *spoken* one after the other, with no physical boundary between.

When a situation arises, however caused, where a sequence of sounds occurs which is not among those normally occurring in that place in the language, it is likely that the language will make some adjustment to bring the sequence into line with its normal patterns—perhaps by omitting one of the sounds of the sequence, perhaps by *metathesis* (exchange of position between two sounds) or *epenthesis* (the development of a new vowel and, consequently, a new syllable). Thus, modern Irish has no -*ks*- or -*ts*- sequence, so when borrowing from English words containing these sequences, it customarily metathesizes the two consonants: thus *bosca* from "box," *cóiste* from "coach." Italian never has three consecutive consonants, unless the first is *s*; therefore, *in Spagna* must become *in Ispagna*.

6.   "Prosodic" features

There are many things which can be observed about an utterance besides the speech sounds of which it is composed. One speaker talks very rapidly, another very slowly; an angry man usually talks more loudly ("raises his voice") while conspirators proverbially whisper; some speakers enunciate clearly, others seem to "swallow their words." All these well-known phenomena, and quite a few more, can be defined and measured by the physicist. They are not part of the information, or message strictly so called, which is conveyed by the language; yet they communicate a great deal, whether we call it "message" or not: they aid or hinder our grasping the message; they tell us much about the speaker—whether he is excited or calm, sincere or hypocritical.

These features have been variously named. They have been called *prosodic*, suggesting that they bear the same relation to the content of speech as the metre of poetry to its thought. The term *supra-segmental* has been used, suggesting that they are superimposed on the "segmental" features, that is, the phonemes as segments of the "chain of speech." From a certain point of view, the aggregate of the features here under consideration might be considered the raw material of the ancient art of *elocution*.

Are prosodic features properly in the area of investigation of the linguistic scientist? They normally do not affect the *meaning* of an utterance, but do convey *information* concomitantly with the information transmitted by the meanings of the words used. What is expressed prosodically on one occasion conceivably could be expressed lexically on another: a man may declare, "I am very cold," or he may show by the way he utters the statement "It is four o'clock" that he is very cold while uttering it. Whenever someone says, "I didn't object to what he said, but the *way he said it*," he is distinguishing between meaning and prosodic features.

To consider the whole range of prosodic features would require writing a textbook on elocution. This, to be sure, would be a useful thing to do, and the book might be even more helpful and accurate if written by a scientific linguist than by one who had practiced the art successfully without conscious knowledge of, or ability to explain, the principles he had followed; but this is not within the province of linguistics in its strict sense. Among the phenomena which elocution embraces, however, there are two or three which are essentially only quantitative variations of features which really do affect, if not determine, message meaning, and which might well be argued to be phonemes in their own right. These the linguist must treat.

These features are *accent, pitch, voice cadence,* and *pauses*. What we call *accent* may be defined as any device by which a language marks one syllable in a sequence of syllables as distinct from the others. It may be marked by having greater amplitude (i.e., being louder), in which case we speak of *stress accent,* or by having a fundamental note of higher or lower frequency (i.e., spoken on a higher or lower pitch), in which case we speak of a *pitch accent*. This mark is prosodic, that is, it is added to a given syllable without affecting what it means with or without the added feature; for example, the word "you" in the phrases "what do you think?" contrasted with "what do *you* think?" The pitch accent may be illustrated by the jump in pitch on the first syllable of the word *tutti* in the Italian phrase, *me lo dicono tutti,* said with emphasis.

The acoustic phoneticians, however, find it difficult to define accent in physical terms. Some experiments, indeed, suggest that stress and pitch may be ultimately the same thing: that the stressed syllable always has a higher pitch, and that a high-pitched syllable is always stressed. In any case, it is clear that we are dealing with relatives, not absolutes: it is not a certain *proportion* between the frequency of one syllable and that of the others; it is not a certain degree of loudness that makes stress, but the *extent* to which one syllable is louder than others. Thus it seems that "accent" is not an objective reality subject to physical measurement, but a *concept*—based, of course, on facts of physics—and therefore part of the code comprising the language: not part of the *matter* of language, but part of the form; hence, belonging to phonemics (see the next chapter) rather than phonetics.

In the nomenclature of accent phenomena it is traditional to say that a syllable has an *acute accent* when its pitch is *higher* than the average pitch of the other syllables in a word, and a *grave accent* when its pitch is lower. Several languages claim to have a *circumflex* accent—

234

and tone languages regularly have one or more syllabic "tones"—under which the pitch of the syllable first rises, then falls (or moves in some other direction). Phonetically, in such a case, the "pitch of the syllable" must be the pitch of the vowel, and if this changes pitch it is equivalent to saying the vowel twice in succession, on two different pitches—like the "Oh" at the beginning of the *Star Spangled Banner,* which is sung on two different notes. But, as we have just observed, we are not really in the realm of phonetics in matters like these, and many descriptive linguists prefer to say that a single vowel is divided into one or more "morae," each with a different pitch, the movement of pitch from the first "mora" to the last being the complex accent of the vowel.[19]

When we consider the contour formed by a succession of pitches, we are in the domain of "voice-melodies" or "cadences." In languages with stress accent, such voice melodies are variable, but it seems that at least a few are learned as part of the language, signal something definite, and are regularly used; failure to conform to this usage clearly marks a foreigner. According to one view these cadences usually come at the end of utterances and involve only the last two or three, or at most four syllables; others believe that a pattern can be found throughout the utterance. Everyone knows the reputed voice-cadence of the Mexican-American, when he says, "He will be here tomorrow, I think," or of the Swedish-American who says, "I bane come from Minnesota." The upswing of the voice of the English speaker on a question ("You do think so, don't you?") in another example. The investigation of this phenomenon is still going on, and may be considered one of the frontiers of linguistics. Different systems of notation have been tried; the one used for the examples above is one of the more popular.

No one will deny the importance and effect of the placement of *pauses.* The early English play, *Ralph Roister Doister,* turns on the point that the meaning of a message can be completely reversed by changing the places where pauses occur; and more recently, we have heard children play a game in which a humorous effect is gained by misplacement of a pause ("What's that in the road—a head?"). But this is part of the phenomenon of *juncture,* which will be given special treatment in Chapter XIV, 5.

All the prosodic features just enumerated strongly affect, and indeed, often determine meaning. In languages with stress accent, putting the stress on a different syllable may change a word into a different word (e.g., *differ/defer*), and, of course, in tone-languages, to pronounce a word with the wrong tones makes it either a different word or meaningless. Juncture evidently affects meaning as a boundary sign, and it seems likely that accent—whether of the stress or pitch type—originated to serve the same purpose. But because of their close connection with the conveyance of meaning, these features should be investigated by the linguist. In the past they have been almost totally neglected, and study of most aspects is still in its infancy, or at any rate early adolescence. But when this branch of the science has reached maturity, we shall have an important addition to the range and scope of our instruments for describing languages fully, accurately and scientifically.

Notes to Chapter XIII

1. Kircher (1601–1680) actually came close to deciphering Egyptian hieroglyphics more than a century before Champollion; but his *Lingua aegyptiaca restituta* was dismissed by the learned, though Kircher was a competent Orientalist. Kempelen, incidentally, built a "talking machine" in 1788 which, it was said, could actually produce comprehensible speech mechanically.

2. The Bell Telephone Laboratories have done much significant work in this area. Cf. R. K. Potter, G. A. Kopp and H. C. Green, *Visible Speech,* New York: Van Nostrand, 1947.

3. For example, the higher pitch of female voices is due to the fact that the larynx is smaller and the vocal cords consequently shorter. But in each system there is a range of normal variation, so that some men actually have higher voices than some women.

4. In transcription of such languages into Roman characters, the apostrophe is usually used to indicate the glottal stop, e.g., *insha'allah,* "May God grant (it)." The "smooth breathing" of classical ancient Greek was probably a glottal stop.

5. The symbols indicate dental vs. alveolar articulation. English *t*'s, *d*'s and *n*'s are alveolar—the tongue does not touch the backs of the upper front

teeth in pronouncing them. In most other languages it does, giving *dental articulation.*

6. This has already been explained; see page 71, note 20.

7. In certain languages, like Russian and Irish, there are two *t*'s, two *n*'s, two *k*'s and so on; in French there are two *n*'s, *n* and *gn* (*n mouillé*). The precise character of the "palatalized" articulation is fully described in many text-books on phonetics.

8. Affrication is defined as a sequence of consonant sounds consisting of a stop followed by the homorganic spirant—i.e., a spirant articulated at the same point. This stop + spirant sequence is frequently derived from a single phoneme and remains, phonemically, a single phoneme, as in English *church, bridge,* Italian *amici.*

9. The *slit* or *groove* in question is formed by the tongue, as can be shown by "palatograms." See Grammont, *Traité de phonétique,* 48–50.

10. For example, the *f* of Japanese *Fujiyama* (see page 217) corresponds to the *b* of Spanish *Cuba.* In Welsh a voiceless *l* occurs, written *ll*, as in *Llangollen.* (To pronounce the latter name as *lang gollen* is a barbarism in Wales.)

11. See above, Note 10.

12. The number of repetitions or "taps" varies from a great many per second (as in the Scottish burr) to only one, as in the British pronunciation of *very,* which is sometimes transcribed by Americans as *veddy.*

13. This is, of course, quite an oversimplification, yet essentially accurate.

14. Cf. Gleason, 212.

15. Quoted from Funk & Wagnall's dictionary, under "syllable."

16. *Ibid.*

17. Cf. Jakobson, *Kindersprache, Aphasie und allgemeine Lautgesetze,* 1–12.

18. Note the use of dashes. It is a convention among linguists to indicate a form quoted from a word in which something follows with a following dash, as *p*-; and, conversely, to indicate something that was final in the word from which it is quoted with a preceding dash: *-p*. Naturally, something that was in the middle of the word would have dashes on both sides.

19. It should be needless to observe that the "accents" of French are not pitch accents, but mere orthographic devices to differentiate different vowels: *é* = [e], *è* = [ɛ], *e* = [ə].

Supplementary Readings to Chapter XIII

Grammont, *Traité de phonétique, passim.*
Rousselot, *Principes de phonétique.*
J. Forchhammer, *Die Grundlage der Phonetik.*
Pike, *Phonetics.*
Jones, *Outline of English Phonetics.*
Delattre, *PMLA* LVI, 864–75.
Jakobson, Fant and Halle, *Preliminaries to Speech Analysis.*
Joos, *Acoustic Phonetics.*
Gleason, 187–204, 205–20.

Chapter XIV

THE ATOMS OF LANGUAGE (PHONEMICS)

We have already observed that two principal lines of development led to the emergence of that concept which more than any other single theory or discovery is the foundation-stone of modern descriptive linguistics: the concept of the phoneme (Chapter IV, 3). On the one hand was the teaching of De Saussure: if we divide language into *langue* and *parole* (see Chapter II, 3), the speech sound, as studied by phonetics, becomes the natural unit of *parole*, and a parallel unit in the domain of *langue* is called for.

On the other hand, phonetics soon discovered that its original concept of the word as a series of distinct, precisely definable sounds was getting lost in the infinity of physical data that could be observed and recorded for the sound emanating from any given source at any given moment. In other words, there is no real scientific justification for our saying that a *b* in one word is the same objective entity as the *b* in another word; for instrumental observation will invariably establish that they are, scientifically speaking, quite different—the more so, in fact, the more sensitive are the instruments of measurement employed. Indeed, it is really quite obvious that the structural unit of the word is a *concept*, not any specific sound.

1. The phoneme

The point of view of modern linguistics, then, is that the unit of word-structure is an *idea of a sound*, quite distinct from any actual sound. When speaking, the user of language seeks to objectivize this concept by producing an actual sound which is a "realization" of his concept; and if he is successful, other speakers of the language will find it a realization of theirs, and each will recognize, in what the speaker has said as a realization of the concept of, say, *b*, what he, too, considers a *b*. The concept of the sound evidently must exist in the speaker's mind before he produces an actual sound, and also in the hearer's mind before he hears the actual sound which he identifies as the *b* of his language.

This concept of a unit of sound, this abstraction which is the real unit of word construction, is the *phoneme,* and is the first unit of the branch of linguistics generally called *phonemics* (in Europe, *phonology*).[1] The actual sound emitted by a speaker on any given occasion in an effort to "realize" this concept may be called the *phone* or *speech sound,* and is the basic unit of the science of *phonetics.*

To say that a formant or word is made up of phonemes is rather like saying that a fleet is made up of ships: the term "ship" is a similar abstraction. In a particular fleet, sighted at sea on a given morning, we shall be able to identify several ships; but no matter how minutely we describe each of these (like the phonetician describing the sounds in an utterance), these particular ships are not the units of all fleets, nor are we to expect that some of these same ships will be found in every other fleet we see.

Since the phoneme is a concept rather than a particular sound, different particular sounds may equally well "realize" the concept of a phoneme. Thus, in English, the *p* of *pot* has a distinct *h* after it—distinct enough to blow out the flame of a match—while the *p* of *spot* does not have this "aspiration." In the English speaker's concept of *p*, however, aspiration is not relevant; so we identify both sounds as our *p*-phoneme, and do not "hear" ("hearing" being half interpretation) that one has a feature which the other one lacks.

Now, in a different language, different features might be relevant for the *p*-phoneme, and the speakers of that language might "hear" the actual sounds quite differently. There are quite a few languages (e.g., ancient Greek) in which p^h and *p* are two different phonemes, and a speaker of those languages would "hear" the difference every time.[2] English speakers, however, would be deaf to it even when talking the other language, and by using *p* or p^h indiscriminately, would cause all sorts of confusion and betray a foreign accent.

From this we can draw an important conclusion: the language you already speak is bound to influence the language you are learning, and we cannot teach the latter with maximum efficiency unless we take into account the sort of interference the former is likely to create.[3]

Some additional examples are the following. In English we have two high front vowel phonemes, the [i] of *machine* (also written *ee*— as in *see*—and various other ways), and the [ɪ] of *hit*. Spanish has only one such phoneme. Hence, to a native speaker of Spanish, *sheep* and *ship* are the same word; in all sincerity, the Spanish speaker will aver that he came to the United States on a *sheep*. French, including Canadian French, likewise has only one /i/ phoneme; but in Canada the sound of [ɪ] in *hit* has been introduced, probably because of the influence of English; it is not yet, however, "phonemic"—as we say— so it makes no difference whether you say one or the other. Thus, *huit* and *ville,* pronounced with [i] in France, are frequently pronounced with [ɪ] in Canada.

In German, voiced phonemes do not occur at the end of a word or syllable if there is a corresponding voiceless one—or we might say that final *b* is always pronounced as *p*, final *c* as *k*, and so on. As a result, we have the sad case of the young German-born immigrant who told his boss he could not get along without a *raise,* whereupon the boss offered to meet him in the parking lot alongside the factory and *race* with him.

It will be clear from these cases that a "foreign accent" is merely the carry-over into a second language of habits of articulation from one's first language. A native speaker of French can have only a French accent in English—never a German one; and so on. By the same token, a person who knew several of the characteristic habits of a language could assume the accent of that language at will. To pronounce *w* as *v*, to pronounce *s* for *th*, and to silence final voiced consonants will quite well establish a German accent.

Since the unit of the word is a concept, not an actual sound, different actual sounds—as in the case of p^h/p, mentioned above—may be sufficiently close to the archetype to satisfy a native speaker that it is a "realization" of his archetype for that phoneme. Such objectively different sounds, all of which constitute only one structural unit—one phoneme—as far as the operation of the language is concerned, are called *allophones.*

Examples of allophones in English are the *p* of *pot* and the *p* of *spot* (which are different phonemes in some languages); the *t* of *top* and the *t* of *butter;* the *k* of *keen* and the *c* of *cold;* the *l* of *silly* and the *l* of *fall*. Many more could be cited. In each case, if one listens very sharply, he will hear that the two *p*'s, *t*'s, *l*'s or whatever are not identical in sound—although he may never have noticed this before, because English has only one *p*, *t* or *l* phoneme, and both of the sounds or "phones" are *allophones* of it.

Some observers may, in fact, still be unable to "hear" any difference, even after listening very keenly; but the difference could be proved in the phonetics laboratory with instruments. A very simple experimental proof is to hold a lighted match close to the mouth; the match will be extinguished by the puff of air after the *p* of *pot*, but will remain lit during the pronunciation of *spot*. Note that in a word like *chophouse* the same sequence of sounds occurs, but this time [h] is a phoneme, hence we "hear" it.

Allophones are bound to arise, if for no other reason, because any given sound is influenced by the sounds adjacent to it in a sequence such as a word. All languages tend to economize both material and the effort of the speaker; or, to put it another way, each individual speaking his native language unconsciously seeks for ways of speaking faster. Thus, if the set-up of the vocal organs required for the production of a given phoneme has to be greatly changed for the production of the next one in the word, there will be a tendency to modify one or the other to reduce the magnitude of the shift and the physical effort involved in making it. So, for example, the *k* of *keen* has a point of contact between tongue and palate nearer the front of the mouth than the *k* of *cold*—because the *ee* vowel is pronounced in the front.

This process, called *assimilation,* is one of the processes which causes linguistic change over a period of time. If a change of this sort does not take place over the whole area over which a language is spoken, it leads to dialectical differentiation, and perhaps ultimately to an altogether new language.

2. Identifying the phoneme

How do we know that two sounds suspected of being allophones are that and not distinct phonemes? The criterion here, as elsewhere in the realm of phonemics, is relationship to meaning: what expresses or affects meaning is "phonemic"; what does not, belongs to a different branch of our science. Our tool for ascertaining whether each of a given pair of sounds differently affects the meaning conveyed by the segment of language in which they occur is, again, commutation, as embodied in a *minimal contrast*.

A minimal contrast or minimum opposition exists between two words which have different meanings, but differ in physical form from each other *only* in the feature under investigation—proving that it must be that difference, and no other, which is responsible for the difference in meaning. For example: suppose we are suspicious that *p* and *f* are allophones of the same phoneme in English. We discover the pair of words *pit* and *fit*, which are identical with each other except for the presence in one of *p* where the other has *f*. Since these two words have entirely different meanings (note that we do not have to find out *what the meanings are*, only that they are different), we may conclude that the difference between *p* and *f* is phonemic, hence that *p* and *f* are distinct phonemes. In Japanese, however, such a minimally contrasting pair could not be found, since *p* occurs where *f* does not, and *vice versa*.

Another way of putting this is to say that, if substitution of one sound for another will produce a different word, the substituted sound is in "phonemic opposition" to the one for which it is substituted. Thus, substituting *k* for *t* in *top* gives us *cop*, a minimal contrast (since the remainders of both words are identical), and shows that *k* and *t* are different phonemes.[4] But if we pronounce the *p* of *spot* as an aspirated *p* (*sp*ʰ*ot*), though it may sound strange, no native speaker of English will recognize it as any other word than *spot*. Therefore, in English, *p*/*p*ʰ is not a phonemic opposition, and *p* is not a distinct phoneme. The difference between *p* and *p*ʰ is not, as we say, *relevant* in the English *p*-phoneme, though *p*ʰ occurs more often than *p*.

Because of the way in which allophones usually arise (see Section 1 of this chapter) it is unlikely that a given allophone or variant will occur in a location other than that in which it originated. Hence, each allophone usually occurs in one set of linguistic surroundings, but not in those in which any of the other allophones occur. The term used in linguistics to describe this situation is *complementary distribution*: we say that each allophone is in "complementary distribution" with the others. As a matter of fact, any allophone, however it originated, *must* be in complementary distribution with other allophones of the same phoneme. Commutation shows that if a given sound can occur in the same circumstances as another, there is at least a possibility that two different but minimally contrasting words may occur, one containing one of the sounds, the other one the other.

It has frequently happened in the historical development of languages that what began as a positional variant became phonemic when it became possible for this variant and what had formerly been an allophone to occur in opposition to each other. In later Latin, for instance, the affricated pronunciation of *c* as [ts] or [tʃ] was at first nonphonemic, since it never occurred before back vowels (*a, o, u*). But when it became possible for [k] to occur before front vowels, it became possible for Italian *ci* and *chi* to be different words—and /c/ was thenceforth a phoneme. If two sounds are not in complementary distribution, the opposition between them may or may not be phonemic (the language will not necessarily take advantage of every possible opposition), but *if we know that the difference is phonemic, the allophones must be in complementary distribution.*

We have just alluded to the fact that a language does not necessarily take advantage of all the phonemic oppositions possible to it to construct words for its vocabulary. The number of pairs of words distinguished by a given feature is the measure of how much a given language uses that particular opposition. This is called *functional yield.* The lower the functional yield, the more possible it is to eliminate the phonemic opposition involved.

For instance, some native speakers of English do not pronounce [h] before [w] or [j], and thus in their dialect the word-pairs *where* and *wear, whale* and *wail, which* and *witch, what* and *watt,* and so on, become homonyms or homophones. But in the speech of many other native English speakers, the opposition *wh/w* remains fully phonemic, and these words could not possibly be mistaken for each other. Evidently the number of such pairs (the "functional yield" of the opposition *wh/w*) is low enough so that the phonemes *wh* and *w* could be merged in a given dialect of English without causing too much confusion. But if we tried to eliminate the opposition *p/b*, making identical such word-pairs as *pull/bull, peas/bees, pen/been* (for those who do not say [bin] or [bɪn]), and so on, the amount of confusion—due to the high functional yield—would evidently be so great as to prevent this development.

A distinction which is phonemic in one position is not necessarily phonemic in all positions. It not infrequently happens that a language will have, say, ten distinct vowel phonemes in the accented syllables of words, only five in unaccented syllables, and only three in final syllables. For certain consonants in contemporary German, for instance (as we mentioned above), the opposition *voiced/voiceless* is phonemic only initially; *within* words, either could occur without altering the meaning, and in final position only voiceless variants occur. (Even the initial opposition is foregone in some dialects, e.g., Alemannic and Alsatian,[5] where one may say *deutsch* or *teutsch, Bier* or *Pier, Kuh* or *Guh;* in these dialects, therefore, the opposition is totally nonphonemic.)

In situations like this, we say that a phonemic distinction is *neutralized* in certain positions. In such a position the neutralization can be effected by always using one phoneme and never the other, or by using a special phoneme which is neither the one nor the other. In either case, the phoneme used is called the *archiphoneme,* replacing the two phonemes normally distinct.

It may occur that, in some certain position, a variant of a phoneme A may be identical with a variant of another phoneme B in the same position. This is essentially the same situation. For example, in English the long vowels are distinguished before final r or $r+$ consonant (*far, for; farm, form*), but all short vowels become identical (*fern, fur*). In such a case we may say that either phoneme A or phoneme B, or a third phoneme, is the only one that can occur in that position, and that all other phonemes merge with it there. In the example cited, the sound actually heard is entirely different phonetically from any other English vowel, and the most economical analysis would probably be to list it as a variant of one of the short vowels, say /ɛ/, and state that the oppositions between /ɛ/ and /ɪ/, /ɚ/, /ʌ/ and /ʊ/ are neutralized, with this variant of /ɛ/ as archiphoneme.

To show that two sounds are in phonemic opposition in a minimally contrasting pair of words proves that both are phonemes in the language in question, even if it should appear that one or both do not appear in all possible positions, or that the opposition between them has a low functional yield. (Of course, the basic phonemes of the language are the terminals of many strong phonemic oppositions of very high functional yield, as will be seen directly.) This clinching proof is not always possible to obtain, and a variety of analytical and descriptive procedures have been developed to enable the scientific linguist to establish with reasonable certainty what the phonemes of the language are, even in the absence of entirely adequate data, or in cases where experts might take different points of view. It is not within our scope in this book to go into detail in this direction (this would really be the content of a first course in phonemics). It will suffice to refer the student to several basic textbooks in this area.[6]

3. Phonemic systems

By now the student will no doubt appreciate that it is impossible to define a phoneme adequately without taking into account all the phonemes to which it is opposed. As a matter of fact, this is all that gives the phoneme its identity; for if a difference between it and any other sound is *not* phonemic, that feature is irrelevant as far as the phoneme is concerned, and in respect to that particular feature, no phoneme exists in the language under investigation.

This fact creates a fundamental difference in point of view between a newer and an older approach to the study of language. The neo-grammarian, believing that every *b,* for instance, was identical with every other *b,* sought merely to give as accurate as possible a description of this objective physical phenomenon, much as the chemist finds the same chemical properties and behavior in every sample of sodium chloride. The neo-grammarian was attempting to make linguistics a natural science; but language is not a phenomenon of nature, it is a work of man. Because of his attitude, the neo-grammarian would take up each sound of a language in turn, giving anything from an inadequate to an exhaustive description of it, but it never occurred to him to consider the relationship between any of these units and any other. It would never occur to him that the long *ā* was long only in relation to a short *ă.* He would be more likely to say that "the *a* in French is *x* milliseconds long." It is important to understand the neo-grammarian point of view, since almost all textbooks for the study of any language that are currently available are written from that point of view.

The descriptive linguist begins, of course, by observing physical "phones," and noting them down in his phonetic transcription of the text to be analyzed. But when he begins to work out the phonemic system, he can postulate a phoneme only on the basis of phonemic oppositions. While one valid opposition establishes a phoneme, it is hard to imagine a language in which any phoneme would be in phonemic opposition to only one other phoneme; for one thing, such a language would have only two phonemes, and we do not know of any language with so restricted an inventory.[7] Each phoneme, therefore, contrasts with every other phoneme, and theoretically, in a statement of the phonemic system of a language, each such opposition should be demonstrated.[8]

This means that each phoneme is the terminal of many oppositions, and that all the phonemes together form a network—a structure—in which, as in a brick wall or the steel framework of a building, each unit supports another and is in turn supported, directly or indirectly, by all the others. The modern linguist is keenly interested in the nature and characteristics of this structure, study of which reveals basic inner workings of language, just as an understanding of atomic structure has led to the discovery of basic secrets of nature. The linguist seeks to set up spatial arrangements on paper of the phonetic symbols for phonemes which will fairly accurately reflect the relationships existing in reality among these concepts, and, of course, among any specific sounds which are their objective "realizations."

For example, *p* and *b* have, as we have seen (Chapter XIII, 3), the same articulation; the difference between them is solely that *b* adds the sound of the voice to the features present in *p*. But the same is true of the opposition *t/d* and the opposition *k/g*. When we have, as in this case, a series of oppositions based on the same feature, we call the series a *correlation,* and name it by the feature in question. Hence we would say that, in English, there is a *correlation of voice* which includes the following phonemes:

p	t	k	ch	s	f	th (as in *thin*)	sh
b	d	g	j	z	v	th (as in *these*)	zh

Now, it is evident that some of these phonemes also participate in a *correlation of nasality:*

b	d	g
m	n	ng

Vowels also may participate in correlations, e.g., the *high-mid correlation:*

```
        i              u
        e              o
```

or the *close-open correlation:*

```
        i              u
        ɪ              ʊ
```

We may also distinguish the *correlation of spirantization:*

```
        p        t        k
        f        th       h
```

And, of course, many more. Normally, each phoneme is a member of several correlations; for example, *p* is opposed to *b* by the feature of voice, but it is opposed to *t* because, while both *p* and *t* are voiceless stops, the former is labial and the latter dental. Of course *b* and *d, f* and *th, v* and *th* are opposed on the same basis. Hence, we may postulate a *labial-dental correlation:*

```
    p          b          f          v
    t          d          th         th
```

Since *p* and *b* are already in the correlation of voice, we may try to plot these features in the same figure, perhaps as follows:

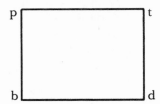

In this square figure, the vertical lines represent the correlation of voice (and, of course, the individual oppositions on this basis), while the horizontal lines represent the labial-dental correlation.

Since, however, all these phonemes also belong to the correlation of spirantization, we may try to work this into the figure by going into another dimension:

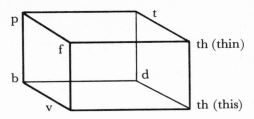

Now the lines from *p* to *f, t* to *th,* and so on, will represent the new correlation, while those from *f* to *v, th* to *th,* will represent the correlation of voice in a new series of phonemes (as if we had plotted the correlation of voice from left to right, then taken the right-hand half and placed it *in front of* the left-hand half).

Since there are only three dimensions, and even the third can be expressed on paper only with difficulty and by making use of arbitrary convention, much ingenuity can be expended on these designs, and even then an entirely satisfactory figure frequently cannot be achieved. Nevertheless, to one who understands what these spatial arrangements seek to represent, a glance at one of them gives a clearer idea of the phonological structure of a language—of its phonemic units and their relations to one another—than, perhaps, a whole volume of *Lautlehre* written from the neo-grammarian point of view.

In a thorough introductory course in phonemics, such as Troubetzkoy's, all the various possible kinds of correlation and series of correlations would be determined and classified, and such matters as prosodic features, neutralization and functional yield would be studied in detail; techniques of establishing phonemic units, of deciding whether to interpret sequences of sounds as one phoneme or more (depending, of course, upon the language), of determining distribution and syllable structure, and all the other devices that have been worked out for constructing a phonemic analysis, would be presented and demonstrated.

4. The dynamics of phonemic systems

Once we have established the phonemic units of a language and plotted the system they form, we can often see the direction in which the system is tending, or the organic reason for linguistic changes which have taken place in the period just concluded.

Why this is so will begin to be evident if we put forward the proposition—which will probably not be argued—that the more correlations a phoneme is a member of, the more integral and indispensable it is in the system. It follows as a natural corollary that a phoneme which occurs in a limited number of situations (only in the middle of words, for instance, never at the beginning or end), and contrasts with only a few other phonemes, stands, as it were, on the periphery of the system, and would not be too greatly missed if the speakers of the language began to neglect or neutralize the oppositions which give it existence. Practically every language "has a little list" of phonemes like this, which "never would be missed."

In this connection we must remember that every phonemic system has a *tendency toward balance,* and that a *tendency to economy* prevails throughout every language. It is probable that the native speaker of a language appreciates the symmetry of paradigms and phonemic systems quite as much as the scientist, but, of course, on a subconscious level. There are many indications of this. Suppose a language has among its phonemes *b, k, g, t,* and *d,* but no *p;* surely the native speaker subconsciously draws the proportion $k:g = t:d = x:b$ and the "hole in the pattern" as we call it, created by the absence of /p/, tends to get itself filled. (This is what would traditionally be called a change due to "analogy.") Conversely, some development which would introduce a new phoneme that crowded the pattern would create a pressure to simplify. If the system builds up to a very complex one, with many phonemes and innumerable phonemic distinctions, it will tax the subconscious memory of native speakers and occasion a trend to cut corners and discard a few of the less necessary phonemic distinctions.

On the other hand, alterations which upset the symmetry and balance of a system may be followed by complementary alterations which tend either to maintain the original balance, or to establish a new one; for, as we have said, the native speaker seems to appreciate symmetry and prefer it (and, indeed, most structures in nature are symmetrical). Linguistic change is thus often a see-saw between the tendency toward economy, which occasions a certain development, and the tendency toward symmetry, which initiates another development to compensate for the first.

Indo-European, for instance, undoubtedly had gemination—that is, phonemic doubling of consonants (so that, for instance, a sequence *ata* would contrast phonemically with a sequence *atta*). Several of the descendants of Indo-European eliminated gemination; only *ata* would occur, even where *atta* had formerly been pronounced. We might view this as a development initiated by the trend to economy, since it reduces the total number of phonemes (by eliminating the geminates), and since it takes less effort to pronounce one *t* than two. We assume, also, that the functional yield of the opposition is not so high that an unworkable number of homophones are created by elimination of the opposition *t/tt* (which would have been a little weak in the first place, since it probably would not have occurred initially or finally).

But at this point, a tendency arises in the languages in question to shift the single medial consonant to a spirant: i.e., *ata* tends to become *atha*. This is a change that evidently seeks to restore balance— to keep distinct the words that used to be distinguished from each other by the opposition *ata/*atta*, though they will now be distinguished by the opposition *ata/*atha*. Though the *basis* of one opposition has changed, the opposition remains, and the *system of oppositions* is still in balance and effectively unchanged. This process is prominent in the Celtic languages, and is known as *lenition*.

Similarly, when Latin and Saxon gave up the opposition between *long* and *short* vowels, this opposition was largely exchanged for one between *diphthongs* and *single vowels* in Old French and Middle English. On the other hand, when Latin eliminated the opposition *c/k*, *k/q*, and later the opposition *c/q*, the resulting homophones were, generally speaking, allowed to fall where they might, except that the phoneme /q/ was largely replaced by /kw/. (This was not possible, of course, before /u/ or /v/, with the result that in Livy we read *ecus* for *equus* and *quum* for *cum*.)

This kind of phenomenon was partly what we had in mind when we observed earlier that to one who understands the figures constructed by the modern linguist to represent in spatial arrangement the interrelationships of a phonemic system, a glance at such a figure reveals much about the fundamental nature, past history, and probable development of a language. A whole new field in the study of and research into language is then opened up. This history of every language could (indeed, must) be rewritten, taking into account this new point of view;[9] and when that has been done, whole new vistas of insight into the etiology of the development of language will surely begin to appear.

5. Juncture

Before we can feel that our tools for the scientific description of a language are complete, two final questions must be answered: (1) How are the boundaries between linguistic structures marked? (2) Having ascertained the devices used as boundary markers, how are we to classify them—as phonemes, or in some other category? The answers to these questions by the American school of linguists are somewhat characteristic and are treated in that school under the title of *juncture,* which we shall here use to cover the same phenomena, though not necessarily following the approach of the majority of American linguists. (One is tempted to write what would, in effect, be a critique of the American system, which would be a poor substitute for an independent study of the data.)

An obvious boundary for linguistic structures is *silence.* When a person who is using language ceases to speak, and continues silent for some considerable amount of time, this certainly constitutes a distinct and unmistakable boundary between what he uttered before the silence and what he commences to say after it. This boundary we have used already (Chapter VIII, 1) to discover complete structural units. We should think it would be safe to presume that an utterance followed by the kind of boundary just mentioned would be of a final nature and structurally complete, unless the speaker had been interrupted or had interrupted himself. In the former case, the circumstances should make the fact sufficiently clear; the latter would surely be of such infrequent occurrence that in a sufficiently large body of material its abnormality would be evident.

But is silence—perhaps of varying duration—the only boundary between linguistic structures? It would be convenient, and would greatly simplify analysis, if we could adopt this proposition; but it is doubtful whether we can. When we have learned how a language is constructed, we might *a priori* suppose that boundaries might be wanted between *words,* between *endocentric structures,* between *exocentric structures,* and between *groups of exocentric structures.* But the *a priori* reasoning does not seem to give satisfactory results here, for this does not seem to be the system formed by boundaries actually observed.

It seems clear that in normal speech, words follow each other without any pauses at all. The name "New York" was probably not pronounced differently when it was written "New-York."[10] If we have a clear enough concept of the word to separate words in writing, that concept would appear to be based on structural criteria,[11] not on observable boundary signs. The same holds for complexes of exocentric structures; if German orthography conventionally punctuates a pause at the beginning of every subordinate clause, this pause does not express anything in the pronunciation, either in German or in English.

Apparently there is a structural and (at least occasionally) observable boundary between syllables: we are occasionally unsure whether the conductor has said "West Eighth Street" or "West State Street," whether the professor referred to "a known poet" or "unknown poet."[12] We really do not have as yet all the experimental data necessary for dealing adequately with these cases: specifically, it is not yet possible to say definitively whether the native speaker's consciousness of the syllable boundary rests on some objective, acoustic feature that is instrumentally observable and measurable, or is based purely on his knowledge of the language's structural patterns. What appears to happen is that a consonant originally belonging to a following syllable crosses the boundary and becomes part of the preceding syllable, or *vice versa*; but the problem is to define scientifically both the syllable boundary and what constitutes "crossing over." This is what the American school calls "internal" or "plus juncture," and symbolizes $/ + /$.[13]

Here, again, there seems to be no physical pause. Some suggest that the loudness of the voice decreases toward the end of the syllable and starts to pick up with the new syllable, so that the low point of this fluctuation would be the objective syllable boundary. Others relate this phenomenon to the pulses of breath; but it seems clear that there is no regular correspondence between the muscular mechanics of refilling the lungs and any linguistic boundary: the normal linguistic boundaries apparently provide as much opportunity for this as is necessary. The present writer's tentative conclusion is that the boundary is purely structural, and that the minimally contrasting pairs that are cited would be regularly confused with each other in the absence of any structural context.

The placing of the boundary *between structures* can produce minimal contrasts in cases like the following:

"I expect her _____."
"To behave herself. Naturally."
"To behave herself naturally."[14]

Here Tracy's observation is equivalent to "I naturally expect her to behave herself," Dexter's to "I expect her to behave herself naturally." The same device was used, as already mentioned (Chapter XIII, 6) in the old play *Ralph Roister Doister,* where a message, read with the wrong punctuation, conveys exactly the reverse of the intended meaning.[15]

What we are concerned with here can readily be identified as a *pause*; but it is not so easy to say with scientific accuracy what a pause is. Off-hand, one would probably define it as a "momentary silence," and it could then be regarded as some fraction of the maximum silence. But it is not so easy to show that any silence actually occurs in this juncture; and it is hard to dissociate the juncture from accompanying prosodic features, particularly changes in pitch and stress. It has been suggested that there may be prolongation of a phoneme, signaling a boundary after the prolonged sound,[16] or that a glottal stop is introduced, or that there is an abrupt slowing of the tempo of speech (as measured in syllables uttered per second).

With the data presently available, it would be rash to try to isolate definitively the phonemically relevant feature of this juncture, which is the one called "level" or "single bar" juncture and is symbolized $/|/$. Whatever that feature is, however, it is probable that the kind of boundary used at the end of a declarative sentence (called "terminal juncture" or "double cross," symbolized $/\#/$, and in general parlance often named "falling inflection") is more of the same. Now, the terminal juncture certainly involves silence, either actual or virtual (the latter proved by the fact that, even if the next sentence begins "without pausing for breath," the last phoneme of the preceding one will undergo any changes which take place in this language before silence). Hence, we might be permitted to argue back to the proposition that single bar is, after all, basically a silence.

The remaining juncture is called "double bar" (expressed $/||/$) and is the familiar "rising inflection" given to an interrogative sentence:

Where's Bill? ||
He went home. #

It should be kept in mind that the "cadences" or pitch contours of these sentences are, at least theoretically, distinct from the juncture.

It will be noted that there is a general correspondence between the "junctures" identified and marked by linguists of the American school and the conventional marks of punctuation:

Question mark	?	||	Double bar
Period	.	#	Double cross
Dash — or Comma	,	|	Single bar
Unmarked pause		+	Internal juncture

Under this system the semicolon, colon and parentheses would be alternative to the dash or comma—useful in terms of typographic composition, since otherwise there would have to be a great many commas, which would risk causing confusion; also, the dash and parentheses can be used in correlated groups of two. In other times, however (the eighteenth century, for instance), there *was* a tendency to overwork one punctuation mark or another, without, apparently, any difference in the pronunciation.

It appears, too, that the American system classifies the "junctures" as phonemes.

The present writer must confess to doubts as to whether the four junctures are the most economical way to classify the phenomena which they embrace. We are inclined to feel that boundary-signs in language can be reduced to two classes—*structural,* where there is no observable physical sign of the boundary, but one is constituted by the occurrence and distribution of phonemes (it follows that these would not be detectible to an observer not intimately acquainted with the language); and *objective,* where phonetic features which can be observed and measured by instruments correspond to the boundary.

In our view, syllable boundaries and internal juncture would belong in the first class; "single bar," "double bar," and "double cross" in the second. But it seems to us that it would be more efficient to detach the boundary signal from the tone-formant; then the three junctures would differ from each other only in length—in other words, there would be only one boundary signal (we can call it "pause," bearing in mind that the term is not as yet accurately defined), which varies in length and is often associated with one sequence of tones when conclusion is signaled, with a different sequence when the utterance is a question. (There are several formants to signal a question, and frequently two or more are used concurrently.) We would be disinclined to classify boundary signals as phonemes, however, on the same principle that we do not count the spaces between words as letters.

It is important to stress, in conclusion, that the subject of this section is one that went completely uninvestigated by traditional "grammar," and is still somewhat of a frontier for modern scientific linguistics. Until more studies and experiments have been made, we must consider any conclusions in this area tentative. Here, indeed, as so often in linguistics, is worthwhile work to be done, even for the newcomer to the field, as soon as he finishes his professional training.

Notes to Chapter XIV

1. See Chapter I, Note 1.

2. In a language where aspirated *p* was *never* used (e.g., French), it would be equally evident.

3. Cf. N. Brooks, *Language and Language Learning,* p. 175; *PMLA* LXX (1955), no. 4, Part 2, 46–49, 51–65.

4. We are here assuming that the reader has gone through Chapter XIII, and knows that the letters *c* and *k* (and *q*) express the same sound.

5. Alsatians do the same in French, so that someone imitating an Alsatian accent in French will say *ah! que c'est un choli bedid homme.*

6. Particularly recommended are De Saussure, Gleason, Troubetzkoy and Pike. The last two are a little hard to read.

7. Except, perhaps, the language of children at a certain period, when the child's only phonemes may be C vs. V. Cf. Jakobson, 32 ff. Of course, any language may have certain specific contexts in which only two phonemes are possible, or even only one.

8. In practice this is not done; cf. Appendix A. The nature of allophones being what it is (cf. 241–242), allophones of a phoneme normally fall into the same phonetic category, or a similar one, and we may go on the working assumption that we do not expect phones of very different phonetic nature to be allophones of each other.

9. For example, Meyer-Lübke's comparative grammar of the Romance languages, and Brugmann's comparative grammar of *all* the Indo-European languages, rest upon neo-grammarian descriptions of the individual languages.

10. Where a difference in pronunciation exists, it appears to be either a matter of stress (as *blackbird* vs. *black bird*; the difference is in the stress of the second syllable), or of acceleration of the prevailing speed of speech, as measured in syllables uttered per second.

11. For example, what clusters can begin a word or close one, but will not be tolerated within one: cf. 230–233.

12. Other cases are cited in Hill, 25.

13. Cf. Hill, 24–26.

14. Philip Barry, *The Philadelphia Story,* Act III.

15. Nicholas Udall, *Ralph Roister Doister* (1550), III. iv, v.

16. Cf. Hill, 24.

Supplementary Readings to Chapter XIV

Martinet, *Description phonologique,* 16–47.
Alarcos Llorach, *Fonología española,* 9–18.
Gleason, 158–186.
Bloomfield, 74–108.
De Saussure, 63–93.
Martinet, *Phonology as Functional Phonetics.*
Martinet, *L'Économie des changements phonétiques,* 39–152.
Pike, *Phonemics, passim.*
Troubetzkoy, *Principes de phonologie,* tr. J. Cantineau, 1–15, 31–33.
Twaddell, *On Defining the Phoneme.*

Chapter XV

FRONTIERS AND APPLICATIONS
OF LINGUISTICS

We have now concluded our survey of the basic principles of scientific linguistics. The student will realize, of course, that a survey of the whole field in one volume necessitates some cursoriness in the treatment of particular branches. Specifically, little has been said on *comparative* and *historical* linguistics, since descriptive linguistics is basic to these two areas and presumed by them. The task of comparative linguistics has been stated in Chapter IV, 1: the comparison of languages at a given period to formulate some idea of the earlier language from which the languages compared are derived, and the comparison of successive stages of the same language to determine the nature of such derivation. Both comparisons presuppose satisfactory *descriptions* of the different languages or dialects, or of their different stages, as the case may be.

For the student ambitious to become a specialist in this field and to pursue a soundly planned course of studies leading in that direction, the next step would be to study the various specific branches of linguistics whose fundamental problems have been broadly sketched in the preceding pages: *phonetics* (acoustic and articulatory); *phonemics; morphophonemics* or *structural analysis;* the *history of linguistics;* the *linguistic history of specific languages;* the *history of writing and the alphabet* (including palaeography); the *influence of languages on one another* ("languages in contact"); field techniques and the use of informants; *Indo-European comparative linguistics,* and whatever comparative work is available for other language families; and, finally, certain areas of psychology and philosophy, and (for some specializations) communications theory, computer theory, and certain areas of mathematics and engineering. The readings suggested at the end of each chapter in this book would be a good start in this direction; basic books on all these subjects are listed in the general bibliography. It has been our intention and hope that, having assimilated the contents of this book, a student will enter these specific branches with no feeling of strangeness or perplexity, or of being "beyond his depth," but rather with a feeling of confidence born of an understanding of the scope, purposes, and fundamental problems of each branch, and its relation to the whole science.

Needless to say, the really serious student should, concomitantly with all this, be perfecting his knowledge of at least half a dozen languages besides his own. Ideally, he should have a really thorough knowledge of all the basic European tongues and of at least one language in each basic structural type, and should be well on the way to becoming an authoritative scholar in a particular linguistic area— Germanic (like Bloomfield); American Indian (like Sapir); Slavic (like Troubetzkoy); Indo-European (like Meillet; this of course requires proficiency in the classical tongues); Turkic; Caucasian; Celtic; linguistic geography; and so on. We shall not mention the names of living contemporaries in the field; but for all who enjoy a measure of repute, such a field of specialization could be listed.

1. Frontiers of linguistics

As we have often stressed, this book is only an exposition of the basic preliminaries of linguistics, for the most part below the level at which different "schools" separate from one another—in the main constituting those things which practically all linguists agree should be learned by every serious recruit before he hopes to do independent work.

The beginner, standing before the first of the many steps we have listed as leading toward the mastery of these fundamental branches, will doubtless view linguistics as a mature science—even a little too mature, perhaps. But the more advanced linguist is acutely conscious that his field is still in the pioneering stage. Its frontiers are still advancing—though in many places impinging on adjacent fields, showing that it is beginning to fill its own proper area.

On the higher levels, contemporary linguists engage in lively controversy at meetings and in the professional journals[1] on such theories as "glottochronology,"[2] "transformational analysis,"[3] "glossematics,"[4] statistical linguistics and linguistic statistics,[5] mechanical translation,[6] "glossodynamics,"[7] "information theory"[8]—the titles (by no means an exhaustive list) suggest the amount of research and theorization which is going on, and the number of schools and subschools, apostles and disciples which have emerged.

To attempt to summarize or explain the work of these schools would be inappropriate in a book of this nature and scope. It may be said in general, however, that the description of the phonological structure of a language is out of its "barnstorming days," and new research nowadays is generally aimed at finding the most efficient ways of analyzing and describing the grammatical structure of languages, or at estimating the nature and rate of linguistic change; and a great deal of work is being done in the direction of attempting to describe both phonology and structure in mathematical language, as a step toward possibly using electronic computers to process linguistic data, and perhaps translate mechanically. Other topics which appear in the titles of contemporary research papers are, of course, new contributions in the basic categories—descriptive studies of languages not hitherto adequately analyzed, or particular aspects of familiar languages; studies in comparative and historical linguistics; proposed explanations of particular linguistic changes, and so on.

The outer frontiers of linguistics have begun to approach the borders of related disciplines, so that it becomes a little uncertain where to draw the boundary between, for example, linguistics and psychology; and "twilight zones" (such as "psycholinguistics" and "anthropological linguistics") where two sciences overlap have come into being. The linguist who pursues the nature of the mental concepts of which language is the symbol soon finds himself at, if not beyond, the border of psychology; the one who becomes especially interested in how and whether language expresses culture before long feels that he may be duplicating work already done by the anthropologist. Meanwhile the anthropologist (though not, so far, the sociologist) has come to feel that ethnic habits and the behavior of society cannot be adequately investigated without taking account of that foremost of social habits, language; and he has felt the need to become acquainted with what has been discovered about language by those who have long devoted their energies to its study.

These developments seem to tend in the direction of research teams, composed of linguists and psychologists, or, as the case might be, anthropologists, operators of calculators, literary critics, and so on. Many questions could hardly be investigated adequately except in this way; even though, occasionally, one who had qualified himself as a productive original scholar in, say, anthropology, might later take up linguistics and become more than an amateur in that field, this must certainly always be the exception. But the linguist who has only a smattering of psychology (for instance) knows—or should know—that he is likely to be basing his explanation of linguistic problems on principles or theories which professional psychologists consider long since exploded;[9] while sociologists, for example, may either seek to establish their systems without reference to language (which ultimately proves impossible) or, in the absence of knowledge of the discoveries of linguistics, continue to follow concepts of "grammar" that are grossly out of date.

This *rapprochement* of disciplines, whatever form it takes and whatever the machinery by which it is worked out, has an additional advantage of no mean importance. As this book goes to press, the maturity and importance of the discipline of linguistics is daily gaining increased recognition in the better educational institutions: state colleges for the preparaton of teachers are more and more generally requiring the subject in the program of those preparing to be language teachers, and the leading universities that do not already have graduate departments of linguistics are thinking about setting them up. The difficulty in both cases is financial; will there, for some time yet, be enough students to defray at least a reasonable fraction of the expense?

The solution already adopted by several universities is to combine linguistics with another subject, so that the two together will almost surely enjoy adequate support. Thus, several universities now have professors of Linguistics and Psychology, Linguistics and Anthropology—and so on. The writer's view is that the best solution is to set up a *Department of Languages and Linguistics* for the teaching of linguistics and the elementary and intermediate levels of any language

261

(including English "grammar" and English as a second language): existing language departments could then continue to be departments of French literature, German literature, and so on.[10] This would ensure students enough for the new department, while the *littérateurs* of the old departments would be relieved of the always irksome burden of teaching the first steps in their respective languages and would continue to enjoy the support of those students who are their most faithful and satisfying members, together with additional recruits well-prepared in their respective languages by the Department of Languages and Linguistics.

2. Linguistics and the teaching of languages

It is an ancient fallacy to assume that a scientist who has made notable discoveries in a certain branch of knowledge is, or would be, *ipso facto* a better teacher of that subject than those who have made a profession of teaching it. Indeed, it is largely to this fallacy that we owe the hitherto futile teaching of language skills in the United States; for books intended (like this one) to present facts discovered by scientific investigation about the nature and operation of language were taken as textbooks for the teaching of Latin and, on its model, of other languages.

The weakness of a language textbook so designed was not entirely evident as long as the skilled teacher did not depend too much on the book; but when the situation arose, as it did in this country, where the teacher himself knew nothing of the language except what he had been able to glean from a similar book and an equally ill-prepared teacher—and when teachers of all subjects were so poorly rewarded that ordinarily only the less brilliant and less able went into teaching—the utter futility of the method was both revealed and cloaked in a nation's conviction that its people simply had "no talent for learning languages."

It is legitimate to expect that the discoveries of linguistics will somehow lead to improvement in the teaching of languages (and indeed they have already done so, as will be shown), but it is at the same time unreasonable to expect the linguist *per se* to be a better teacher of languages, or even to turn aside from his study of language to search for the applications of that study to teaching them. We must not expect that the document in which a linguist describes a language for other linguists will be a teaching textbook of that language. The true linguist, in short, is devoted to basic research, and the application of linguistics to language teaching comes under the heading of "applied science."

These conclusions do not in any degree diminish the need for applying the discoveries of linguistics to language teaching; they only explain why so little has as yet been done along this line. The fact is that *applied linguistics* constitutes an area of research distinct from linguistics as such, calling for researchers who will make this their specialty, who will stand to pure linguists in the relationship, for instance, of industrial chemists to research chemists; they should be scholars who combine a full training in linguistics with theoretical and practical knowledge of the art of teaching.[11]

The teachers colleges or state colleges should probably be the natural home for this type of specialist, who would answer the earnest demand for this sort of work (to which the linguist is often accused of turning a snobbish nose and a deaf ear) and would reap the greater rewards generally offered to those who find "practical" applications for the discoveries of pure science. The courses taught by such persons would no doubt become part of the specifically professional preparation required of teachers in the field of language (which would include the teaching of English both as a second language and to native speakers).

Meantime, the applications of linguistics to language teaching will probably be found chiefly in the unformulated practice of experienced language teachers who have made a fairly deep study of linguistics. It is, perhaps, possible to suggest two or three specific practices which such teachers might be found fairly generally to follow.

First, *commutation and minimal contrast* prove to be practical teaching methods as well as tools for analysis. The feature (of phonology, for example) which is to be taught to the student is presented as one member of a minimal contrast, either in a pair of words, or in contrasting sentences. For example, let us suppose that we wish to teach the pronunciation of the German *ach-Laut*. The students, if they are native speakers of English, will tend to pronounce *ch* as *ck*; in fact, they may not *really* realize there is a difference—for we must not forget that the average individual, listening to speech sounds in any language, identifies phonemes only within the framework of the language he already knows, his native language. Hence, we can give the student such pairs of words as *doch - Dock, stechen - stecken, Strich - Strick,* stressing the difference of meaning in each case and exploring the ridiculous possibilities in substituting one word for another. Or a sentence may be presented in which substitution of the other word in the pair produces hilarious results, e.g., *Gnädiges Fräulein, möchten Sie heute nackt*[12] *mit mir spazieren?*

An extension of this same principle is to present paradigmatic forms as minimal contrasts. The traditional make-up of paradigms contrasts *persons* with one another; would it not be much more important to contrast *tenses,* by opposing the same person in different tenses?—giving a paradigm like the following:

> er spricht
> er sprach
> er spreche
> er wird sprechen
> er hat gesprochen

Exercises might be given where a series of sentences in the present tense are to be rewritten in the future, and so on.[13]

The linguist, trained to look at a language without preconceived notions, will often re-organize the "paradigms" for the most efficient learning, instead of following the rationale (if any) by which they are traditionally presented. Thus, neo-grammarian textbooks of Sanskrit and Old Irish present numerous "declensions"—not on the basis of any logical classification of forms in either language, but according to a classification into which the *presumed ancestors of the words fell in Indo-European!* If we depart from that classification, we can reduce some twelve "declensions" to three or four. The Latin declensions are set up according to the way the word forms its genitive—meaning that you must know part of the declension of a word before you can know what declension it belongs to. The lack of logic of this sort of thing naturally makes learning difficult for the student; whereupon he is told that the difficulty is inherent in the language, and that struggling with it is good mental exercise for him.

The influence of linguistics will be seen in the teaching of pronunciation: here the linguistically knowledgeable teacher distinguishes the question of *what the phonemes are* from that of *how they are expressed orthographically*. Often it turns out that a language which is said to be "difficult to pronounce" is really quite easy to pronounce but is spelled erratically. German, for instance, has only about four phonemes which are not very similar in articulation to corresponding English phonemes (the two languages, after all, are closely related); but students have difficulty pronouncing German because it often uses the same Roman letters we use, but with different values (e.g., $z = ts$, $w = v$, $v = f$, etc.).

The linguistically trained teacher will not list the letters of the alphabet of the foreign language and dismiss them by saying, "the following . . . are pronounced as in English, and the following . . . can be learned only from a native." A book which treats pronunciation in this way is fifty years out of date, and so is a teacher who cannot explain the articulation of a non-English sound and devise articulatory exercises for the student who cannot acquire the sound by pure imitation. The linguistically trained teacher would certainly teach Latin in such a way that the student would realize that vowel length was phonemic, and would hear the difference between ā and ă.

In applying the important principle that linguistic description must start with "transferred" utterances,[14] linguistically trained teachers will have to junk the great majority of exercises in today's foreign language grammars. These exercises are based on the assumption that language developed from the expressions found in immediate situations; hence, having created highly artificial immediate situations (e.g., the American student talking to his Spanish friend), they overwork the least frequent forms of the language, having one speaker ask for, or convey, information already evident ("Are you tall or short? Are you a student?" etc.). The vast disinterest which this awakens in students reminds us that language is purposeless when not communicating information.

The "linguistic" language teacher will adopt what might be called a *morpheme-formant approach*. Here, reflecting what we have learned about the structure of language, the up-to-date teacher will teach separately *formants* and the *morphemes* which they express, instead of (as formerly) teaching formants only, apparently for their own sake. Many a student has become letter-perfect in repeating the conjugations of French verbs, and has received his A in French for this, though he translates every verb form which he is able to recognize for such as third person singular past tense. He has learned forms because he was required to learn forms. He was not required to learn what the forms meant, or whether they had any meaning; and he did not. How often has a teacher said wonderingly, "I can't understand it; he knows all the Rules of Grammar, but he can't translate or converse. He must be lazy; he must know how, but won't let on that he knows!"

In the linguistic approach, the teacher endeavors first to make sure that the student understands what the language is trying to express (the *morpheme*) before he endeavors to learn the form which expresses it (the *formant*). Suppose, for instance, we are teaching the subjunctive. We can arrange the subjunctive forms in a "paradigm" and force the student to memorize them in this form, and a number of rules as to when the subjunctive is to be used. Will he then understand the subjunctive and be able to use its forms correctly? Hardly, as any experienced language teacher can testify.

But suppose we first explain that the subjunctive is a form used by the speaker to alert the hearer to the fact that the statement he is making is not necessarily true; hence it is naturally used in conditional statements and wishes—where the statement does not report what is happening or has happened, but what *may* happen *if* the condition is fulfilled or the hope realized; in expressions of opinion, which *may* not be true; or in certain expressions of negation, where the possibility that a certain thing *might* happen is denied. The student may then appreciate that certain constructions in English, like *let us*, he *may, might, should*, etc., express "subjunctive" morphemes. The forms themselves may then be presented in contrasting sentences, like the one cited above (page 175), *Long live the Queen/Long lives the Queen.*

Traditional language teaching went on the (unproved) assumption that if the student were brought to comprehend the principle governing the selection of forms, and made to commit the forms themselves to memory, he could, for any occasion, select the proper forms in accordance with the principle. But we know now that language is neither constructed nor spoken in this way: rather, a linguistic construct or structured pattern is learned as an automatic, subconscious response to a situation, and the speaker can vary the content of this pattern (in response to varying situations) by substituting units within it—by substituting formants expressing different message morphemes. Comparison of different patterns gradually yields a *subconscious* realization of the principles of structure.[15]

These principles have far-reaching implications for the task of constructing a new formula for the "grammar" of a language—not the description of it for scholars, but the book for teaching it to students—based on the discoveries of linguistics and newly discovered fundamental principles of language. Little has been done along this line as yet, but we may venture the prediction that a "linguistic grammar" will be largely based on what is becoming known in the "language laboratory" as "pattern drill": that is, grammatical structure will be presented by starting with fundamental patterns, drilling these by substitution of message morphemes until they can be used automatically, then gradually expanding them (following the same procedure at each step) until all the grammatical structure has been presented and assimilated, without taking any time for theoretical discussion or the introduction and application of technical names.

Before teaching-grammars based on linguistic science are generally available, however, we shall probably have a considerable time to wait. Experimental versions must be prepared, tested in the classroom and laboratory, and improved in accordance with the results. These stages will be delayed by the fact that few are working in this area. It would seem that only when the number of linguists in the country has been greatly increased; when this increased number has trained future teachers of languages in linguistic science; and when such teachers have generally applied their linguistic training to the problems of language teaching—only then will the student of a foreign language fully benefit from the discoveries of linguistics.

3. The language laboratory

As these pages are written, the language laboratory is making a triumphal progress through the schools of the United States. Typically, a university president or a superintendent of schools, laying plans for expansion—a new hall or a new high school—decides that since the new facility must be up to date in every department, it must have a language laboratory, and authorizes or requests the language department to negotiate for one. The language teachers have heard of these things, but perhaps have no concrete ideas whatever on the subject.

They are not even sure they want one; but, not to look a gift horse in the mouth, they select a manufacturer (sometimes on the basis of what color wood he uses for the booths) and are guided entirely by him on the educational values and uses of the language laboratory. Finally, having got it installed, they look at the shiny chromium switches and wonder what to do with this thing.

Discussion of the language laboratory might not seem, on the face of it, to be within the scope of a book on linguistics; but although the language laboratory can be and often is used merely as a teaching machine or an occasional audio-visual aid—with no reference to linguistics, by teachers who never heard of the subject—it originated in an attempt by teachers trained in scientific linguistics to meet a specific need. As with all teaching machines, its effectiveness is directly proportional to, if not identical with, the kind of program prepared for use on the machines; and, in the best language laboratories, programming is done by persons familiar with scientific linguistics.[16]

During World War II it was thought necessary to train certain soldiers and sailors in certain languages very little known in this country. It often turned out that there were no teachers of these tongues in the United States, and only a few native speakers, who were not teachers. Ultimately a solution was worked out: whatever native speakers were available were used as "informants," and scientific linguists from the universities,[17] who had worked with languages of very unfamiliar structure, went before classes with the "informants" and, in effect, made a descriptive analysis of the language for the benefit of the students.[18] The arrangement of the matter was therefore more for scientific study than for effective teaching; but efforts were made to be as "teachable" as the professors—often teachers with many years' experience—could make it. The influence of linguistics was, naturally, paramount. When electronic recording equipment was available, it was possible to preserve the utterances of the informant and dispense with his actual presence in the classroom; and thus the language laboratory was born. (At the famous U.S. Army language school at Monterey, California, live informants are still used.)[19] The sensational results achieved with the language laboratory as a teaching tool at Georgetown University's Institute of Languages and Linguistics, and later in the undergraduate college, soon spread through the academic world.

While much of the unprecedented success of early post-World War II language teaching was due merely to allowing more time in the curriculum for language instruction, there was ample evidence that the language laboratory did greatly improve the degree of success achieved by the language teacher; and such also is the testimony of most teachers who have had experience working with a language laboratory. The manufacture and installation of language laboratories has become a profitable and competitive business, and some publishers have been able to revitalize the sale of obsolete textbooks by supplying recordings of their neo-grammarian exercises; but, considering the rarity of linguists and of teachers who have had any training in linguistics, the construction and use of laboratories has gone further and further along its own road, growing in its own direction quite independently of the development of linguistics. When used as an application of linguistics to language teaching, however, the language laboratory may be said to offer the following features:

(1) *It provides for the student's imitation, as models, the voice of an authentic native speaker.* (This point cannot be overemphasized. Much can still be learned by simple imitation; when the teacher does not speak the language, however, the student cannot learn to speak it better than the teacher. *Nemo dat quod non habet.* If the student learns to associate the meaning of a word with a pronunciation thereof meaningless to a native speaker—or indeed to anyone but himself—there is obviously a great waste of effort.)

(2) *It drills each student for every minute of the class period.* In the long run, a language can be learned only by a great deal of practice or drill. Each expression, or linguistic response, must be drilled until its association with a certain situation, or with the speech which calls it forth, is subconsciously automatic.

(3) *It makes certain that the student associates meaning with sound.* Under traditional methods of teaching, the student often associated the meaning of a word not even with his own notion of how the word sounded, but with the graphic figure composed of the letters which spell it. This is soon evident to the teacher in the language laboratory; some of the students who got straight A's in high school for "translating" cannot translate at all from a spoken text.

(4) The language laboratory is probably, of all teaching situations, the one best adapted to what would probably be the characteristics

of a true "linguistic method" of teaching languages—presentation of *authentic specimens of purposeful communication between native speakers,* to be imitated until within tolerable variations from native norms; *presentation of basic patterns* to be learned until the student can produce them automatically, easily making such commutations as are necessary to convey his message; gradual *cumulation of these patterns, with constant drill,* until the student subconsciously grasps the principles of grammatical structure, and can apply them creatively.

Other applications of linguistics to language teaching can be made either in or out of the language laboratory. As the present writer has discussed the techniques specific to the laboratory elsewhere,[20] there is no need to repeat the data here. Let it be noted, however, that the most successful language laboratories will invariably be found to be operated by linguistically trained teachers, which gives good grounds for suspicion that it is their application of linguistics at least as much as the nature of the laboratory that is responsible for the results.

4. Other applications of linguistics

It would be manifestly impossible to catalogue in this chapter all imaginable applications of linguistic science. Some of the most important applications, in fact, may not yet be guessed or imagined, as is always the way with any pure science and its applications; such a potent "application" as the hydrogen bomb began with the almost idle curiosity, thirty years before, of a professor of physics about some spoiled photographic plates;[21] and, indeed, the whole industrial revolution can be regarded as the "application" of the idea which occurred three hundred years ago to Francis Bacon, that we should make extensive use of *a posteriori* reasoning, for a change. Hence, we propose to conclude this volume with just a few of the examples of possible applications of linguistics which are the most immediately evident.

Language engineering, a term apparently originated by G. A. Miller of the Massachusetts Institute of Technology,[22] covers "the application of scientific knowledge to any sphere of human experience where greater productivity and efficiency can be attained thereby, whether machines are involved or not."[23] Now that a body of scientific knowledge about language has been built up, the directions in which that knowledge may be used for "engineering" in this sense are many, and we need not be surprised to find one or more professions developing along these lines.

Missionaries, of course, have for some time realized how linguistics facilitates establishing communication with inhabitants of remote areas, and often require prospective missionaries to take training in linguistics.

The *advertising* field has lately been calling on linguists for help in conveying sales messages to speakers of other languages, and *public-opinion polling* has found that accuracy in this field is virtually impossible without knowledge of linguistic principles.

Manufacturers of *communications equipment* have found it worth while to maintain laboratories[24] in which some of the research is into the linguistic aspects of communications.

Activities relating to *cultural exchange, international relations* (whether on the part of a government or of a private concern which finds itself much involved in a foreign country) and *international cooperation* (the development of underdeveloped regions) require, in the first instance, an understanding of an unfamiliar culture: linguistics is involved here indirectly, insofar as it is able to facilitate understanding the language, which in turn is one of several keys to the culture. While linguists are not necessarily specialists in these areas, it is probable that the most successful specialists will be linguists, or at least linguistically trained.[25]

The field of what may be called *communication theory*[26] is primarily directed toward finding ways to express information in binary-number units (called "bits") so that it can be mathematically processed by data-processing machines using punched cards or tapes—notably computers. By such processing, accurate measurement of the amount of information put into a system of communication (such as a language) and the amount received at the output—hence, of the efficiency of the system, with obvious implications for the system's operation and improvement—is made possible. This is really a self-contained field in which linguistics occupies only a corner, by virtue of the fact that language is a system of communication. Nevertheless, those scholars who are at work in this corner—those seeking to develop the theory of communication in its applications to language—form a large and very important fraction of contemporary linguists. Special glamor has been lent to this type of linguist by the exciting vision—possibly an El Dorado or Northwest Passage—of "translating machines." True to American "practicality" and inability to see the implications of anything moderately abstract (like liberal education, for instance), there appears to be a contemporary trend to pour the majority of money currently available for research into this area of linguistics.

The teaching of English to native speakers of the language—universally conceded to be the core of liberal education in English-speaking countries—is, we are certain, destined to be profoundly influenced, and in no small degree altered, by the past and future development of linguistics.[27] We have no doubt that this prospect will be welcomed with excitement and enthusiasm by the true scholars in the English field.

The professor of English is presumably teaching (1) how to speak and write "correct" English, (2) how to appreciate great writing, (3) how to write well. Now, it is certainly not necessary to dwell upon what linguistics can do toward establishing an objective, scientific, measurable definition of "correctness" for native speakers,[28] and toward devising really efficient means for teaching students how to acquire whatever dialect is decided to be "correct," and to give up their native speech in its favor.

In the field of criticism, one has always been troubled by the subjectivism of critical standards, according to which so many of the writers ultimately recognized as belonging among the greatest were adjudged worthless by critics upon their first appearance: a scientific approach might do much to bring criticism into agreement with itself and with the truth. One has also been disturbed by the fact that professional writers and professors of English are so much at odds—that the student who is most proficient in the "writing" class seldom accomplishes anything worthy of notice in either literature or journalism, and so few of the professors who teach writing can themselves write readable, clear and interesting copy.[29] Linguistics can be of help here, too: it will not be too long, we are sure, before the linguists will eventually develop a scientific technique for the delicate and precise definition and description of style—delicate and precise enough so that one could, at will, reproduce the style of any given author. Not that this in itself would be a particularly desirable achievement; but it would then be possible to compare the styles of various authors universally acclaimed as great, and find some least common denominator which could serve as a concrete definition of good style. Something like this, to be sure, is what we have always endeavored to do: but it has been the author's observation that, in practice, the English instructor consciously or subconsciously takes as the embodiment of "the best" writing either his own or his favorite author's; the latter may have written in a style contemporary in his time but now archaic by at least a century, whereas the former is vulnerable to G. B. Shaw's cruel but famous remark.[30]

The teaching of speech is an increasingly important task in these days when a man's ability to sway audiences may win or lose him a dictatorship or a presidency. Yet, increasingly, it is leaving the core curriculum and the educational institutions altogether, and becoming the domain of professional, nonacademic coaches and their schools. The reason, we believe, is that in schools this task was generally agreed to belong to the English department, which struggled unsuccessfully with it for a while, and then decided either to unload it on a special department or forget it altogether. The cause of the failure, again, would be the fact that the training of most English teachers includes nothing relating to the nature of language as such, and very little relating to English itself *as a language*. Again the first, perennially unsolved question is, how to decide on a standard of "good" spoken English? The speech teacher usually either adopts a tradition foreign to himself and his students (e.g., London British, or that taught in some school of acting), or takes his own speech (which may not merit the choice) as a norm. Usually the students, while not openly expressing rebellion, simply cannot be induced to give up their native speech for something so artificial. Supposing, however, that we could arrive at a standard dialect which all could accept, the linguist could, we believe, develop precise, scientifically accurate descriptions of what constitutes good elocution—descriptions which would be much easier to comprehend and teach than an experienced speaker's efforts to formulate, with some difficulty, what he himself perhaps understands only by instinct.

The degree to which linguistics can influence *lexicography* is no doubt evident. New dictionaries have often been made merely by revising old ones, hence are always seventy-five years behind: in most dictionaries of modern European languages you can find the expression for "reef the top-gallant sail," but not the one for "check the oil and water." Linguistics contributes not only accurate etymologies, but new discoveries about meaning and the nature of words, how to ascertain "meanings," even how to determine what a word is. The leading publishers of dictionaries are now availing themselves of the knowledge and skills of linguists.

These, then, are a number of specific applications of the knowledge about the first prerequisite for education, science and civilization which, over the past two centuries, has been collected and here presented as *the Science of Language*. For those interested only in the "practical" aspect of things, there should be enough here to justify the study of linguistics. But, of course, to anyone who understands the nature of science and how human progress has been achieved, it needs no justification, and never did. The enlargement of man's knowledge in any field is justification unto itself.

Notes to Chapter XV

1. Leading professional journals are *Language* and *Word* in the United States, and in Europe, *Lingua, Archivum linguisticum, Bulletin de la société de linguistique de Paris, Norsk tidskrift for sprogvedenskap,* and the *Sbornik s jazykoznanie* of the *Akademija Nauk.* The journals devoted to specific languages or language families also frequently include articles on linguistic questions in these fields.

2. Cf. S. C. Gudschinsky, "The ABC's of Lexicostatics," *Word* XII, 2 (August 1956), 175–210.

3. Cf. N. Chomsky, *Syntactic Structures.*

4. Cf. L. Hjelmslev and H. J. Udall, *Outline of Glossematics.*

5. Cf. Whatmough, *Language,* 199–210.

6. Cf. *Mechanical Translation,* a journal published by the Massachusetts Institute of Technology since 1954, and H. P. Edmundson (ed.), *Machine Translation,* 1961.

7. Cf. Whatmough, *loc. cit.*

8. Cf. G. A. Miller, *Information Theory and the Study of Speech.*

9. For example, behaviorism, which is the school from which many linguists have taken and still take their psychological postulates, has undergone a great deal of development in the last thirty years, and many new viewpoints have arisen in psychology during that period. Cf. Carroll, 74 ff., 81 ff.

10. Cf. J. P. Hughes, "The Administrative Organization of Language Teaching," *Modern Language Journal,* XL, 4 (April 1956), 178–81.

11. For the application of linguistics to language teaching we can cite L. Bloom-field, *Outline Guide for the Study of Foreign Languages;* C. C. Fries, *Teaching and Learning English as a Foreign Language;* R. Lado, *Linguistics Across Cultures;* and H. L. Smith, Jr., *Linguistic Science and the Teaching of English.* All of these books have met with massive resistance from both teachers and publishers who have strong vested interests in traditionalism.

12. *nackt* = naked; correctly, *Nacht* = night.

13. These could be tied in with the language laboratory; see next section (XV, 3).

14. See page 156.

15. See page 151.

16. Cf. J. P. Hughes, "The Machine Age in Language Teaching," *Catholic School Journal,* LVIII (September 1958), 63–68.

17. M. Haas, "The Linguist as Teacher of Languages," *Language,* XIX, 3, 203–8.

18. This was what had a brief celebrity as "The Army Method."

19. One weakness of the laboratory is that the informant is no longer able to tell the student that his imitation is not acceptable.

20. See above, Note 16.

21. In the laboratory of Prof. Robert Millikan at the California Institute of Technology. This got Millikan working on cosmic rays, for which work he won a Nobel prize, and the publications which came out of his cosmic-ray work in turn interested other scientists in the source of cosmic rays and their nature.

22. Cf. Carroll, 121.

23. *Ibid.,* 196.

24. For example, the Bell Telephone Laboratories; Haskins Laboratories in New York City; the Ramo-Wooldridge laboratories in Los Angeles.

25. This, it will be remembered, was the original idea behind the setting up of the Institute of Languages and Linguistics in the School of Foreign Service at Georgetown University.

26. For an excellent explanation of which, see Carroll, 199 ff.

27. This has already taken place in the area of the teaching of English as a second language.

28. When the linguist says that the native speaker is always correct—one of the findings of linguistics which most horrifies English teachers—he is not

really using "correctness" in this sense; or, to put it more "correctly," the English teacher is not really teaching *correct* (i.e., true, authentic) English, but *acceptable* English, according to an admittedly arbitrary standard— very much like "good" manners.

29. Cf. B. de Voto, *Minority Report*, 336 ff.

30. "He who can, does. He who cannot, teaches." Shaw, *Maxims for Revolutionists*.

Supplementary Readings to Chapter XV

Whatmough, *Language*, 199–220.
Hockett, *A Course in Modern Linguistics*, 512–38.
Carroll, *The Study of Language*.
Stack, *The Language Laboratory and Modern Language Teaching*, 7–47, 84–134.
Barzun, *Teacher in America*, 132–47.
Weinreich, *Languages in Contact*.
G. A. Miller, *Language and Communication*.
O'Connor, *Oral Drill in Spanish*.

APPENDIX A

A MODEL STATEMENT OF PHONOLOGY

1. Introduction

This statement is based on studies made by the author on field trips to Inishmore in the Aran Islands in 1947 and 1953, and on a monograph published in 1952.[1] The dialect described, therefore, is one of the Connaught (northwestern) dialects, which in general are more archaic and more conservative than most other forms of Irish. Because of limitations of space, this statement is considerably abbreviated, but the reader is referred for all details to the fuller monograph.

The purpose here is chiefly to provide the reader with a model for the statement in which the linguist might report to the profession what his studies of a language have established about its phonology and phonemic system. It must be stressed (and the distinction should always be kept rigidly) that this is *not* a description of the language for someone who wishes to master it as a tool of communication; in some places the difference from such a statement is not great, but in others the difference from a description organized for teaching is substantial.

2. The phonemic system

The phonemes of the Irish dialect here presented form the following system:

Vowels (12)

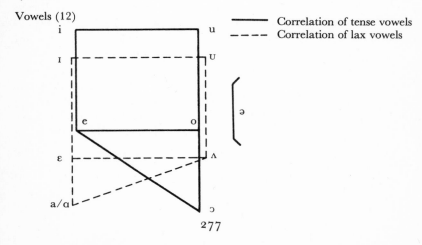

——— Correlation of tense vowels
– – – Correlation of lax vowels

Consonants (36)

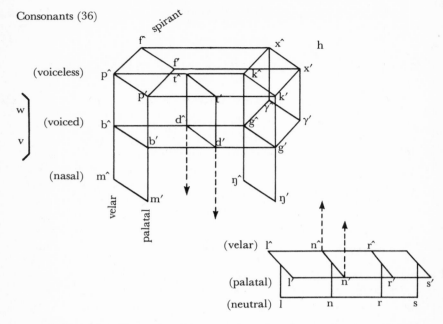

It is evident from the diagrams that the phonemic system is some-what complex. There are 48 phonemes, 36 nonsyllabic (consonantal) and 12 syllabic (vowels). (There are no diphthongs: as is shown be-low, there are sequences of phones which would be diphthongs in English or other languages, but which in Irish are successive pho-nemes.)

Each phoneme participates in several correlations and is well inte-grated into the system, the only peripheral phonemes being /w/, /v/ and /h/. (In other dialects the first two may be classified as /vˆ/ and /v'/, and thus these also would become integrated.)

Most important of the many correlations is that of *palatalization,* almost every phoneme in the language occurring as one of a pair *velar/palatal.* With so complex a system we should expect, in *parole,* a good deal of deviation from norms (which proves to be true), and many neutralizations and dissociations, which are also encountered.

3. The phonemes: (A) syllabic, (B) nonsyllabic

The phoneme /pˆ/; minimum oppositions—
with /bˆ/—pˆɔnə 'pane of glass'/ bˆɔnə "white' (adj. plural)
with /pˆ/—kɑpəl 'horse'/ kapˆɪl' 'horses'
with /fˆ/—pluːr 'flour' / fluːr 'my flour'
with /tˆ/ —pˆor 'race' / t'or 'give!'[2]

A voiceless, velarized labial stop, in the pronunciation of which the lips are loose and somewhat protruded. As the phoneme is of rather less frequent occurrence than others, oppositions are somewhat hard to locate. A slight [w] glide can be heard after /pˆ/ initially and medially before high front vowels.

The phoneme /p'/; minimum oppositions—
with /pˆ/—pˆin' 'a jot' / p'in 'penny'
with /f'/—p'iən 'pain' / f'iən 'wine'
with /bˆ/—p'iən 'pain'/ bˆiən 'hostel'
with /b'/—p'iən 'pain'/ b'iən 'they usually are'
with / fˆ /—p'ɑn 'pen' / fˆɑn 'weary'

A voiceless, palatalized bilabial stop; it is normally aspirated, and the lips are usually tensed and retracted during production of the sound.

The phoneme /m'/; minimum oppositions—
with / mˆ /—m'ir' 'part' / mˆir' 'the sea'
with / n' /—m'i 'month' / nˆi 'thing'
with / p' /—m'iən 'desire' / p'iən 'pain'

A labial nasal, palatalized with copalatal articulation.[3] The lips are normally tense and retracted.

It occurs before /i/, /ɪ/, /u/, /ʊ/, /o/, /ɔ/, /ʌ/—a slight [j] glide being heard after it when the back vowels follow. In final position the palatalization may be omitted, but the /m'/ is attacked through an [ɪ] glide if a back vowel precedes—i.e., it is actualized as [ᶦm]. Elsewhere (i.e., before /e/, /ɛ/, /ə/ and /ɑ/), the opposition mˆ/m' is neutralized, an [m] without velarization or glides appearing as the archiphoneme.

[Space does not permit going through the whole inventory of phonemes, but it is hoped that the above examples will serve as a model for the establishment and description of individual phonemes.]

4. Syllabic structure and distribution of phonemes

The syllable in Irish is built around a high point of sonority constituted by one of the syllabic phonemes. None of the others can constitute a syllable, and none of the syllabic phonemes occurs as nonsyllabic (which is to say, there are no syllables containing diphthongs or triphthongs). Syllables in Irish may be structured in any of the following ways:

v	vc	vcc
cv	cvc	cvcc
ccv	ccvc	ccvcc
cccv	cccvc	[No example of cccvc has been found.]

Any of these structures can occur as constituent syllables within polysyllabic words, but not in such combinations as to create clusters of more than three consonants. (A list of the possible three-consonant medial clusters is given in the original monograph.)[4]

Any of the nonsyllabic phonemes except /r'/ can occur singly at the beginning of a word or syllable. The phonemes /fˆ/, /f'/, and /γ/ do not occur finally, and /γˆ/ does not occur medially. All other consonantal phonemes can occur singly in medial position, although the neutral phonemes are more frequent than the palatal or velar ones in this position. (Some speakers, however, do not use [ŋˆ] or [ŋ'] singly in medial position, always following them by [gˆ] or [g'] respectively.)

In any consonant cluster within a word, all the consonants are of the same quality, whether velar, palatal or neutral. In initial two-consonant clusters, the second consonant is usually /rˆ/, /r'/, /r/ or /lˆ/, /l'/, /l/; less frequently /p/, /k/, /m/, /n/.[5] In final two-consonant clusters, the last phoneme is usually /tˆ/, /t'/, /kˆ/, /k'/, rarely /s/; and the first is generally /ŋ/, /s/, /s'/, /l/, sometimes /x/. Final two-consonant clusters are relatively infrequent.

The only three-consonant initial clusters are /skˆlˆ-/, /s'k'l'-/. /s'k'r-/, /str-/, /spr-/, /s'p'r'-/, /spˆlˆ-/, and /s'p'l'-/. In an initial three-consonant cluster, /s'/ or /s/ is always the first; the second is always a voiceless stop, and the third is /r/ or /l/.[6]

There are no clusters consisting of the same consonant repeated, i.e., no geminates. Vowel sequences do not, within words, exceed two vowels, and are always disyllabic: hence there are no diphthongs. (But there are sequences [ɑγ'] and [ɑw] in which /γ'/ and /w/ are fully phonemic.) In two-vowel sequences, the first is always stressed and tense; the other may be unstressed, lax, or *schwa* /ə/. There are no interior vowel sequences consisting of the same vowel repeated, hence there is no correlation of long *versus* short vowels.

The lax vowels occur only in closed syllables. In open syllables which are not stressed, therefore, the inventory of vowel phonemes is reduced. The stress of Connaught Irish is a stress accent, which is nonphonemic since it is normally fixed on the first syllable of each word. In this first, stressed syllable all vocalic phonemes may occur. The next syllable normally has minimum stress, therefore only the phoneme /ə/ appears. The third syllable has secondary stress, and, if open, admits only /i/, /u/ and /ə/ (with a few rare exceptions).[7] As words are seldom longer than three syllables, this is normally the final syllable.

5. Neutralizations and dissociations

Some of the many neutralizations and phonemic dissociations of Irish are best treated under the individual phonemes affected. A few cases, however, should be highlighted as general principles. Here, however, the descriptive linguist must be careful to define his point of view and stick to it, for in the complexity of Irish phonology it is easy to be led down side paths in diachronic or areal linguistics.

From this point of view we shall say that, although there are indications of its weakening in some dialects, the correlation of phonemic distinctions between velar and palatal sounds is fully maintained. In certain positions the distinction may be shifting its basis in such a way that /b^/ vs. /b'/ is no longer [b^] / [b'] but [b] / [bʲ]. For Aran Irish, however, this can still be questioned, and in any case [bʲ] would still be phonemically /b'/.

The basic principle of the language that consonantal phonemes have their strongest (*fortis*) articulation at the beginning of words, and a weaker one (*lenis, lenition*) medially and finally, turns out to be outside the scope of the linguist concerned with synchronic description; for, although we may have /p/ or /ľ/ most frequently in initial position and /f/ or /l/ most frequently in medial-final, the stop-spirant

and velar-palatal correlations are not weakened, since such oppositions as p/f and p̂/p′ can still occur in all positions.

In the case of a/ɑ we apparently have, not a neutralization, but
the beginning of a dissociation.[8] A genuine neutralization may be seen,
however, in the fact that the opposition of voice to voicelessness cannot
be distinguished after /s/. In other words, [sgɑr] and [skɑr] would
not be distinct words, nor would [ə'mask] and [ə'masg]. In this case,
the voiceless variant is the archiphoneme. All consonant oppositions
appear to be neutralized between initial /s/ and /r̂/, as well as the
r̂/r opposition, for we cannot distinguish str from sr, nor sr from sr′-;
in all these cases we get as archiphoneme a variant of /r/ which sounds
like a voiceless [r̥′], and nothing else is admitted in this position. If
the initial consonant is /s′/, however, all possible distinctions are
made, although of course we do not expect combinations like /s′r̂/.

In the first syllable after the stressed one, which admits only /ə/,
the /ə/ is to be regarded as the archiphoneme of all the vowels, for
all vocalic oppositions are neutralized in such a syllable. . . .

[It should be evident that the complete statement of the phonology
and phonemic system of a language is a fairly lengthy document. Since
a representative portion of each of the most important sections has
been presented, we terminate this illustration here.]

Notes

1. John P. Hughes, *A Phonemic Description of the Aran Dialect of Modern Irish*
   (Diss. Columbia U., 1952).

2. To save space, only one minimal contrast is given. Normally one should
   present at least one each for initial, medial, and final position.

3. For the term *copalatal,* see the original publication, pp. 7–9.

4. Which see, p. 67.

5. When we write /p/ etc., without special marks, it stands for /p̂/, /p′/ and
   /p/, and so on.

6. See Note 5. With regard to /r/, see under Section 5.

7. See the original publication, p. 47.

8. See the original publication, p. 58.

APPENDIX B

A Model Statement of Grammar

[As a counterpart to the statement of phonology, a corresponding statement of the grammatical structure of a different language was originally planned. Considerations of space prevent this; but the list of headings is given to show how the modern linguist might organize the material. Again we stress that this is *not* the outline of a book designed for teaching the "grammar" of a language; such a teaching "grammar," however, should be based on a scientific description of this sort.[1]]

1. Introduction

History of the investigation; the language studied—by whom spoken; the area in which the language is used; other languages or dialects of which it is a dialect, or to which it is related; methods of the investigation; the materials collected, etc.

2. Typological statement

General characterization of the structure of the language under investigation, identifying the typological category in which it belongs, and giving a general outline of the chief principles of structure.

3. Basic-sentence patterns

The *exocentric* structures. There should be some half a dozen, to which all sentences met with in the language can be reduced, by taking account of the equivalency of single-word with multiverbal structures. (In polysynthetic languages the number may be greater, since sentence patterns are also word patterns.) Possible positional variation must be studied for its significance, if any.

---

[1] For additional examples and discussion of the grammatical statement, see C. Hockett, "Two Models of Grammatical Description," *Word* X, 2–3 (Aug. 1947), 216–34.

4. Sentence-component structures

The *endocentric* structures, which do not make sentences, but organize sequences of words into sentence-component structures equivalent to single words in basic sentences. (In polysynthetic languages this category would not exist, since there are no structures less than a sentence.)

5. Sentence-functional word classes

If the language marks words to indicate their function in the sentence—which, of course, creates form-classes of words similarly marked—such classes are listed here with their characteristic marks. This section will most nearly resemble the lists of "paradigms" of which traditional grammars consist. The roots of these words convey most of the content of messages transmitted by the language.

6. Determinants and structural words

Here will be listed words whose sole or principal function is to establish structural patterns, and any others which contain little or no message information. They will, of course, be organized into categories which pattern alike and have the same function.

7. Nonbasic structural morphemes and formants

a) grammatical "gender" and bonding or "agreement" in general
b) "number"
c) person
d) tense
e) aspect
f) mood and voice
(The precise terms would vary somewhat, of course, with the language.)

8. Word structure (see Chapter XII).

9. Complex sentence patterns (see Chapter XI).

10. Texts with analysis.

BIBLIOGRAPHY

The Bibliography has been compiled to accomplish three purposes: (1) to give full bibliographical data on all books and articles mentioned or referred to in the Text, Notes and Readings (for this reason, details have usually been omitted at the place of citation); (2) to list other books and articles on the topics treated in the text which are worthy of the reader's attention, though not so immediately relevant as to have been specifically cited, or to have found a place in the Supplementary Readings; (3) to give as thorough as possible a list of the contemporary journals devoted to linguistics, in which new research first appears. Items starred are on the list of required readings for candidates for the M.A. in Linguistics at Columbia University.

The Bibliography is in four sections: (A) books; (B) articles; (C) linguistic journals; (D) other journals.

Bibliographic completeness has not been aimed at. Some titles have been intentionally excluded because they belong to a more advanced level, are hard to obtain, are too specialized, and for similar reasons.

A. Books

Adams, Joseph Quincy (ed.). *The Chief Pre-Shakespearean Dramas.* Boston, Houghton Mifflin Co., c1924.

Alarcos Llorach, Emilio. *Fonología española (según el método de la escuela de Praga).* Madrid, Editorial Gredos, 1950.

——— *Gramática estructural de la lengua española (según la escuela de Copenhague).* Madrid, Editorial Gredos, 1951.

Aristotle. *The Rhetoric of Aristotle,* with a commentary by Edward M. Cope, revised and edited by John Edwin Sandys. 3 vols. Cambridge, at the University Press, 1877.

Barry, Philip. *The Philadelphia Story;* a comedy in three acts. New York, Coward-McCann, Inc., c1939.

Barzun, Jacques. *Teacher in America.* Boston, Little, Brown and Co., 1945.

Baudouin de Courtenay, Jean (1845–1929). *Niekotorye otdiely "Sravnite'noi Grammatiki" slovianskikh iazykov.* Warsaw, M. Zemkevich, 1881.

——— *Otryvki iz Lektsiy po Fonetike i Morfologii Russkago Iazyka.* Voronezh, 1882.

——— *Zur Kritik der künstlichen Weltsprachen.* Leipzig, Veit, 1908.

*Bloomfield, Leonard. *Language.* New York, Henry Holt, 1933.

*——— *Outline Guide for the Study of Foreign Languages.* Baltimore, 1942.

——— *Sacred Stories of the Sweet Grass Cree.* Ottawa, F. A. Acland, 1930 (Canada. Dept. of Mines. National Museum of Canada, Bulletin No. 60).

*Boas, Franz. *Handbook of American Indian Languages.* 3 vols. Washington, Government Printing Office, 1911–22. (Vols. 1–2 are Bulletin No. 40 of the Bureau of American Ethnology.)

Bopp, Franz (1791–1867). *Ueber das Konjugationssystem der Sanskritsprache in Vergleichung mit jenem der griechischen, lateinischen, persischen und germanischen.* Frankfurt am Main, K. & J. Windischmann, 1816.

Brooks, Nelson. *Language and Language Learning; theory and practice.* New York, Harcourt, Brace and Co., c1960.

Brücke, Ernst Wilhelm, ritter von. *Grundzüge der Physiologie und Systematik der Sprachlaute, für Linguisten und Taubstummenlehrer.* Vienna, 1865.

*Brugmann, Karl (1849–1919) and B. Delbrück. *Grundriss der vergleichenden Grammatik der indogermanischen Sprachen.* 2d ed. Strassburg, Trübner, 1897–1916. 2 v. in 7.

Budge, E. A. Wallis. *First Steps in Egyptian; a book for beginners.* London, Kegan Paul, Trench, Trübner & Co., 1895.

Byron, George Gordon Noel. *The Poetical Works of Lord Byron,* ed., with a memoir, by E. H. Coleridge. London, John Murray, 1905.

Carrell, James, and William R. Tiffany. *Phonetics; theory and application to speech improvement.* New York, McGraw-Hill, 1960.

Carroll, John B. *The Study of Language; a survey of linguistics and related disciplines in America.* Cambridge, Mass., Harvard University Press, 1955.

Ceram, C. W. *The Secret of the Hittites; the discovery of an ancient empire.* Tr. . . . Richard & Clara Winston. New York, A. A. Knopf, 1958.

Chakravarti, Prabhatchandra. *The Linguistic Speculations of the Hindus.* Calcutta, University of Calcutta, 1933.

Chomsky, Noam. *Syntactic Structures.* The Hague, Mouton & Co., 1957.

Clemens, Samuel L. ("Mark Twain"). *Mark Twain's Autobiography,* with introd. by Albert Bigelow Paine. New York, Harper & Bros., 1924.

Collins, Wilkie. *The Moonstone* and *The Woman in White* . . . with a Foreword by Alexander Woollcott. New York, The Modern Library, 1937.

Cordier, Mathurin (1479–1564). *Colloquiarum scholasticorum libri IV.* Edinburgi, excudebant haeredes Andreae Hart, 1632.

*Dauzat, Albert. *La Géographie linguistique.* Paris, Flammarion, 1922.

—— *Les Noms de lieux; origine et évolution.* Paris, Delagrave, 1939.

DeVoto, Bernard. *Minority Report.* Boston, Little, Brown, 1940.

*Delbrück, Berthold. *Das Vergleichende Syntax der indogermanischen Sprachen.* 3 v. Strassburg, Trübner, 1893–1900. (Part of Brugmann, *Grundriss der Vergleichenden Grammatik,* see above.)

*Diringer, David. *The Alphabet; a key to the history of mankind.* New York, The Philosophical Library, 1948.

Dumézil, Georges. *L'Héritage indo-européenne à Rome.* Paris, Gallimard, n.d.

Edmundson, H. P., ed. *Proceedings of the National Symposium on Machine Translation.* Englewood Cliffs, N.J., Prentice-Hall, 1961.

Eighth International Congress of Linguists. *Reports.* . . . Oslo, 1957.

*Février, James G. *Histoire de l'écriture.* Paris, Payot, 1948.

*Finck, Franz N. *Die Haupttypen des Sprachbaus.* Leipzig, Teubner, 1910.

Firth, J. R. *Papers in Linguistics,* 1934–1951. London, Oxford University Press, 1957.

Forchhammer, Jörgen. *Die Grundlage der Phonetik; ein Versuch, die phonetische Wissenschaft auf fester Sprachphysiologischer Grundlage aufzubauen.* Heidelberg, C. Winter, 1924.

Freeman, Kenneth (1882–1906). *Schools of Hellas; an essay on the practice and theory of ancient Greek education from 600 to 300 B.C.* Ed. M. J. Rendall. 3d ed., London, Macmillan, 1922.

*Fries, Charles C. *The Structure of English: an introduction to the construction of English sentences.* New York, Harcourt Brace, 1952.

——— *Teaching and Learning English as a Foreign Language.* Ann Arbor, University of Michigan Press, 1945.

Ganss, George E. *St. Ignatius' Idea of a Jesuit University.* Milwaukee, Marquette University Press, 1954.

Gilliéron, Jules, and E. Edmont. *Atlas linguistique de la France.* 35 parts, Paris, Champion, 1902–1910.

Gleason, H. A., Jr. *An Introduction to Descriptive Linguistics.* New York, Henry Holt and Co., 1955.

Gouin, François. *The Art of Teaching and Studying Languages.* Tr. . . . Howard Swan and Victor Bétis. 5th ed. London, G. Philip and Son, 1896.

Grammont, Maurice. *Traité de phonétique.* 3e éd., rev. Paris, Delagrave, 1946.

Gray, Louis H. *Foundations of Language.* New York, Macmillan, 1939.

*Greenberg, Joseph H. *Studies in African Linguistic Classification.* New Haven, Yale University Press, 1955.

Haarhoff, Theodore J. *Schools of Gaul; a study of pagan and Christian education in the last century of the Western empire.* London, Oxford University Press, 1920.

Halliday, W. R. *Indo-European Folk Tales and Greek Legend.* Cambridge, at the University Press, 1933.

*Heffner, Roe-Merrill S. *General Phonetics.* Madison, University of Wisconsin Press, 1949.

Herodotus. *Herodotus,* with a translation by A. D. Godley. 4 v. London, Heinemann, 1931. (Loeb Classical Library.)

Heyerdahl, Thor. *American Indians in the Pacific.* New York, Rand McNally, 1933.

Hill, Archibald A. *Introduction to Linguistic Structures; from sound to sentence in English.* New York, Harcourt Brace, 1958.

*Hirt, Herman (1865–1936). *Die Indogermanen: ihre Verbreitung, ihre Urheimat, und ihre Kultur.* 2 v. Strassburg, Trübner, 1905–1907.

Hjelmslev, Louis. *Principes de grammaire générale.* Copenhagen, 1928.

————, and H. J. Uldall. *Outline of Glossematics: a study in the methodology of the humanities, with special reference to linguistics.* Copenhagen, Nordisk Sprog- og Kulturforlag, 1957.

*———— *Prolegomena to a Theory of Language.* Baltimore, 1953. (Supplement to *International Journal of American Linguistics,* XIX, 1.)

Hockett, Charles. *A Course in Modern Linguistics.* New York, The Macmillan Company, 1958.

Hrozný, Bedrich. *The Ancient History of Western Asia, India, and Crete.* Tr. Jindrich Procházka. New York, The Philosophical Library, 1953.

———— *Die Sprache der Hethiter.* Leipzig, Hinrichs, 1917.

Hsi-en Chen, Theodore, and W. Chung-chen. *Elementary Chinese Reader and Grammar.* South Pasadena, Calif., P. D. and Ione Perkins, 1945.

Hughes, John P. *A Phonemic Description of the Aran Dialect of Modern Irish, with a detailed consideration of problems of palatalization.* New York, Diss. Columbia University, 1952.

Jackson, Kenneth H. *Contributions to the Study of Manx Phonology.* Edinburgh, Thomas Nelson & Sons, 1955.

*Jakobson, Roman. *Kindersprache, Aphasie und Allgemeine Lautgesetze.* Uppsala, 1942. (Uppsala Universitetsårsskrift, No. 9.)

*————, Gunnar Fant, and Morris Halle. *Preliminaries to Speech Analysis. The distinctive features and their correlates.* Cambridge, Mass., Acoustics Lab., M.I.T., 1952. (Massachusetts Institute of Technology. Acoustics Laboratory. Technical Report. No. 13.)

*Jespersen, Otto. *Language; its nature, development and origin.* London, Macmillan, 1922.

———— *How to Teach a Foreign Language.* Tr. Sophia Yhlen-Olsen Bertelsen. London, Allen & Unwin (1956).

———— *A Modern English Grammar on Historical Principles.* Completed by Niels Haislund. 7 v. London, Allen & Unwin, 1927–1949.

*Jones, Daniel. *Outline of English Phonetics.* 6th ed. New York, E. P. Dutton & Co., 1948.

*Joos, Martin. *Acoustic Phonetics.* Baltimore, 1948. (*Language* Monograph No. 23.)

*————, ed. *Readings in Linguistics: the development of descriptive linguistics in America since 1925.* Washington, American Council of Learned Societies, 1957.

Joyce, Patrick W. *Origin and History of Irish Names of Places.* Dublin, McGlashan and Gill, 1875. 2 vols.

Kempelen, Wolfgang von. *Mechanismus der menschlichen Sprache, nebst Beschreibung seiner sprechenden Maschine.* Wien, J. V. Degen, 1791.

Kipling, Rudyard. *The Works of Rudyard Kipling.* One volume ed. New York, Walter J. Black, n.d.

Kircher, Athanasius, S. J. (1602–1680). *Lingua Aegyptiaca restituta.* Rome, 1643.

Kuipers, Aert H. *Phoneme and Morpheme in Kabardian (Eastern Adyghe).* The Hague, Mouton and Co., 1960.

*Kurath, Hans. *Handbook of the Linguistic Geography of New England.* Providence, R.I., Brown University, 1939.

*Lado, Robert. *Linguistics Across Cultures; applied linguistics for language teachers.* Ann Arbor, Michigan, University of Michigan, 1957.

Langer, Susanne K. *Philosophy in a New Key. A study in the symbolism of reason, rite and art.* Cambridge, Mass., Harvard University Press, 1942.

*Lehmann, Winifred P. *Proto-Indo-European Phonology.* Austin, Texas, University of Texas, 1952.

*Leopold, Werner F. *The Speech Development of a Bilingual Child: a linguist's record.* 4 v. Evanston & Chicago, Northwestern University, 1939–1949.

Lepsius, Karl Richard (1810–1884). *A Standard Alphabet, for reducing unwritten languages and foreign graphic systems to a uniform orthography in European letters.* London, Williams & Norgate, 1863.

Lewis, M. M. *How Children Learn to Speak.* New York, Basic Books, 1959.

Locke, John. *Locke on Education.* Ed. R. H. Quick. Cambridge, Cambridge University Press, 1880.

MacDonell, Arthur Anthony (1854–1930). *Vedic Mythology.* Strassburg, 1917. (In *Grundriss der Indo-Arischen Philologie und Altertumskunde,* Vol. 3, No. 1a.)

*McMillan, Brockway, ed. *Current Trends in Information Theory.* Pittsburgh, University of Pittsburgh, 1953.

Mallinson, Vernon. *Teaching a Modern Language.* London, Heinemann, 1953.

*Martinet, André. *La Description phonologique, avec application au parler... d'Hauteville...* Paris, M. J. Minard, 1956.

——— *Économie des changements phonétiques; traité de phonologie diachronique.* Berne, éditions A. Francke, c1955.

——— *Phonology as Functional Phonetics.* London, Oxford University Press, 1949.

*Meillet, Antoine. *Introduction à l'étude comparative des langues indo-européennes.* Paris, Librairie Hachette, 1922; 8th ed., 1937.

———, and M. Cohen, ed. *Les Langues du monde.* Nouvelle éd. Paris, H. Champion for CNRS, 1952. (With 26 maps.)

*——— *Linguistique historique et linguistique générale.* 2 v. Paris, 1936–1938.

Mencken, Henry L. *The American Language, Supplement I.* New York, Alfred A. Knopf, 1945.

*Miller, George A. *Language and Communication.* New York, McGraw-Hill, 1951.

Montaigne, Michel de. *Essais,* ed. Pierre Villey. Paris, Alcan, 1922.

Müller, Johannes. *Handbuch der Physiologie des Menschen.* 2 v. Coblenz, J. Holscher, 1838–1840.

Murra, John V., Robert M. Hankin, and Fred Holling. *The Soviet Linguistic Controversy*. New York, King's Crown Press, 1951.

Nida, Eugene A. *Morphology: the descriptive analysis of words*. 2d ed. Ann Arbor, University of Michigan Press, 1949.

——*Outline of Descriptive Syntax*. Glendale, Calif., 1951.

O'Connor, Patricia, and Ernest F. Haden. *Oral Drill in Spanish*. Boston, Houghton Mifflin Co., c1957.

O Cuív, Bríain. *Irish Dialects and Irish-Speaking Districts*. Dublin, Institute for Advanced Studies, 1951.

O Faoláin, Seán. *The Story of Ireland*. London, Collins, 1946.

*Ogden, Charles K., and I. A. Richards. *The Meaning of Meaning*. London, 1923.

Ogg, Oscar. *An Alphabet Source Book*. New York and London, Harper & Bros., 1940.

—— *The 26 Letters*. New York, T. Y. Crowell and Co., 1948.

*Osgood, Charles E., ed. *Psycholinguistics, a survey of theory and research problems*. Report of the 1953 Summer Semester. Baltimore, Waverly Press, 1954. (Indiana University Publications in Anthropology and Linguistics, Memoir No. 10.)

Osgood, Cornelius, ed. *Linguistic Structures of Native America*. New York, 1946. (Viking Fund Publications in Anthropology, No. 6.)

*Pedersen, Holger. *Linguistic Science in the Nineteenth Century; its methods and its results*. Tr. J. W. Spargo. Cambridge, Mass., Harvard University Press, 1931.

*Pei, Mario. *The Story of Language*. Philadelphia, Lippincott, c1949.

—— *The World's Chief Languages*. New York, S. F. Vanni, 1945.

*Pike, Kenneth L. *Phonemics: a technique for reducing languages to writing*. Ann Arbor, University of Michigan Press, 1947.

*—— *Phonetics*. Ann Arbor, University of Michigan Press, 1943.

*Pop, Sever. *La Dialectologie; aperçu historique, et méthodes d'enquêtes linguistiques*. 2 v. Louvain, chez l'auteur, 1950.

*Potter, Ralph K., G. A. Kopp, and H. G. Green. *Visible Speech*. New York, Van Nostrand, 1947.

Rashdall, Hastings. *The Universities of Europe in the Middle Ages*. Ed. F. M. Powicke and A. Emden. 3 v. Oxford, Clarendon Press, 1936.

Rask, Rasmus Kristian (1787–1832). *Undersøgelse om det gamle nordiske eller islandske sprogoprindelse*. Kjöbnhavn, Gyldendal, 1818.

Roberts, Paul. *Patterns of English*. New York, Harcourt Brace, 1956.

*Robins, Robert H. *Ancient and Medieval Grammatical Theory in Europe, with particular reference to modern linguistic doctrine*. London, G. Bell & Sons, 1951.

Rousseau, Jean-Jacques. *Émile, ou de l'éducation*. Paris, Garnier, 1951.

Rousselot, Pierre Jean, abbé. *Principes de phonétique expérimentale*. Nouv. éd. 2 v. Paris, Didier, 1924–1925.

*Sapir, Edward. *Language*. New York, Harcourt Brace, 1921.

Bibliography

*Saussure, Ferdinand de. *Cours de linguistique générale,* publié par Charles Bally et Albert Sèchehaye. 4th ed. Paris, Payot, 1949.

*——— *Mémoire sur le système primitif des voyelles dans les langues indo-européennes.* Leipzig, Teubner, 1879.

*Schleicher, August. *Compendium der vergleichenden Grammatik der indogermanischen Sprachen.* Weimar, 1861.

Schulze, Wilhelm. *Tocharische Grammatik . . . im Auftrag der preussischen Akademie der Wissenschaften bearbeitet . . . von Emil Sieg und Wilhelm Siegling.* Göttingen, Vandenhoeck, 1931.

Shaw, George Bernard. *Man and Superman; the Revolutionist's Handbook; Maxims for Revolutionists.* New York, Brentano's, 1905.

——— *Androcles and the Lion; Overruled; Pygmalion.* New York, Brentano's, 1916.

Siertsema, B. *A Study of Glossematics.* The Hague, Nijhoff, 1955.

Sievers, Eduard (1850–1932). *Grundzüge der Lautphysiologie, zur Einführung in das Studium der Lautlehre der indogermanischen Sprachen.* Leipzig, Breitkopf und Härtel, 1876.

Skeat, Walter William. *Principles of English Etymology.* 2 v. Oxford, Clarendon Press, 1887–1891.

——— *The Science of Etymology.* Oxford, Clarendon Press, 1912.

*Smith, Henry Lee, Jr. *Linguistic Science and the Teaching of English.* Cambridge, Mass., Harvard University Press, 1956.

Snell, Bruno. *Der Aufbau der Sprache.* Hamburg, Claassen-Verlag, c1952.

Stack, Edward M. *The Language Laboratory and Modern Language Teaching.* New York, Oxford University Press, 1960.

Sturtevant, Edgar H. *A Comparative Grammar of the Hittite Language.* Philadelphia, University of Pennsylvania for L.S.A., 1933.

*——— *The Indo-Hittite Laryngeals.* Baltimore, Linguistic Society of America, 1942.

——— *An Introduction to Linguistic Science.* New Haven, Yale University Press, c1947.

——— *Linguistic Change; an introduction to the historical study of language.* Chicago, University of Chicago Press, c1917.

Suetonius. *Suetonius,* with an English translation by J. C. Rolfe. 2 v. London, Heinemann, 1928. (Loeb Classical Library.)

Tacitus. *Tacitus: The Histories,* with an English translation by Clifford H. Moore; *The Annals,* with an English translation by John Jackson. 2 v. London, Heinemann, 1931. (Loeb Classical Library.)

Taylor, Isaac, *Words and Places.* New ed. London, Macmillan, 1882.

Thompson, Edward A. M. *An Introduction to Greek and Latin Palaeography.* Oxford, Clarendon Press, 1912.

*Trager, George S., and H. S. Smith, Jr. *Outline of English Structure.* Norman, University of Oklahoma, 1951.

Troubetzkoy, Nikolai S. *Principes de Phonologie*. Tr. J. Cantineau. Paris, Librairie C. Klincksieck, 1949.

Twaddell, W. Freeman. *The English Verb Auxiliaries*. Providence, R.I., Brown University Press, 1960.

*—— *On Defining the Phoneme*. Baltimore, 1935. (*Language* Monograph No. 16.)

Udall, Nicholas. *Ralph Roister Doister*. (See Adams, J. Q., ed.)

*Weinreich, Uriel. *Languages in Contact: findings and problems*. New York, Linguistic Circle of New York, 1953. (LCNY *Publications,* No. 1.)

Whatmough, Joshua. *Language; a modern synthesis*. New York, St. Martin's Press, 1956.

*Whitney, William Dwight. *Language and the Study of Language*. 7th ed. New York, 1867.

—— *The Life and Growth of Language: an outline of linguistic science*. New York, D. Appleton, 1875.

Wrede, Ferdinand. *Deutscher Sprachatlas, auf Grund des Sprachatlas des deutschen Reichs* von Georg Wenker, begonnen von F. Wrede, fortgesetzt von Walther Mitzka und Bernhard Martin. 2 v. Marburg (Lahn), Elwert, 1927–1956. 128 maps.

B. Articles

Adams, J. Donald. "Speaking of Books," *New York Times Book Review,* January 31, 1960.

Bloomfield, Leonard. "A Note on Sound Change," *Language* IV (1928), 99–100.

Bolinger, Dwight. "Linguistic Science and Linguistic Engineering," *Word* XVI, 3 (Dec., 1960), 374–91.

*Bonfante, Giuliano. "The Neolinguistic Position," *Language* XXIII (1947), 344–75.

Chatman, Seymour. "Immediate Constituents and Expansion Analysis." *Word* XI, 3 (Dec., 1956), 377–85.

De Voto, Bernard. "The Good Teacher," *Woman's Day,* February 1948, 47, 122–30.

*Delattre, Pierre C. "The Physiological Interpretation of Sound Spectrograms," *PMLA* LXVI (1951), 864–75.

Dillon, Myles. "The Hindu Act of Truth in Celtic Tradition," *Modern Philology* XLIV (1947), 137–40.

Ellegård, Alvar. "Estimating Vocabulary Size," *Word* XVI, 2 (August, 1960), 219–44.

*Gudschinsky, Sarah. "The ABC's of Lexicostatics," *Word* XII, 2 (August, 1956), 175–210.

Haas, Mary R. "The Linguist as a Teacher of Languages," *Language* XIX, No. 3 (July 1943), 203–8.

Haas, W. "Linguistic Structures," *Word* XVI, 2 (August, 1960), 251–76.

*Hall, Robert A., Jr. "American Linguistics, 1925–1950," *Archivum linguisticum* III (1951), 101–25; IV (1952), 1–16.

*Harris, Zellig S. "From Phoneme to Morpheme," *Language* XXXI (1955), 190–222.

Hjelmslev, Louis. "Principes de grammaire générale," Kongelige danske Videnskabernes Selskab, *Historisk-Filologiske Meddelelser* XVI, 1 (1928), 1–363.

*Hockett, Charles F. "Two Models of Grammatical Description," *Word* X, 2–3 (Aug.-Dec., 1947), 210–34.

Hughes, John P. "The Administrative Organization of Language Teaching," *Modern Language Journal* XL, 4 (Apr. 1956), 178–81.

—— "The Machine Age in Language Teaching," *Catholic School Journal,* LVIII (Sept., 1958), 63–68.

—— "What Are the Liberal Arts?" *Association of American Colleges Bulletin,* XLI, 4 (Dec., 1955), 614–25.

Lees, Robert B., review of Noam Chomsky's *Syntactic Structures, Language* XXIII (1957), 406.

*Lounsbury, Floyd G. "The Varieties of Meaning," Georgetown University *Monograph Series on Languages and Linguistics,* No. 4.

Martinet, André. "Elements of a Functional Syntax," *Word* XVI, 1 (Apr., 1960), 1–10.

*O'Connor, J. D., and L. M. Trim. "Vowel, Consonant, Syllable—a Phonological Definition," *Word* IX (1953), 103–22.

*Pokorny, Julius. "Substrattheorie und Urheimat der Indogermanen," *Mitteilungen der anthropologischen Gesellschaft in Wien* LXVI (1936), 69–91.

Troubetzkoy, Nikolai. "Caucasian Languages," *Encyclopaedia Britannica,* 14th ed., 1929, v. 5.

Waters, Leonard A., S. J. "Progressivist Attack on Grammar," *America* XCIX (Apr. 12, 1958), 56–58.

*Wells, Rulon S. "Immediate Constituents," *Language* XXIII (1947), 81–117.

—— "Meaning and Use," *Word* X, 2–3 (Aug.-Dec., 1950), 235–50.

C. Linguistic Journals

Acta linguistica, v. 1 (1939)–   Copenhagen, Munksgaard, 1939–   .

Archivum linguisticum, v. 1 (1949)–   . Glasgow, 1949–   .

Association pour l'étude et le développement de la traduction automatique et de la linguistique appliquée. *La traduction automatique,* v. 1 (1960)–   . The Hague, Mouton & Co., 1960–   .

Beiträge zur vergleichenden Sprachforschung . . . v. 1 (1856)–8 (1876). Berlin, Dümmler, 1858–76.

Bulletin de la société linguistique de Paris see Société. . . .

Center for Applied Linguistics *see* Modern Language Association of America.

Cercle linguistique de Copenhague. *Travaux*, v. 1 (1947)–   . Copenhagen, 1947–   .

Cercle linguistique de Prague. *Travaux*, v. 1 (1928)–8 (1939). Prague, 1928–39.

Conférences de l'institut de linguistique see Paris. Université. Institut. . . .

General Linguistics, v. 1 (1955)–   . Lexington, Ky., 1955–   . (University of Kentucky.)

Georgetown University. Institute of Languages and Linguistics. *Monograph Series on Languages and Linguistics*. Washington, D.C., 1951–59.

International Journal of American Linguistics, v. 1 (1934)–   . Baltimore, 1934–   (University of Indiana.)

International Journal of Slavic Linguistics and Poetics, v. 1 (1958)–   . The Hague, Mouton & Co., 1958–   .

Language see Linguistic Society of America.

Language Learning; a Journal of Applied Linguistics, v. 1 (1948)–   . Ann Arbor, Mich., Research Club in Language Learning, 1948–   .

Lingua; International Review of General Linguistics, v. 1 (1952)–   . Haarlem, North Holland Publishing Co., 1952–   .

Le lingue del mondo; unica rivista italiana di cultura linguistica, v. 1 (1947)–   . Firenze, 1947–   .

Linguistic Circle of New York. *Word*, v. 1 (1947)–   . New York, 1947–   .

The Linguistic Reporter see Modern Language Association of America.

Linguistic Society of America. *Language*, v. 1 (1925)–   . Providence, R.I., 1925–   .

Mechanical Translation, v. 1 (1954)–   . Cambridge, Mass., Massachusetts Institute of Technology, 1954–   .

Modern Language Association of America. Center for Applied Linguistics. *The Linguistic Reporter*, v. 1 (1959)–   . Washington, D.C., 1959–   .

Moscow. Akademiia Nauk. Institut Iazykoznany. *Trudy*, v. 1 (1952)–   . Moscow, 1952–   .

Norsk Tidskrift for Sprogvidenskap, v. 1 (1928)–   . Oslo, W. Nygaard, 1928–   .

Paris. Université. Institut de linguistique. *Conférences*, v. 1 (1933)–   . Paris, Klincksieck, 1934–   .

——— *Travaux*, v. 1 (1956)–   . Paris, Klincksieck, 1957–   .

Revue de linguistique et de philologie comparée, v. 1 (1867)–48 (1916). Paris, Maisonneuve, 1867–1916.

Société de linguistique de Paris. *Bulletin*, v. 1 (1869)–   . Paris, 1871–   .

Die Sprache; Zeitschrift für Sprachwissenschaft, v. 1 (1949–   . Vienna, 1949– . (Wiener Sprachgesellschaft.)

Der Sprachforum; eine Zeitschrift fur angewandte Sprachwissenschaft, v. 1 (1955)–   . Köln, Böhlau-Verlag, 1955–   .

Studia linguistica; revue de linguistique générale et comparée, v. 1 (1947)– .
Lund, Gleerup, 1949– .
La traduction automatique see Association pour l'étude, etc.
Travaux de l'institut de linguistique see Paris. Université.
Travaux du cercle linguistique de Copenhague see Cercle linguistique. . . .
Travaux du cercle linguistique de Prague see Cercle linguistique. . . .
Travaux du cercle linguistique de Vienne see *Die Sprache.*
Trudy instituta iazykoznaniia see Moscow. Akademiia Nauk. Institut. . . .
Word see Linguistic Circle of New York.
Zeitschrift für vergleichende Sprachforschung, v. 1 (1852)– . Berlin, Göttingen,
1872 .

D. Other Journals

America; a Catholic review of the week, v. 1 (1909)– . New York, The Ameri-
can Press, 1909– .
Anthropologische Gesellschaft in Wien. *Mitteilungen,* v. 1 (1870)– . Vienna,
1870– .
Association of American Colleges. *Bulletin,* v. 1 (1913)– . Lancaster, Pa.,
1914– .
The Catholic School Journal, v. 1 (1900)– . Milwaukee, Wis., The Bruce Pub-
lishing Co., 1900– .
The Modern Language Association of America. *Publications,* v. 1 (1885)– .
Menasha, Wis., 1885– .
The Modern Language Journal see National Federation of Modern Language
Teachers' Associations.
Modern Philology, v, 1 (1902)– . Chicago, University of Chicago Press,
1903– .
National Federation of Modern Language Teachers' Associations. *The Modern
Language Journal,* v. 1 (1916)– . Menasha, Wis., 1916– .
Woman's Day, v. 1 (1937)– . Greenwich, Conn., Fawcett Publications,
1937– .

INDEX

INDEX

38, 452

Hughes, John Paul

The science of
language

Date Due

BJJH
